In the Shadow of the Beartooth

Clark, Wyoming

In the Shadow of the Beartooth

Clark, Wyoming

By
Art Kidwell

Published by:
DESERT MOON PRESS
P. O. Box 121
Powell, Wyoming
82435

Printed by:
Artcraft Printers
Billings, Montana

Dedicated
to all
Clark residents

Past, Present and Future

Table of Contents

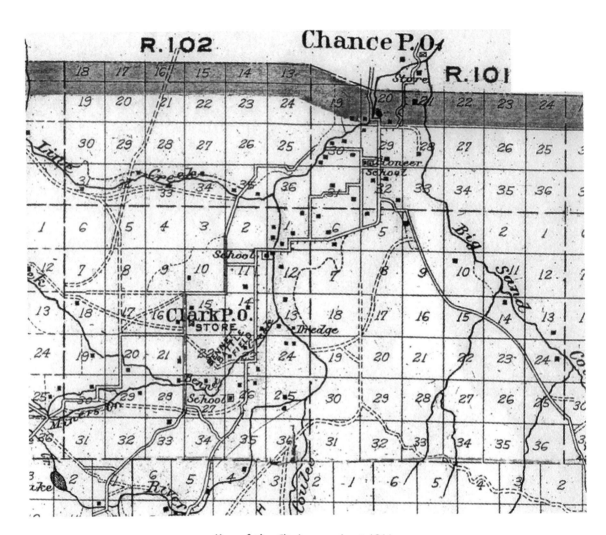

Map of the Clark area about 1916

1

The Road to Clark

*"Clark, a small town and post office in Park County, 35 miles north
of Cody, the county seat. Belfry, Montana is the nearest railroad and
banking point. Farming and stock raising are the principal industries.
Population of neighborhood is 250. Altitude 4,500 feet."*
Wyoming State Business Directory, 1921

The last 38 miles of Wyoming Highway 120 extends between the city of Cody and the Montana border. Travelers on their journey north pass the old fish hatchery seven miles north of town. Then the road climbs toward the summit of Skull Creek Hill, after which it winds down its slope.

To the left of the highway is the beginning of the small creek, which gave its name to this location. Beyond it are the remnants of the original dirt road winding back and forth through the sagebrush and across small gullies on its way up to the summit. For decades that old road with its rocks and chuckholes provided the way for those on horseback, horse-drawn wagon, and later on by motor vehicles until a new paved route was cut into the hill.

Few of those crossing the hill today realize that in much earlier times travel to Cody or in the opposite direction to Montana could consume a whole day or even longer. Rain made the old dirt road slick, and heavy snowfalls often stopped travel completely requiring an alternate route. Alva Trask, who lived at the summit of Skull Creek Hill until the early 1950's, often assisted wagons and motor vehicles to the top. [1] Today county road crews keep the new route plowed and sanded even during the heaviest winter storms.

After descending the hill, the highway winds north toward Montana. At mile marker 116.5 is the turnoff to the Chief Joseph Scenic Highway, which leads to Sunlight, Crandall and Cooke City. Off in the distance to the west across an irrigated field are the buildings and main house of the Two-Dot Ranch headquarters. Its beginnings back in 1878 make it one of the oldest ranches in northwestern Wyoming.

For the next 11 miles north the highway passes through just a small part of this magnificent ranch whose open range on both sides of the highway extends as far as the eye can see. Along the way hundreds of Black Angus cattle can often be seen grazing behind the wire fencing that protects them from the roadway as it climbs up and travels across the Chapman Bench, named for the original owner of the ranch. With over 200,000 acres, the Two-Dot is also one of the largest spreads in Wyoming.

Soon the highway descends from the Bench, crosses the Quick Bridge over the Clarks Fork River, and passes Mile Marker 129. Almost immediately a County Road sign announces "Clark" and points to the left. Here County Road 1AB leaves the highway and heads west toward the mountains. In their shadow lies the community of Clark, straight ahead.

Clark

In the beginning there were no roads here. There was no post office, store, or schools. No group of buildings could be called a town or even a village. Most of its first residents were homesteaders who came to get land and saw that their future lay in farming and ranching. Others were gold seekers who hoped to get rich. All saw a chance to start new lives.

The nearest town was Red Lodge. Cody and Powell didn't even exist when the first settlers came with dreams that could only be achieved through hard work and perseverance. There was land to be cleared, cabins and houses to be built, roads to be blazed, and irrigation ditches to be dug.

Where there is isolation and lack of conveniences, there is a pooling of limited resources. The need for neighborliness drew strangers together into a warm bond of cooperation, friendship, and helpfulness toward one another to accomplish what could not be done alone. Those with little shared with those who had nothing. All of these values helped to turn this land into a community.

Acknowlegments

My journey to discover the story of Clark, its pioneers and their history began six years ago when I first moved here, and has been gathered from many sources. Some of it was found in the records kept at the Montana Historical Society, Helena; the Carbon County Historical Society, Red Lodge, Montana; the Park County, Wyoming Courthouse; the Park County Historical Archives; and the Wyoming State Archives in Cheyenne. Much of it was gleaned from newspaper articles in Cody, Powell, Red Lodge, and Billings newspapers.

While area newspapers reported news worthy events occurring here, it was the periodic columns submitted by early area correspondents, Charlie Snow, Mary Say, Emma Simpson, Virginia Bunn Teichert, and Iva Bunn Kelsey who provided the more personal side of life of this rural area. Often their writings documented events reported nowhere else.

Some of Clark's past is also recorded in the memories, family documents and photographs held by the descendants of early Clark residents, many of whom do not live here today. I can not say thank you enough to the following for their much appreciated help and friendship: Nona West Allen, Ina Moore Badura, the late Margaret Weathermon Bailey, Marian Fricke Bainter, Louise and Earl Black, Hank and Betty Bratsky, Frances Heimer Brown, Clara Sirrine Brown, Carol Brown Christiansen, Hazel Cochrane, Jim and Rose Weathermon Cox, Ada Weathermon Eckerman, Rayola Teichert Fink, Roberta Bunn Gairrett, Viola Bunn Gairrett, Juanita Gordon, Ina Fricke Haines, Virginia Stinson Hoiness, Noralee and Wilda Hoefer, Felix Hoff, the late Carol Briggs Joy and Stan Joy, Iva Bunn and Everett Kelsey, the late Phyllis Bosley Lovercheck, Bob and Doris Marney, George and Betty Hogan Moore, Juanita Smith Moore, Dorothy Cochrane Napier, Mickey Obert, Ramon and Phyllis Hoff Sammons, Howard Sparhawk, Mildred Petit Taylor, Oscar and Jane Riddle Thompson, Jackie and Don Tolman, Steve and Agnes Thull Torczon, Linda Torczon, Melvin Torczon, Dave Vickery, Marilyn Hardee Wardell, Lee Weathermon, Mark Weathermon, Dorothy Pearson Williams and Joise Denney Wolchesky.

I also appreciate the assistance of others who helped me locate former residents or needed research documents. They include: Bruce Blevins, Park County Assessor Doug Brandt; Park County Clerk Karen Carter and members of her staff, Chris Eck, Sophie Deleon, Kay Lundstrom and Mary Lou Mills; Cindy Brown at the Wyoming State Archives; Judy Buckingham at St. Barbara's Church, Powell; Frances Clymer, Lynn Houze, Lillian Turner, and Dr. Juti Winchester at the Buffalo Bill Historical Center; Tom Egenes, owner of Flash's Photography, Red Lodge; Dee Heny at the Office of the Powell District Schools Superintendent; Ann Johnson, Yellowstone Nat. Park Archaeologist; Superintendent Dave Miller, John Chaffey, Chester Bettger, Brian Blutt, and John Burns at the Clarks Fork Fish Hatchery; Jeanne Parker and Penny Collins Redli at the Carbon County Historical Society Archives, Red Lodge, MT; Rhonda Spaulding, Pat Haines, Marylin Schultz, and Krystal Hazen at the Park County Historical Archives; Rowene Giarrizzo and Christina Brown at the Homesteader Museum, Powell; Cheryl Schock at the Riverside Cemetery, Cody; Joan Andersen, Rusty Blough, Stu Conner, Agnes and Nick Cowger, Shirley Cox, Pearl Deville, Ken Feyhl, Donna Harkness, Dave and Susan Hoffert, Kurt and Lavonne McNabb, Janice Kuntz, D. Rosalie Miller, Ester Johansson Murray, Ruby Reno, and Patti Yedlicka.

I would also like to thank Roy Close for allowing me to use his original drawing of his family's former ranch home on the Clarks Fork River for the inside cover page. Uncredited drawings and photos throughout the text were drawn or taken by the author.

Lastly, I would like to acknowledge the major contributions of five area pioneers who provided a wealth of information, advice, and photographs, and worked continually with me from the beginning of this project. Their vivid memories of earlier days in Clark, as well as their patience with my seemingly endless questions laid the foundation for all of my research. I am particularly indebted to: Barbara and Elmer Bunn, Georgia Frame Close, Irma Chance McLuskie, and Clytie Fuson Williams and thank them for their much appreciated and valued help.

This book is an overview of Clark history, and as such, does not record everything that has occurred here in the past century. Other events will be documented in a second planned volume on the early Clark families. Hopefully what is related in these pages will remind pioneer residents of days gone by, and give newer residents an appreciation of those who lived here before us. Whether they lived in the Bennett Creek, Clark, Line Creek, Pioneer, Paint Creek or Pat O'Hara areas, they like us, called this place in the shadow of the Beartooth Mountains – home.

Chapter 1 notes:

[1] Alva Trask wasn't the only one who helped travelers up steep Skull Creek Hill. In about 1923 or '24 when Howard Sparhawk was eight or nine years old, he and his father rode their mule, Jack from Clark to Cody spending a night at John Kirkpatrick's cabin on Skull Creek. The next day as they were riding up Skull Creek Hill, they encountered a car that was having trouble making the grade. Frank Sparhawk took his rope and hooked it onto the car and attached the other end to his saddle and "helped it get over the hill." Then they continued on their way to Cody where they had lunch at the Irma. Afterwards, Frank bought his son a pair of wool chaps and some cuffs while they were in town. (Howard Sparhawk, interview with author, Clark, Wyoming, June 10, 2002.

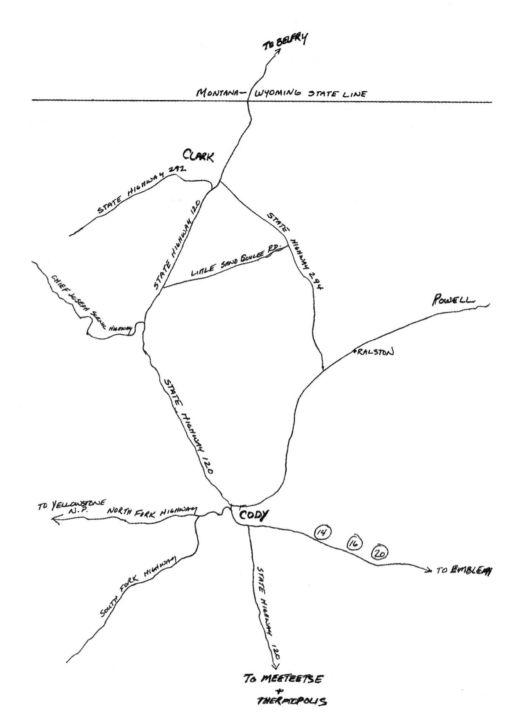

General area map showing Clark and its relationship to Powell, Cody and the Montana border.

2
Where the Heck is Clark?

Clark is a small, rural community lying in the shadow of the Beartooth and Absaroka Mountains . It has an elementary school, two churches, a tax-supported recreation center and cemetery, and a scattered population of about 325 full-time and part-time residents. [1] The mountain ranges to the west form a dramatic backdrop for those who live on the sage brush-covered valley floor or in the upper Line Creek valley about 1,000 feet higher.

While today's Clark includes a much larger geographic area than it did in the past, its population has not varied too much since the early 1890's when the first homesteaders spread across the valley. Census figures indicate that by 1900 there were 129 residents living here. Ten years later the population had grown to 390 residents, and then declined to 302 by 1920.

The drought of 1918 and continued economic decline during the 1920's across Wyoming and elsewhere was also felt here. Many residents who made their livelihood as farmers and ranchers were unable to repay banks for real estate and livestock loans, and as a result, lost not only their investment, but also their property. The 1930 census population of 254 area residents reflects those changing economic times here. [2]

Rivers and Creeks
The Clarks Fork of the Yellowstone is the most important watercourse in the area. It is one of only a few rivers in Wyoming that flow into the state and then out in a different direction.

Beginning on the west side of the Beartooth Mountains in Montana, the river flows through Crandall and the Sunlight Basin and then into and through the Clarks Fork Canyon. The canyon marks the division between the Beartooth Mountains on the north, and the Absaroka Mountains on the south. [3]

Leaving the canyon it flows out onto the valley floor, meandering south and then east before turning north again on its final journey to join the Yellowstone River, south of Laurel, Montana.

Other smaller watercourses running through this area include: Bennett, Line, Little Rocky, Lake, Newmeyer, Pat O'Hara and Paint Creeks.

Warren Sirrine Names Clark
The naming of the Clark community originated with the establishment of the first post office here on February 27, 1891. Warren O. Sirrine who had arrived in the area with his family in 1888 made application to establish the post office on his Clark Fork River ranch "20 yards from said river on the south side of it." [4]

The Sirrine ranch located south of the Wyoming-Montana border and a little west of the Meeteetse Trail was an ideal location for a post office. For centuries, this well-traveled route had been used as a migration and hunting trail by prehistoric Indian groups. By 1889 a regular stage route was operating over it from Red Lodge to Meeteetse, carrying mail as well as passengers with two stops enroute at Dilworth and Corbett.[5] Warren Sirrine, in filing his application for the post office, decided "the proposed office to be called Clark." [6]

The following year his wife, Mary Coates Sirrine, succeeded him as postmaster serving until July 1902 [7] when her husband's declining health forced her to give up the position. The Clark post office with its name intact was then moved about nine miles away to the William Barber ranch south of Bennett Creek in the northeast quarter of Section 28.[8]

More Homesteaders Arrive

As more homesteaders moved into the valley, specific areas had their own names. The area closest to the Montana border was initially called Sirrine, named for Warren and members of his large family who had property here. In 1904 when the Sirrine school district was renamed Pioneer,[9] the name eventually replaced the former one for the area too. Today this area is still known as Pioneer.

Other areas became known as Bennett Creek, Line Creek, Paint Creek and Pat O'Hara, being named for the watercourse passing through the areas where early homesteaders had chosen acreage. These early valley residents toiled clearing the land of rocks and sagebrush, and building cabins in order to full-fill government-mandated requirements to get title to their land.

To the Lindquist store in Clark they traveled to purchase food and supplies, and to get and send mail. Dances, church services, and meetings were held at the school buildings in Pioneer, Bennett Creek, Clark, Line Creek, Paint Creek and Pat O'Hara. These social gatherings attracted residents from all over.

Neighbors helped each other with road and bridge building, land clearing, and threshing operations in those early days. There was a spirit of cooperation and unity throughout the valley. While each area had its own name identity, Cody, Powell, and Red Lodge newspapers more often referred to the entire area as the "Clarks Fork" without mentioning specific geographic locations.

Clark's Legal Boundaries

After Park County was created from Big Horn County by a special election in May 1909,[10] its officials eventually set specific formal boundaries for determining school, cemetery, election, fire, and property assessment districts. The southern areas of Paint Creek and Pat O'Hara areas were placed in a separate district from those of Pioneer, Line Creek and Clark, which were merged into the area officially known as Clark today.

Today Clark's legal boundaries include an area encompassing one hundred twenty-three thousand acres or 193 square miles. [11] Its southern boundary begins on Chapman Bench north of County Road 7RP and extends west to the Beartooth and Absaroka Mountains including parts the Shoshone National Forest. Its eastern boundaries include part of the arid lands of Badger Basin, while the Wyoming-Montana border marks its northern one. The exact boundary described in great detail can be found in this chapter's footnotes.[12]

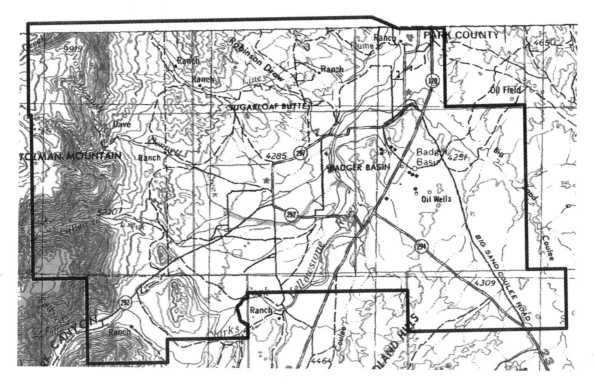

Clark's legal boundaries encompass an area of 193 square miles and are used in determining school, cemetery, election, fire, and property assessment districts. Overlay map computed from legal description and drawn by Rusty Blough of Holm, Blough, and Company, Cody.

Clark Now

Today's Clark community is very different from that of the past. While cattle ranching and farming continues, many ranches are larger in size but smaller in number. Large-scale sheep operations terminated in the 1970's. Within the past year a couple ranches, which had raised bison instead of cattle, have terminated this production due to a fall in bison meat prices. A number of former ranch properties and BLM land have been subdivided into smaller acreage home sites for the increasing influx of new residents.

While Clark's present population is roughly the same as in the past, the age demographics have shifted toward retirees who moved here from elsewhere to enjoy its beautiful location and peaceful life style.

In the past where there were five area elementary schools, now only one is necessary to educate less than 25 students yearly. Only a handful of residents can boost that their family was here a hundred years ago. As a result, today's newer residents are mostly unaware of its history and its heritage.

Snow-capped Beartooth Mountains overlook the entrance to the Clarks Fork Canyon.

Chapter 2 notes:

[1] This population estimate is based on information collected in March 2004 concerning the number of registered voters, the number of Clark youth enrolled at the Clark Elementary School, the Powell High School and Belfry (Montana) High School, and the number of mail delivery locations in the community. A few residents are part-time and divide their time between Clark and another location.

[2] **1900** – 37 households and 129 residents, *12th U.S. Census, Big Horn Co., Wyoming*, (Clark Precinct, E.D. 72), p. 189B – 191A; **1910** – 93 households and 390 residents, *13th U.S. Census, Park Co., Wyoming*, (Painter Precinct, Clark Precincts # 1 and 2, and Paint Creek Precinct, E.D. 28), p. 134A – 137B; **1920** – 73 households and 302 residents, *14th U.S. Census, Park Co., Wyoming*, (Election Districts 1 and 10, E.D. 101), p. 65A – 68A; **1930** – 54 households and 254 residents, *15th U.S. Census, Park Co., Wyoming*, (Election Dist. 1, E.D. 15-1), p. 1A – 3B; T. A. Larson, *History of Wyoming*, 2nd ed. Revised, (Lincoln and London, University of Nebraska Press, 1990) p. 411-418.

[3] Robert Harold Brown, *Wyoming – A Geography*, (Boulder, Colorado, Westview Press, 1980), p. 100.

[4] Application to Post Office Department, Office of the First Assistant P.M. General, Washington, D.C., dated February 13, 1891 signed by Warren O. Sirrine; Post Office Department, Topographer's Office document dated April 29, 1891 signed by Warren O. Sirrine.

[5] "Mail Was Carried Daily by Stage Between Red Lodge, Meeteetse," *Carbon County News*, August 27, 1964; Ester Johansson Murray, *Red Lodge-Meeteetse Trail*, 1995, p. 1- 7.

[6] Sirrine post office documents, February 13 and April 29. 1891.

[7] Post Office Department, Topographer's Office, Washington, D.C. document signed by Mary E. Sirrine on April 09, 1900; Ltr. to Bronson Tolman from Miss Jane F. Smith, Acting Dir. Social and Economics Records Div., General Services Administration, National Archives and Records Service, Washington, DC 20408, dated October 17, 1966; Ltr. To Ms. Debra J. Eddy from Rita L. Moroney, Research Administrator/Historian, Office of the Postmaster General, Washington, DC 20260-0011, dated July 21, 1988.

[8] Smith letter to Bronson Tolman, October 17, 1966; Ltr to U. S. Post Office Topographer's Office from Alice M. Barber, postmaster, dated July 11, 1902.

[9] Janet Hanson, *Pioneer School 1904 to 1969*, manuscript compiled in 1992, from the Park County Historical Archives.

[10] Special Election to create new county held on May 4, 1909. (*Park County, Wyoming Commissioners' Records*, Book 1, p. 5).

[11] Computed from legal description on area USGS topographical maps by Rusty Blough, Holm, Blough, and Co., Cody, Wyoming, February 26, 2003.

[12] It's legal boundary is as follows: "Beginning at the northwest corner, T.58 N., R. 103 W (unsurveyed); thence south to the southwest corner of T. 57 N., R. 103 W. (unsurveyed); thence east to the northwest corner of T. 56 N., R. 103 W.; thence south to the southwest corner of Sec. 18, T. 56 N., R. 103 W.; thence east to the southeast corner of Sec. 16, T. 56 N., R. 103 W.; thence north along the section line for about ¾ of a mile; thence east on a line projected west from the south lines of Tracts 54, 55, 184, 183 and 182 to the west line of T. 56 N., R. 102 W.; thence north to the north line of Tract 155, T. 56., R. 102 W.; thence west along said north line of Tract 155 to the Clark's Fork River; thence north and east along said river to the west line of T. 56 N., R. 102 W.; thence north to the midsection line of Sec. 6, T. 56 N., R. 102 W.; thence east on the midsection lines to the east line of T. 56 N., R. 102 W.; thence south to the southeast corner of Sec. 12, T. 56 N., R. 102 W.; thence east to the southeast corner, Sec. 12, T. 56 N., R. 100 W.; thence north to the northeast corner of said township; thence west to the southeast corner of T. 57 N., R. 100 W.; thence north to the northeast corner of said township; thence west to the northwest corner of Sec. 3 of said township; thence north to the north boundary of Wyoming; thence west along said boundary to the point of beginning." (Description in assessment records used for creation and establishment of Clark Cemetery District signed by Ronald R. Christie, Park County Assessor, January 17, 1985; also recorded in *Park County, Wyoming Commissioners' Record*, Book 12, p. 297; also boundaries for the Clark Fire District, in *Park County, Wyoming Commissioners' Record*, Book 8, p. 473).

3
Weather

Everyone who has ever lived in the Clarks Fork Valley has experienced the erratic wind conditions that occur here from time or time. Prevailing westerly movements of colder, denser air pass over the higher elevations of the Absaroka and Beartooth Mountains can accelerate to high speeds on their journey down to the valley floor. During winter months the prevailing wind can also shift from the north as Arctic air originating in Canada blows across the Clark landscape making frigid temperatures feel even colder.

Children who grew up here in the 1920s and '30s remember long stretches of bitter cold nights and days during winter months, which made for unpleasant walking or horseback rides to school. Viola Bunn Gairrett shared her childhood memories of going to school:

"We walked by ourselves or rode horseback. In the wintertime Dad would usually go with us because of ice on the field ... clear back to Granddad Bunn's place. And he'd walk the horse on that ice.

"We started one time and Uncle Fred was going with us. Our sister Iva got cold and we just got over to Granddad Bunn's place when we said,' I think we'd better turn around and go back.' Fred was going with us to make sure we made it.

"Well, we went back and Iva's fingers were white clear down to the knuckles. We found out afterward it was 20 below. Often we couldn't get to school, because it would be so darn cold. We just couldn't make it." [1]

Winters of the past were long in Clark. Snow blocked roads and cancelled schools sometimes for a week. Temperatures of –30 degrees were not uncommon. Photo courtesy of Ina Badura.

What Newspapers Had to Say About Early Clark Winters

As early as 1909, local newspapers reported the weather in Clark. Winters conditions with subzero temperatures and heavy snowfalls, road blockages, no mail delivery, and school closures were common. The following are a sampling of weather conditions reported in Cody newspapers from 1909 to 1958:

January 1909 - "The deepest snowfall seen in this vicinity since 1896 visited us the forepart of the week. There were 20 inches on the level." [2]

February 1909 - "This is the coldest winter Wyoming has experienced since the season of 1886-87." [3]

February 1910 -"In the weather report for 1910 just issued by the Weather Bureau, the vicinity of Clark the lowest (temperature) was 23 below zero on Feb. 22..." [4]

November 1922 -"Fourteen inches of snow fell at the Two-Dot ranch during the recent storm..." [5]

January 1924 -"Paint Creekers have a new occupation this week of digging tunnels into their igloos and roads in and out of their ranches since the big blow..." [6]

April 1924 -"O.C. Bevelhymer arrived in Cody Tuesday from Paint Creek. He says this is the first time for the past six months he has been able to come to town on account of the heavy snowfall in the Paint Creek district." [7]

April 1926 - "Eighteen inches of snow fell in the Clarks Fork section during the last storm." [8]

December 1926 - "44 below zero was registered in our vicinity last Monday..." [9]

April 1927 -"The snow storm of the past week was one of the worst of the season. At least three feet of snow fell in our vicinity. The roads are in very bad shape again... [10]

April 1927 - "We are sure having a wonderful spell of winter weather this spring, nearly a foot of snow on the level at Paint Creek." [11]

February 1929 – "Last Wednesday night was one of the coldest nights here this winter. At the Hopkins ranch it registered 40 below zero and at least 30 below everywhere else in this community." [12]

February 1929 - "The winds a week ago drifted the snow into the roads so that there has been no car travel all week. The mail is being brought in on a sled." [13]

February 1929 - "We are still having very cold and stormy weather. Gentle breezes, lots of snow. Drifts so dense in some places car travel is impossible in this part of the country and

Ralph Fouse house in Pioneer area after a snowstorm. Photo taken
on January 15, 1943. Photo courtesy of Noralee Hoefer.

it is difficult to get anywhere with wagons, even when taking a four-horse team." [14]

February 1929 - "The winds a week ago drifted the snow into the roads so that there has
been no car travel all week. The mail is being brought in on a sled." [15]

February 1936 - "The 44 below zero weather and deep snow last Monday morning prevented
the school bus from getting over part of its run and was not able to get near the Stidham
ranch all week." [16]

April 1936 - "The roads between here and Cody are blocked with snow again..." [17]

January 1937 - "There was no school at the Clark school Tuesday owing to the weather and
heating of the building." [18]

February 1939 - "The 26 degree below temperature during the week made most of us
stay close by the fires, so neighbors have not seen much of each other." [19]

January 1942 - "The down to 30 below weather last week kept most of us home..." [20]

March 1948 – "Clark school was again started after three weeks loss by bad road conditions
the U. S. mail was also delayed and at times came by car, truck and horse drawn sled as far
as the P. O. Clark residents getting their mail by breaking snow-drifts and injuring cars by
so doing." [20a]

February 1949 - "There was no school at Clark three days of last week and the first two
days of this week due to the weather. Thermometers out here dropped to 36 degrees
below and 40 degrees below." [21]

April 1953 -"There was no school at Clark for three days because snow blocked roads." [22]

April 1954 - "Winds drifted the snow so no mail to Clark that day and no school busses" [23]

May 1958 - "The snowstorm last Tuesday caused some inconvenience. The electric power around Clark and the Clarks Fork valley was off for twenty-four hours which meant no water, no cooking in a number of places, no heat at the schoolhouse so no school for one day." [24]

Temperatures Are Milder Now

Recorded temperatures during the past forty years reveal that area weather conditions have become milder with less snowfall and rainfall. Data collected and tabulated from the CLARK 7 NE weather station (#481775-1) by the Western Regional Climate Center from 1961 through 2003 reveals an average maximum temperature of 60.8 (F) and an average minimum temperature of 29.7 (F). Average total precipitation was 7.45 inches and an average total snowfall was 24.8 inches. [25]

The highest daily temperatures recorded from 1961 through 2003 were: 102 F (08 Aug 1995), 103 F (01 Sep 1983), 104 F (29 June 1984), and 105 F (26 July 1985). Record daily lows were recorded of -30 F (30 Nov 1975), -37 F (13 Jan 1997), -38 F (02 Feb 1996), and -44 F (01 Dec 1999). [26]

Clark and other northern parts of the Big Horn Basin now share the distinction of being one of the two driest areas in Wyoming. The other is in the Great Basin Divide near Wamsutter off Interstate 80. [27]

The Wind Blows in Clark

Due to our mountain backdrop, light winds are common in Clark throughout the year, but are particularly welcome at night during warm summer months. Just as suddenly, these same winds can grow in intensity and pound the Clark landscape with a strength and vengeance that few new residents have ever experienced elsewhere. Over the years high wind velocities here have resulted in property damage or personal injury, which have been documented in newspaper stories. Here is a sampling.

In January 1911 Mrs. Johnson's frame house on Lake Creek was destroyed by a terrible windstorm, and Matt Wagner's haystacks were blown into the Clarks Fork River. [28] The following year "one of the severest storms ever experienced in this vicinity rolled down off the mountains" and did a great deal of damage to hay and grain in the area. [29]

In 1921 an unidentified Chance, Montana resident coming across the Bennett Creek flat reported that the wind struck the rear of his car "like the main sail of a schooner," and although he immediately shut off the engine and set the car's brakes, "the car flew across the flat at the rate of about a hundred miles an hour." [30]

While Ed Manning was hauling hay, the wind blew the rack and load over throwing him to the ground injuring his back, as well as Fred Schmidt "causing him to go limping around for several days." [31]

Two years later Fred Schmidt had another wind encountered after he left his vehicle at the Broughs and returned to find it blown by the wind on its side into Paint Creek. "Fred Walters, Fred Schmidt, Fred Schultz, Glen and Frank Brough, and Ed Manning worked several hours getting the car out of the creek. Refreshments were then served." [32]

In 1937 a severe wind blew the windows out of the Paint Creek schoolhouse resulted in the school being closed for two days. [33]

Wind coupled with a severe snowstorm in January 1943 stopped the high school bus' trip to Belfry necessitating all of the students onboard to stay overnight at the John McClelland ranch in Chance. Some parents went by horseback to get their children at school, as the weather made vehicle travel impossible. A car and truck buried on Badura Lane necessitated travel across the fields, and no mail delivery to the Clark post office. [34]

On January 19, 1967 a twister wind roared through the Clarks Fork Valley and did considerable damage in Clark. Mickey Fraker's large lambing shed was picked up and thrown 200 yards across the county road into a neighboring field. Sheds at Dave Denney's ranch were destroyed, while his house had windows broken out and the chimney destroyed. "Others up and down the valley had windows broken, granaries blown over, and other buildings damaged." [35]

An almost unbelievable situation occurred in February 1972 when strong winds tore up temporary surfacing on a hundred yard section of the new highway near the entrance to the Clarks Fork Canyon. The wind worked its way under the roadbed, which was moist from melting snow, and ripped up huge chunks of blacktop scattering it all over the road. [36]

Almost two years later in January, hurricane force winds, estimated from between 80 and 100 miles per hour, occurred over three days and two nights. The winds moved and destroyed buildings, snapped off trees, destroyed vehicles, injured residents, closed schools, and started a fire that destroyed a home.

Tony Gordon, who was building a house, lost his construction lumber, which was picked up and hurled across the countryside. It was believed that one piece of the Gordon's lumber crashed through John and Ada Eckerman's living room window some distant away.

At the Clarks Fork Fish Hatchery windows were blown out of residence windows and one and a half inches of sand was blown into the raceways. The newly constructed home of Betty Van Wagoner on Line Creek was destroyed when the windstorm blew out her living room windows spreading the fire in the fireplace. The fire also destroyed a trailer house, a pickup truck and car parked in the yard.

An 8" diameter tree on the Tolman ranch fell on Buster Tolman injuring his shoulder, which required surgery to fix.

Ada Eckerman, then a bus driver for the Clark School, had just made her last student delivery at the Rock Creek Ranch, when the wind blew her bus off the highway. Although injured, she managed to get out of the vehicle and walk back to the ranch for help. The next day it was discovered that the wind had flipped the badly damaged vehicle back up onto its wheels during the night. [37]

Ten years later in early November 1984 winds recorded at 105 miles per hour tore off the roof from the Clark School multi-purpose room and damaged roofing on the remainder of the building. Luckily no students or teachers were injured, as the school was vacant that Friday afternoon due to parent-teacher conferences.

Ada Eckerman, who was still driving one of the school buses and lived near the school, said, "The sand and dirt were blowing around so hard that you couldn't see the schoolhouse or even your neighbors. Things were blowing across our field, including what looked like a tin shed. Then I saw pieces of roof coming off the schoolhouse and blowing across the field. The wind took all the trim off and ventilator tops and bent the school's metal flagpole." [38]

While stories about the wind in Clark abound in Cody, Powell, and other nearby areas, they also experience the wind, which at times can be just as fierce, so it is not unique to us. We can all can joke about it, and get defensive when outsiders complain about it. After a few years in Wyoming, everyone has their own memories of the Wyoming wind, no matter where they call home.

Five-year old Carol Briggs playing in the snow at her grandmother, Hannah Pearson's Pioneer area home in 1949. Photo courtesy of Carol Briggs Joy.

Chapter 3 notes:

[1] Viola Bunn Gairrett, interview with author, Billings, Montana, August 28, 2002.

[2] *Wyoming Stockgrower and Farmer,* January 07, 1909, p. 1.

[3] *Wyoming Stockgrower and Farmer,* February 11, 1909, p. 5.

[4] "In the weather report for 1910 just issued by the Weather Bureau, the vicinity of Clark had 8.94 inches of rainfall, just 3 inches below the general average. An average temperature of 49.6, which is as high as any reporting station in the state. The highest temperature was 102 on July 14, and the lowest was 23 below zero on Feb. 22. Total snowfall 19.3 inches, 57 rainy days, 176 clear days, 116 partly cloudy and 73 cloudy days. The prevailing wind direction was from the north. Of the months that had the most rainfall, April had 1.18 inches, May 2.67 inches, June .79 inches, July .81 inches, August .22 inches, and September .89 inches." (Park County Enterprise, April 1, 1911, p. 6).

[5] *The Cody Enterprise,* November 15, 1922, p. 8.

[6] *The Cody Enterprise,* January 23, 1924, p. 2.

[7] *The Cody Enterprise,* April 02, 1924, p. 8.

[8] *The Cody Enterprise,* April 14, 1926, p. 8.

[9] "Pat O'Hara," *The Cody Enterprise,* December 22, 1926, p.5.

[10] "Pat O'Hara," *The* Cody *Enterprise,* April 20, 1927, p. 8.

[11] "Paint Creek," *The Cody Enterprise and Park County Herald,* April 20, 1927, p. 8.

[12] "Clarks Fork," -"Paint Creek," *The Cody Enterprise,* February 20, 1929, p. 3.

[13] "Clarks Fork," *The Cody Enterprise,* February 27, 1929, p. 6.

[14] "Paint Creek," *The Cody Enterprise,* February 27, 1929, p. 3.

[15] "Clarks Fork," *The Cody Enterprise,* Wednesday, February 27, 1929, p. 6.

[16] "Clarks Fork," *The Cody Enterprise,* February 26, 1936, p. 3.

[17] "Clarks Fork," *The Cody Enterprise,* April 08, 1936, p. 7.

[18] "Clarks Fork," *The Cody Enterprise,* January 27, 1937, p. 6.

[19] "Clarks Fork," *The Cody Enterprise,* February 15, 1939, p. 6.

[20] "Clarks Fork," *The Cody Enterprise,* January 14, 1942, p. 3.

[20a] "Clark Items," *The Cody Enterprise,* March 17, 1948, p. 12.

[21] *"Clarks Fork," The Cody Enterprise,* February 09, 1949, p. 9.

[22] *"Badger Basin," The Cody Enterprise,* April 16, 1953, p. 6.

[23] *"Clarks Fork," The Cody Enterprise,* April 01, 1954, p. 8.

[24] ."Clarks Fork," *The Cody Enterprise,* May 01, 1958, Sec. 2, p. 7.

[25] "Clark 3 NE, Wyoming, Period of Record Monthly Climate Summary," Western Regional Climate Center, (wrcc.dri.edu/cgi-bin/cliRECtM.pl?wyclar).

[26] "Clark 3 NE, Wyoming, Period of Record Monthly Climate Summary," Western Regional Climate Center, (wrcc.dri.edu/cgi-bin/cliGSCStT.pl?wyclar).

[27] Dennis H. Knight, *Mountains and Plains - The Ecology of Wyoming Landscapes,* (New Haven and London, Yale University Press, 1994), p. 27.

[28] *Park County Enterprise,* February 1, 1911, p. 2.

[29] "Clark," *Park County Enterprise,* November 27, 1912, p. 4.

[30] "Chance," *The Picket-Journal,* January 26, 1921, p. 8.

[31] "Paint Creek," *The Park County Herald,* February 11, 1925, p. 4.

[32] "Paint Creek," *Cody Enterprise,* January 12, 1927, p. 9.

[33] "Clarks Fork," *The Cody Enterprise,* January 13, 1937, p. 6.

[34] "Lower Clarks Fork," *The Cody Enterprise,* January 27, 1943, p. 6.

[35] "High Winds Damage Homes, Other Property," "Clark's Fork News by Mrs. Walter Teichert, *The Powell Tribune,* January 24, 1967, p. 2.

[36] "Wind Rips Up Clarks Fork Highway Pavement," *The Powell Tribune,* February 22, 1972, p. 1.

[37] An Unforgettable Wind Storm Lashed Clark Area," "Tree Falls on Man In Storm," "New $50,000 House Leveled By Fire," *The Powell Tribune,* January 17, 1974, p. 1 and "Bus Driver Hurt as Vehicle Flips," *The Powell Tribune,* January 17, 1974, p. 14.

[38] "105 Mile-An-Hour Wind Lifts Roof Off Clark School on Friday," *The Powell Tribune,* November 6, 1984, p. 1.

4
Some Events in Clark Area History

1806 –1807 = John Colter spends winter in Clarks Fork Canyon

1807-1808 = George Druillard travels through area (winter)

1850's – Pat O'Hara begins living on Pat O'Hara creek

1877 – Chief Joseph evades U.S. Army by passing through Clark (Sep)

1878 – Bannock – Miles battle on the Clarks Fork and John Chapman here to establish ranch (Sep)

1890 – Henry, John, and Affie Chapman first to prove up on their land (Jan, May & Dec)

1891 – Clark post office established on Warren Sirrine ranch (Feb 27)

1895 – Sirrine School established

1901 – Bennett Creek School established on R. L. Davis ranch

1902 – John Perry Allison buys Chapman ranch (Jan)
      Post Office moved to Barber ranch and Alice Barber appointed postmaster (May 21)
      Paint Creek School District created (Oct 14)

1904 – Warren Oscar Sirrine, first postmaster of Clark, dies in Chico, California (Nov 1)

1905 – Engineers arrive from Sheridan to survey a planned ditch out of Clarks Fork Canyon (Apr)

1906 – Luce & Benedict's reservoir began (Feb)
      Luce reservoir completed (Sep)

1909 – David Parker appointed postmaster of Clark (April)
      Mrs. Marinda Weathermon dies and is first burial in Bennett Buttes Cemetery (Aug 15)

1909 – Lindquist Store opens its doors (Sep)

1910 – Dredge Ford Bridge and Hopkins Bridge completed (Jul)
      Clark gets a voting place (Jul)

1911 – Work finally begins on the Hubbard Canal on Chapman Bench (March)
      Oscar Lindquist appointed postmaster (Apr 12)
      Line Creek School District established (May)

Post Office moved from Parker Ranch to Lindquist Brothers Store (Jun 1)
Florence Card dies of scarlet fever from tick bite (Jun 5)
William Decker, 19 months old, of Paint Creek, drowns in Clarks Fork (Oct 13)

1912 – Lawsuit filed against Clarks Fork Irrigation Co. for Hubbard Canal failure (Mar 23)

1913 - Bennett Buttes Cemetery Association has cemetery surveyed and lots plotted (May)
Hubbard Canal lawsuit reaches no settlement (Jun 18)
Articles of Incorporation of Bennett Buttes Cemetery Assoc. signed (Nov 18)
Lindquist Brothers move into new store building (Dec)

1914 – Charles B. Hubbard, early Clark pioneer, dies in Cody (Jun 4)
James Hogan, pioneer rancher, dies from a fall (Jul 20)
Pat O'Hara visits Mrs. Manuel Hoffman before leaving area (Sep)

1915 – Dedication dance held at new Pioneer School (Jan 27)

1916 – Gus Barth and Joseph Ganguet buy John Chapman and Martin Jobe ranch (late Mar)
Ernest Arnold arrested for the January murder of Charles Steiner (Mar 21)
Patent for 40 acres for Bennett Buttes Cemetery issued (May 3)

1917 – Rev. Daniel Spencer McCorkle arrives as first area permanent minister (Apr 1)

1918 – Mary Ellen Coates Sirrine, Clark's second postmaster, dies in Billings (Mar 20)
Alice Rosalie Card dies helping father gather coal in cave-in (Mar 23)
Edgar Vickery, first area WWI casualty, dies in France (Oct 15)

1919 – James N. Hunter, Bennett Creek rancher, dies of blood poisoning (May 27)

1920 – Henry A. Luce, Paint Creek area pioneer, dies in San Diego (Feb 10)

1921 – Dollie Brown Petit, early Paint Creek resident, dies in childbirth (Dec 1)

1922 – Telephone line between Cody and R. G. Hopkins ranch completed (Aug)

1922 – Pat O'Hara School dedicated (Nov 3)

1923 – Solomon F. Weathermon, Civil War veteran passes away (Nov 23)
Andy Chapman, pioneer rancher, passes away in Red Lodge (Dec 13)

1924 – Bennett Creek Sheep Company reorganized as a Wyoming corporation (Jan)

1924 – Bennett Creek and Paint Creek Schools were standardized by (May)

1926 – New road to Hopkins Bridge begun (Jun)

1928 – Edgar Stinson shot by Billy Brough (Mar 7)
　　　　Work begins to replace old Dredge Ford Bridge with Marlin Bridge (Mar)
　　　　Mrs. Sarah Frances Cochrane, early Pioneer teacher, dies (Apr 1)

1929 – Crossing by threshing machine destroys new Marlin Bridge (Aug)
　　　　Clarks Fork Bridge at the Hopkins place rebuilt (Oct)

1930 – Clark Justice of the Peace, Charles A. C. Snow dies (Feb 14)
　　　　Bruce Oliver Smith accidentally shot and killed (Mar 22)
　　　　Residents form Clark Fork Community Association (Mar 30)
　　　　Newton H. Castle, Clark rancher, dies on trip to Spokane, Washington (Apr 18)
　　　　Harold Howard Schmidt, 11, dies in gun accident (Sep 12)
　　　　Resolute Oil Co. in Badger Basin strikes gas deposit at 8250 feet (Nov 20)

1931 – Resolute Oil Co. sets record as deepest well ever drilled with cable tools in Rocky
　　　　　　Mountains at 8343 feet (Mar)
　　　　Verne Elmer Smith accidentally shot and killed (Mar 15)
　　　　Resolute Oil well reaches 8670 ft. (Jun)
　　　　David Gloeckner, Pioneer area sheepman, passes away (Jun 28)
　　　　Old-timer Matt Wagner passes away (Oct 7)
　　　　Miss Mary Cravens, former Bennett Creek School teacher, dies in Fromberg (Oct 28)
　　　　Joseph and Josephine Brown celebrate 50th wedding anniversary (Dec 4)

1932 – Mrs. Orpha (Walter) Braten, early Paint Creek pioneer, dies (May 17)
　　　　Edwin Manning, early Paint Creek rancher, dies of a heart attack (Nov 22)

1933 – Mrs. Eliza (Frank) Marlin dies in Powell hospital (Jan 10)
　　　　Nathan Chance, early Chance pioneer, dies (Jan 10)
　　　　Walter Frank Marlin sells his ranch and moves back to Texas (May)
　　　　George Heald and Frank Clark buy Two-Dot Ranch (Aug)
　　　　John W. Chapman, pioneer rancher, dies in Red Lodge (Dec 18)

1934 – Robert Green Hopkins, early Clarks Fork rancher, dies (Jan 22)
　　　　William Bryant Nutting, pioneer rancher, dies (Nov 28)

1935 – Taggart Construction Co. get contract for Skull Creek Road (Apr)
　　　　Taggart Brothers buy Two-Dot Ranch (Jul)

1936 – Area gets heavy snow and 44 below zero temperatures (Feb 24)
　　　　Jean Hogan, 13-year old, dies of scarlet fever (Jun 20)
　　　　Clark School gets a school bus with Frank Thull as driver (Sep)

1937 – William O'Mara, becomes first fatality in the Badger Basin oil field (Dec 1)
　　　　William H. Schmidt, early rancher, dies (Dec 18)
　　　　John W. Harkin, early rancher, dies (Dec 21)

1938 – Andrew Madison, Pioneer area sheepman, dies (Jan 19)
　　　　Marion Poke Stine, old-timer, dies (Sep 13)

William Holthues family moves to Thermopolis (Nov)
Lambert Holthues family moves to Edon, Ohio (Dec)

1939 – Clarence Sirrine, early resident of Pioneer area, dies (Feb 3)
Temperatures drop to –26 during the week (Feb 7)
Earl Durand manhunt comes to Little Rocky Creek in Clark (Mar 27)
Owen Chauncey Bevelhymer, early Paint Creek rancher, found dead in his cabin (Aug 21)
Ordelia Lucas Simpson, early Line Creek resident, dies in California (Dec 2)

1940 – Oscar Lindquist retires as Clark postmaster after serving 29 years (Jan 31)
Clark post office moves to Gallentine ranch with Hulda Gallentine as postmaster (Feb 1)
Contract signed for REA project to bring electricity into Clarks Fork Valley (Sep)
Gerald Glen Briner, 2, drowns in Bennett Creek (Sep 24)
William Holthues, Clark rancher beginning in 1921, dies in Thermopolis (Oct 14)
Frank Badura family buys Cantrell ranch and moves from Loup City, Nebraska (Nov 1)
Alva F. Marney, Clark rancher since 1928, dies (Nov 11)
Granville (George) Berry, stage driver, and Bennett Creek rancher, dies (Nov 19)
Post Office established at Badger Basin store with Mrs. Leo Althoff is postmaster (Dec)

1941 – REA installs electric meters in homes without yard poles. (Apr)
Mrs. Ruth (A. D.) Wilkinson, former Line Creek resident, dies (Jul 13)
Mr. and Mrs. William G. Brough observe 60th wedding anniversary (Oct 5)
George F. Baker, Paint Creek rancher, dies in Cheyenne hospital (Nov 13)

1942 - Catholic Church services conducted at Line Creek schoolhouse by Father Kimmet (Mar)
Taggarts purchase George Heald Ranch holdings and leases (Aug)
Eliza Josephine Brown, early Paint Creek homesteader, dies in Livingston (Aug 31)

1943 - Alvin Bosley, early Paint Creek area rancher, for more than 25 years, dies (Feb 14)
Emerson Bunn, early Clark homesteader and rancher, dies (Feb 16)
Oscar Lindquist, storeowner and former postmaster, dies in Laurel (Feb 18)
Smith Mine disaster at Bearcreek casts gloom over the Clarks Fork valley (Feb 27)
Gordon A. Kneisley, former Paint Creek rancher, dies (Apr 14)
Badura brothers build a big potato cellar using logs from Bald Ridge (Aug)
Mrs. Anna E. Lowmiller dies (Aug 30)
Gerald Glen Briner, 19-month-old son of George Briner, drowns in Bennett Creek (Sep 24)
Sixth well in Badger Basin was brought in at 8600 feet (01 Dec)
Peter Johnson, early Line Creek rancher, dies (Dec 23)

1944 – Eldon Denney and Elmer Bunn auto crash takes down span of Marlin Bridge (Feb 16)
Walter Braten, early pioneer, dies (Mar 19)
Marlin Bridge reopens to traffic (Mar 22)
Peter O. Simpson, area pioneer, celebrates his 91st birthday (May 14)
Harry Grant Simpson, early Pioneer area rancher, dies (May 19)
Two-Dot Company divided into 2000 shares incorporates (May 4)
Joe Harkin fatally injured in Badger Basin boiler explosion (Nov 23)

1945 – Stove at Badger Basin pumping plant explodes and destroys building (Jan 29)
   Two 4-H Clubs, a boys' and a girls', were organized at the Pioneer School (Feb 24)
   Possibility of a road through Clarks Fork Canyon discussed in Cody (Mar 19)
   Clark area donates $221 to the Red Cross
   Red Cross Home Nursing class organized at the Clark School (Apr 20)
   Carl Carlson's barn, sheds, and corrals destroyed by fire (May 25)
   Frank Badura's kerosene refrigerator explodes and burns house down (Jul 17)
   Hopkins Bridge near Paint Creek damaged by two heavy oil trucks (Aug 4)
   Henry Thull, 39, dies in Billings hospital (Nov 4)

1946 – Work starts on repairing Hopkins Bridge (Jan 2)
   William Platte Thompson, 65, dies at old Fred Schmidt ranch ((Jan 14)
   William G. Brough, 92, former Paint Creek rancher, dies (Mar 16)
   Edward Thornton Fuson, 68, long-time Clark rancher passes away (Apr 19)
   Northern Pacific No. 8 well in Badger Basin claims well production record
        at 8,476 feet (Jun 5)
   Mrs. Mary (George) Pointer passes away (Sep 16)
   Drilling in Badger Basin concludes for the winter (Nov 6)
   Clarks Fork Oil Corporation forms in Badger Basin (Dec 14)

1947 – Leo Athoff home in Badger Basin badly damaged by gas explosion (Jan 16)
   Cody meeting consolidates Clark and Line Creek Schools after school year (Jan 17)
   Body of R. H. McHenry found by haystack in Sand Coulee (Feb 15)
   Miss Alice Moore, 73, former Pioneer and Paint Creek School teacher, dies (Mar 15)
   George W. Pointer, Clark rancher, passed away in his sleep (Apr 7)
   Miss Wilda McLaughlin marries Richard Hoefer (Jun 15)
   Former Line Creek School building moves to Clark after consolidation (mid –Jul)
   Electricity current turned on in Clark (early Dec)

1948 – Thomas J. Davenport, 92, early 1900's Paint Creek area rancher, dies (Mar 14)
   Clark school reopens after three weeks closure due to snow-blocked roads (Mar 17)
   Emma Lindquist, 84, former storekeeper, dies in Laurel (Apr 8)
   Free vaccination clinics scheduled in Clark and Pioneer for students (Dec 9)

1949 - Mail deliveries at Clark light due to heavy snowstorms across Wyoming (Jan 12)
   School closed most of the week due to snowbound roads (Feb 9)
   Elmarie Badura marries David Denney (Apr 23)
   James R. Owens, Line Creek rancher, dies (Jun 13)
   Irene Simpson Hogan, early Clark resident, dies (Jul 17)
   Peter Oscar Simpson, early Line Creek resident, dies in California (Dec 1)

1950 – Albert DeForrest Wilkinson, early Line Creek resident, dies (Jan 8)
   Alphia Chapman, former owner of Two-Dot ranch, dies (Feb 14)
   Wind and blowing snow cause travel problems through Sand Coulee (May 1)
   Clark Post Office moved to Lindquist ranch; Florence Lindquist postmaster (mid Sep)
   Pole setting job completed on Paint Creek to bring in electricity (Oct 13)
   Mr. and Mrs. Vernon R. Gallentine celebrate their 50th wedding anniversary (Nov 21)

1951 – Oscar Olson, early Clark homesteader, dies (Jan 19)
      Harold Close sells his ranch on Paint Creek to George Niemi (Feb)
      Chris Schmidt ranch sold to John Eckerman (Feb)
      Steve Torczon family moves back to Clark from Wheatland (Feb)
      Joseph C. Brown, early pioneer of Paint Creek area, dies in Livingston (Feb 21)
      Harold Close buys Norris Gallentine and Dennis Warren ranches (Mar 15)
      Walter Teichert family moves from Badger Basin to Clark (Mar 15)
      Mrs. William (Antje) Holthues dies in Thermopolis (Apr 4)
      Allen Mays family moves to farm near Burlington (Apr 19)
      Norris Gallentine family moves to former May property on Clarks Fork (Apr 19)
      Belfry high school bus was wrecked near the Norris Gallentine ranch (May 11)
      Sabra Marler Hardee, early Paint Creek resident, dies (Jul 4)
      Lena Hogan Marler, early Paint Creek resident, dies (Jul 17)
      Elisha Mosher Clark, early Pioneer area rancher, dies (Dec 15)

1952 – Vernon Gallentine ranch sold (May 25)
      John E. Ricketts, early Clark homesteader, dies in Renton, Washington (Nov 25)

1953 – Line Creek Bridge closed for needed repairs (Jan 8)
      Mrs. Emily (Peter) Johnson, early Line Creek homesteader, dies (Feb 13)
      Much needed work done on Hopkins Bridge (30 Mar)
      Mr. and Mrs. Pete Althoff take over operation of Badger Basin store (Apr 16)
      No school at Clark for three days due to snow blocked roads (Apr 16)
      Resolute Oil Company closes Badger Basin refinery (Jul 1)
      Frank Leslie Clark, early Pioneer area rancher, dies in Billings (Aug 1)
      Russell David Russell, early Line Creek resident, dies (Oct 3)
      Our Lady of the Valley Catholic Church holds first mass (Dec 25)

1954 – Mrs. Emma Garrett Bosley, early Paint Creek resident, dies (Feb 20)
      Clark School wins annual Park County Rural Track and Field Day (May)
      Clark School began serving hot lunches prepared by Mrs. Julia Gairrett (Oct)
      Our Lady of the Valley Church dedicated by Bishop Newell of Cheyenne (Oct 6)

1955 – William H. Fouse, early Pioneer resident and Park County Commissioner, dies (Jan 14)
      Alex Wells, long-time Clark resident, dies (Apr 18)
      Jake Bevelhymer, Paint Creek resident since 1901, dies (Aug 25)
      Frank J. Thull, Clark rancher since 1933, dies in Red Lodge (Sep 8)
      Frank O. Sparhawk, early forest ranger and Clark homesteader, dies in Ohio (Sep 10)
      Clarks Fork fire blazes untamed with over 2,000 acres burned (Sep 15)

1956 – State Game and Fish announce plans to relocate Cody fish hatchery (Jan 5)
      Gustave Hallen, Clark resident since 1926, dies (Feb 7)
      Felix Hoff buys the late Jake Bevelhymer's ranch (Feb 16)
      Explosion destroys Badger Basin office but no one injured (Apr 10)
      David M. Simpson, early Pioneer area rancher, dies (Apr 10)
      Mrs. Augusta (William G) Brough, 94, early Paint Creek pioneer, dies (Jun 30)
      Repair and remodeling work underway at Clark School (Aug 9)

Edgar Simpson, early Pioneer area rancher, dies (Aug 19)
Benjamin Martin Eckloe, Clark homesteader, dies (Sep 5)
Repair work being done on Line Creek Bridge (Nov 1)
Roy Cecil "Shorty" Lowmiller, Clark prospector, dies in mountains (abt Nov 13)

1957 – Clark School tops annual Park County Rural Track and Field Day in Cody (Mary 4)
Harry Clark, Line Creek rancher from 1936, dies in Bridger (May 26)
David William Miller, 71, Clark Canyon ranch hand, dies (Sep 23)
Casper College Mountaineers help string power line across Clarks Fork Canyon (Oct 12)

1958 – Bids let for 9.4 miles of all-weather road from Clark to Montana border (Mar 13)
Clark School wins annual Park County Rural Track and Field Day (May 2)
Mrs. Betsy Elizabeth (Edwin) Fuson, early Clark resident, dies (May 13)
Thomas Bert Stidham, early Paint Creek area resident, dies in Helena (May 20)
Orville Richardson, Clark resident, dies (May 20)
George W. Johnston, Pioneer area farmer beginning in 1902, dies (Jun 21)
Dennis Warren, Clark resident and school bus driver, dies (Oct 5)
Peter Althoff, area farmer and operator of Badger Basin store, dies (Oct 24)

1959 – Clarence A. Pearson, Pioneer area rancher from 1911, dies (Feb 24)
Mrs. Lucy A. (Emerson) Bunn, 1909 resident of Clark, dies (Mar 26)
Clark School wins annual Park County Rural Track and Field Day (May 2)
Work progressing on Clark-Cody road and two Clarks Fork River bridges (Jul 23)
Cody-Clark road open for traffic and bridges complete (Aug 20)
Mrs. Hannah (Clarence) Pearson, 1911 Pioneer area resident, dies (Aug 21)
Wrightis W. Hardee, early Clark resident, dies in Thermopolis (Sep)
George Millard Heald, early Paint Creek rancher since 1909, dies (Oct 2)

1960 – Clark School wins Rural Track Meet in Cody (May 14)
Quick Bridges over Clarks Fork River dedicated (May 28)
Bids let for 4.09 miles of spur road into Clark from Highway 120 (Jun 23)
Mrs. Julia Smith Gairrett, Clark resident since 1937, dies (Jun 23)
15 acres Line Creek put under control (Jul 17)
Vernon R. Gallentine, former Clark resident, dies (early Aug)
Ada Eckerman, takes lunch preparation at Clark School (Sep 01)
Fred A. Bunn, life-long resident of Clark and Cody areas, dies (Oct 10)
Mrs. Hattie Border, widow of Henry Sirrine, early area pioneer, dies in Calif. (Oct 22)
Mrs. Carrie B. (Eli) Vickery, Clark resident in 1893, dies in Billings (Dec 2)
Edward Lindquist, pioneer resident of Clark, dies in Cody (Dec 11)

1961 – John E. Simpson, longtime Paint Creek rancher since 1905, dies in Cody (Feb 17)
Mamie Goff Feyhl, Line Creek teacher in 1921- 22, dies in Cody (Jun 3)
Last stretch of road from Clark to Montana border dedicated (Oct 12)
John Henry Gairrett, Clark rancher from 1937 to 1960, dies in Billings (Nov 30)

1964 – Emma Hasselstrom Simpson, Paint Creek area resident & correspondent, dies (Jan 28)
Thomas Andrew Marler, early Paint Creek rancher and later at Skull Creek, dies (Apr 14)

Martin G. Gloeckner, former Pioneer area sheepman, dies (Jul 27)

1967 - Line Creek Bridge collapses under weight of a herd of cattle (Jan)
      Clark post office discontinued (10 Feb)
      Paul Travis gets contract to deliver mail to Clark from Belfry (Feb)

1968 – Line Creek Bridge is rebuilt and opened again (May 1)

1969 – New Clark School building built
      Eric Alanko, early Line Creek rancher, dies (May 29)

1970 – Clark's Fork Fish Hatchery dedicated (Jun 5)
      Clark School consolidates with Powell
      Edna Mae Smith takes over lunch at Clark School (Sep)
      Old Clark School building torn down

1971 – Leopold C. Bratrsovsky, early Line Creek homesteader, dies in Red Lodge (9 May)

1972 – Ernest Gordon, Paint Creek area resident, dies in tractor rollover accident (Apr 8)
      Emma Clark Carlson, early Pioneer area resident, dies (Jul 11)
      Walter Greenfield Cochrane, early Clark rancher, dies (Nov 9)

1973 – Wilbur Emerson Bunn, early Clark rancher, dies (Oct 5)
      Clark Fire District created by Park Co. Board of Commissioners (Oct 10)
      Bennett Creek Baptist Church dedicated (Nov 25)

1974 – Jesse Earl Bunn, early Clark resident, dies (Jul 10)

1975 – Samuel P. Fouse, early Pioneer area resident, dies (Jan 21)
      Raymond F. Marney, Clark rancher since 1931, dies (Mar 18)

1976 – Beulah Robinson Fouse, Pioneer area resident, dies (Jan 16)
      Former Lindquist store burns down (Spring)
      Carl H. Carlson, early Pioneer area rancher, dies (Nov 25)
      George H. Niemi, Paint Creek area rancher, dies (Dec 29)
      Phyllis Briner Alanko, Clark resident, dies in automobile accident (Dec 30)

1977 – Oscar Noble, Clark rancher, dies (Aug 6)
      Ralph L. Fouse, early Pioneer area rancher, dies (Oct 26)
      Ethel Brown Bunn, early Paint Creek and Clark pioneer, dies (Dec 31)

1978 – Don Oscar Fraker, Pioneer area rancher, dies (Oct 8)

1979 – Dennis Torczon, Pioneer area rancher, dies (Dec)

1981 – Helen Brough Braten Baker, long-time Paint Creek and Clark resident, dies (Sep 2)
      Mail from Belfry terminated – Ken Mees begins to deliver from Powell (Oct 31)

1982 – Virginia Bunn Teichert, long-time area resident, dies (Jul 12)

1983 – Leo Paul Althoff, former owner Badger Basin store, dies (1 Jul)

1984 – Harold Norman Close, early Paint Creek area rancher, dies (Aug 29)
    Edward Pillsbury Pearson, early Pioneer area resident, dies in Oceanside, CA (Dec 24)

1985 – Dominic George Badura, Pioneer area rancher, dies (Jan 5)
    Bennett Buttes Cemetery District created by Park Co. Board of Commissioners (May 21)

1986 – Bronson D. Tolman, Clark rancher and historian, dies (Oct 3)

1987 – Gustave M. Forsman, early oil man and Clark rancher, dies (Jan 2)

1988 – First Annual Clark Reunion held (May 14)

1989 – John Alfred Badura, Pioneer area rancher, dies (Jun 11)

1990 – Florence Neallis Lindquist, last Clark postmaster, dies in Billings (Oct 10)

1991 - Wilbur (Woody) G. Connett, 64, Clark resident, dies (Oct 23)
    Terry Eugene Smith, former Clark resident, dies (Nov 28)

1992 – Maude Wright Tolman, long-time Clark resident, dies (May 23)
    Clark-Pioneer Recreation Center completed (June)

1993 – Norris G. Gallentine, former Clark rancher, dies (Jun 23)
    Leon E. and Virginia B. Sprinkle, Clark residents, die in automobile accident (Aug 31)

1995 – Joana Stalia Badura, Pioneer area rancher, dies (Aug 29)
    Rev. Kurt McNabb becomes permanent pastor of the Bennett Creek Church (Oct)
    John Paul Ranschou, Pioneer area rancher, dies with children in plane crash (Nov 23)
    Rev. Kurt McNabb becomes permanent pastor of Bennett Creek Church (Oct)
    Bennett Creek Church begins its monthly 55-Plus Dinner Program (Dec 14)

1996 – Robert B. Badura, Pioneer area rancher, dies (1 Apr)
    Lloyd E. Thiel, Clark rancher, dies (Apr 19)
    Arthur J. Hoefer, Clark rancher, dies (Dec 18)

1997 – Mary Helen Dahlem Daly, long-time Clark resident, dies (May 1)
    Margaret Thull Torczon, long-time Pioneer resident, dies (Sep 8)

1998 – Richard Theodore Hoefer, Clark rancher, dies (Feb 1)

1999 – Roy Shiffert Daly, 100, Clark rancher, dies (Apr 20)
    Walter Roscoe Hoffman, early Blaine Creek resident, dies in Cody (May 13)

2000 – Hulda Siqveland Gallentine, former Clark postmaster, dies in Livingston (Feb 26)

2001 – Early evening thunderstorm causes Line Creek to flood with widespread damage (Jul 10)
        John George Eckerman, Clark rancher since 1951, dies (Nov 10)

2002 – Ray Bunn, former Clark and Badger Basin resident, dies in Billings (Feb 2)
        Addie Hemmerly Bunn, former Clark and Badger Basin resident, dies in Billings (Sep 5)

2003 – Helen Doyle Wayman, former Clark resident, dies in Red Lodge (Jan 22)
        New Bennett Creek Church building dedicated (Mar 9)
        Deep Lake Fire starts threatening Clark and consuming more than 6800 acres (Jul 16)
        Carmel of the Immaculate Heart of Mary Monastery dedicated in Pioneer (Oct 15)
        Margaret Elise Weathermon Bailey, 83, early Clark resident, dies in Sun City, AZ (Dec 21)

2004 – Ethel May Schmidt Stidham, 99, former long-time Clark resident, dies (Jan 13)

Line Creek School students along Clarks Fork River south of the Line Creek Bridge:
Violet Davis Holthues, Geraldine Green, Marjorie Walters, Neal Holthues, Arthur
Green, Marian Walters, Eileen Jackson, Florence Cantrell, Asa Cantrell, Everett
Cantrell, Cecil Cantrell, Ted Walters, Gerald Spaulding, and Ted Miller. Photo
taken on February 24, 1933, courtesy of Iva and Roberta Bunn Gairrett.

5
Early Visitors

Archaeological Evidence

The first residents and visitors to the Clark and surrounding geographic areas did not have an easy life. Agriculture was not an option for these early prehistoric peoples whose ancestors had crossed over from Asia with the receding of the last glaciers approximately 14,500 years ago and slowly spread out into warmer terrains to the south. [1]

A search of published archaeological articles reveals a lack of documentation for early man sites in the Clark area. Either none have been found, or if found, they have not been published.

Site reports and articles do exist for several sites in areas to the south, east and west not too distant from Clark. One was found near Worland, which contained mammoth remains, spear points and butchering tools which was dated approximately 11,200 years ago. This is the earliest date so far discovered in the Big Horn Basin. [2]

Another location dating about 9,000 years ago, called the Horner site, was found east of Cody. The first excavations there were conducted from 1949 through 1953 by archae-ologists from Princeton University and the Smithsonian Institution. Later excavations were done in 1987 and 1988 by the University of Wyoming, which revealed more bison bones and Eden and Scottsbluff projectile points. [3]

A third important archaeological site for dating early man's presence in the Big Horn Basin is Mummy Cave. Located 40 feet above the North Fork of the Shoshone River east of Yellowstone National Park, this rock shelter site contained 38 occupation levels dating from approximately 9200 to as recently as 300 years ago. The site received its name from an ancient hunter whose mummified remains were found in one of the levels dated at 1300 years old. [4]

The closest discoveries to this area are the Dead Indian Creek site found in the Sunlight Basin just west of the Clarks Fork Canyon, and the Two Dot Flats site located near the base of Dead Indian Hill on the Two Dot Ranch.

The Dead Indian Creek site was a winter camp site which yielded dates of 4400, 4200 and 3800 years ago and contained 565 complete and fragmentary points, scrapers, knives, stone drills and grinding stones. [5] Archaeologists working there during the summers of 1969, 1971 and 1972 found bone remains of 17 mammals, 3 birds, and 3 invertebrates, which had been utilized as food. [6] While three big game species were present – big horn sheep, mule deer, and pronghorn antelope – the percentage of bone material indicated that the mule deer was the prevalent food source for the camp. [7]

The Two Dot Flats site was discovered in 1989 by Wyoming State archaeologists who were investigating the area prior to road construction on Dead Indian Pass. It consisted of what was presumed to be a prehistoric drive line complex containing two main lines and several smaller ones making up a system which extended approximately two miles. The arrangement of the stones in the drive lines indicated that man-made and natural topographical features were integrated during its construction. [8]

These last two sites indicate a high probability that early hunting and gathering peoples were familiar with the Clark area, and most certainly had passed through it on journeys to other areas. The archaeological record for more recent times is much clearer with tipi rings, shell beads, arrow, and other projectile points, as well as a variety of other artifacts have been found over the last hundred years throughout the Clark area. [9] Most of these findings can be attributed with more certainty to later peoples such as the Crow who were known to be in this area.

Mountain Crows or Absaroka

When the first mountain men came into the Clark area in the early part of the nineteenth century, it was already well known to the Mountain Crows or Absaroka tribe who claimed the Clarks Fork valley as part of their hunting ground.

The Crow people trace their ancestry through oral tradition to a group of woodland people who at one time lived in present-day Minnesota or Wisconsin and migrated westward. By 1000 A.D. they had settled into a farming life along the Missouri River in present-day North Dakota, living in villages of dome-shaped earth lodges. Here they became known as the Hidatsa. [10]

During the 1500's small groups of these farming Hidatsa began to spend their winter months hunting out on the plains. By the end of that century some of these groups were traveling further away, and eventually settled and farmed on the river bottoms of what is now eastern Montana. Later, after they acquired a sizeable inventory of horses through trade and theft from the Shoshones, they gave up farming, but maintained ties with their former Hidatsa kin by trading meat and hides to them in exchange for beans, squash and corn and other food crops. [11]

In the early 1700s other Hidatsa hunters also left their villages and migrated west into the upper Missouri River areas of present-day Montana. By 1750 the separation from their farming Hidatsa kinsmen was complete. Both hunting groups took on a new tribal identity calling themselves – Absaroka, meaning "Children of the Large-beaked Bird" in their Hidatsa language. Other tribes who came in contact with them said they were smart and crafty as a bird, possibly a raven. When referring to them in sign language, they would simulate the flapping of bird wings in flight. Interpretation of this hand sign by later explorers was "crow," and thus the Absaroka people became known as the Crows. [12]

The group, which settled along the Yellowstone River and its tributaries, became the Mountain Crows, and the other further to the north became known as the River Crows. These two groups interacted with each other and became a significant force on the Plains by the late 1700's. They cooperated to defend their rich hunting territory against Shoshone from the south, Blackfeet from the north and Sioux hunters from the east.

They gained material wealth by exchanging hides, horses, guns, and tools with these same tribes and others traveling as far west into present-day Idaho and Oregon. Later as an increasing number of fur traders came into their territory, they exchanged beaver, otter and other skins for steel axes, awls, and knifes, as well as beads, flints, smoking tobacco, musket balls, and powder. [13]

John Colter

The fur trade that flourished on the upper Missouri and Yellowstone Rivers and in the mountains to the south followed in the wake of the Lewis and Clark expedition of 1804 through 1806. John Colter, one of the members of this expedition, was the first non-Indian, of which there is definite record, known to have explored the Big Horn Basin.

In early August 1806 as the expedition was on its return trip to St. Louis, it encountered two trappers, Joseph Dixon and Forrest Hancock from Illinois, along the Missouri River. Colter requested permission from Lewis and Clark to terminate his employment with them and to join the two men on their fur trapping endeavors. At the Mandan villages the trapping partnership of the three men started out with about twenty traps, tools for canoe building, ammunition and other equipment and headed back up the Missouri toward the Yellowstone. [14]

From information received from J. K. Rollinson, an early forest ranger in the Sunlight area, the trappers spent the most of the winter on the Clarks Fork of the Yellowstone. Near the mouth of the canyon they "had constructed a combination lean-to and cabin by erecting two walls against the side of a cliff so as to take advantage of a recess in the rock." [15]

As the winter dragged on, Colter became increasing bored with his companions and their temporary shelter. He left both to travel up the canyon and crossed into the Sunlight Basin from where he continued to explore and trap on his own. He walked south to the present Shoshone River north of present-day Cody and saw the sulphur hot springs along the river that he named the "Stinkingwater." [16]

From here his travel route is not definite. One thought is that he walked south of the Owl Creek Mountains then turned west arriving in the Jackson Hole area and then walked north through Yellowstone and back along the Shoshone to the Big Horn River to Fort Manual Lisa.

Another version of his epic walk suggests he traveled east from the Cody area to Yellowstone, then south to Jackson Hole turning east to present-day Riverton before turning north through the Big Horn Basin following the Big Horn River back to Fort Manuel Lisa. [17]

Upon his arrival in St. Louis in May 1810, Colter contacted William Clark. It is not known whether he drew a map for Clark or merely described his extensive travels, but the information that he related was the basis for a map published in 1814 by Clark and three other men, which would be useful to later travelers. [18]

George Drouillard

In the winter of 1807 George Drouillard, who had also been with Lewis and Clark, embarked himself on further explorations. He evidently followed much of Colter's route into the Sunlight Basin and south to the present-day Cody area, up Sage Creek, through Pryor Gap and down Pryor Creek to the Yellowstone River. Upon his return to St. Louis, he also provided Clark with confirming and supplemental information to what had been provided by Colter, which was used in Clark's map.[19]

The End of the Fur Trade

The rugged Rocky Mountains attracted hardy individuals who risked life and limb to suppl[] industry dictated by fashion – the fad for beaver hats in Europe and the eastern United St[] Muskrats, river otter, and deerskins were also highly in demand. Trappers hunted mountain b[] more for food than for their robes, which were too bulky to be transported, by land to mark[] St. Louis. As the number of beaver declined drastically by the 1840's, so did the fur trade. [20]

Pat O'Hara.
Photo by Mrs. Manuelle Hoffman in 1914,
courtesy of Jim Hoffman.

Pat O'Hara

While other trappers undoubtedly came through the Clark area, there is definite documentation of one who actually lived here. Pat O'Hara, a former trapper who was employed by the American Fur Company, came to the Clark area in the 1850's [21] and lived in a cave on the creek that was named for him. In 1913 he helped Frank Sparhawk, the Sunlight Forest Ranger, trap coyotes and related an early experience on the creek when Indians stole his horses. [22]

The following year in July of 1914 O'Hara stopped by the Blaine Creek ranch of Mrs. Manuelle Hoffman and her son, Walter, who was then three years old. He spent the day and night with the Hoffmans and told them that the area was becoming "too civilized," and that he was beginning a journey to Oregon. During his visit he related some earlier events in his own life, and these stores comprise most of the recorded information that historians have on this former mountain man. [23]

Mrs. Hoffman took two photographs of Pat O'Hara before he departed the following morning. She said that he had only a frying pan, coffee pot, blanket, and rain slicker on his horse. When she offered him some provisions for his trip, O'Hara accepted only some coffee, bade them good-bye, and rode away never to be heard from again.

In the 1950's Mrs. Hoffman wrote to Oregon authorities to learn of his death, as well as to Montana where he was known to have a niece. Neither state had a record of his death. [24]

Today Pat O'Hara Creek and Pat O'Hara Mountain are named for this early Clark area resident who was one of the last mountain men.

Pat O'Hara sitting on horseback with young Walter R. Hoffman.
1914 photo by Mrs. Manuelle Hoffman, courtesy of Jim Hoffman.

Chapter 5 notes:

[1] Brian Fagan, *The Great Journey - The Peopling of Ancient America,* (New York, Thames and Hudson Ltd., 1987), p. 138 - 144.

[2] Bob Edgar in *Buffalo Bill's Town in the Rockies;* other co-authors, Jeannie Cook, Lynn Johnson Houze, and Paul Fees, (Virginia Beach Virginia, Donning Company Publishers, 1996), p. 20.

[3] George C. Frison, *Prehistoric Hunters of the High Plains,* 2nd edition, (San Diego and New York, Academic Press, 1991), p. 62 - 66.   For an in-depth study of the archaeological findings of this early man site see: George C. Frison and Lawrence C. Todd, editors, *The Horner Site - The Type Site of the Cody Cultural Complex,* (San Diego, New York, Academic Press, Inc., 1987)

[4] Frison, *Prehistoric Hunters of the High Plains,* p. 67-69; Wilfred M. Husted, *Archaeology of Mummy Cave, An Introduction to Shoshonean Prehistory,* (National Park Service, Midwest Archaeology Center, Sp. Report #4 & Southeast Archaeological Center, Technical Report Series # 9, 2002), p. 1, 2, 29, and 114 and Edgar, p. 20.

[5] Frison, *Prehistoric Hunters of the High Plains,* p. 99; and George C. Frison and Danny N. Walker and others, *The Wyoming Archaeologist,* (Wyoming Archaeology Society, Inc., 27:1-2, Spring 1984), p. 1, 23, 28, 33-38.

[6] The mammals were: mule deer, bison, pronghorn, mountain sheep, black bear, wapiti, wolf, muskrat, porcupine, bush-tailed wood rat, long-tail vole, northern pocket gopher, Unita ground squirrel, red squirrel, snowshoe hare, cottontail rabbit and yellow-bellied marmot; birds: black-billed magpie, blue grouse, woodpecker or flicker; and 2 land snails and river mussels. Karen West Scott and Michael Wilson, "Dead Indian Creek Local Fauna," *The Wyoming Archaeologist,* (Wyoming Archaeologist Society, Inc., 27:1-2, Spring 1984), p. 51-62.

[7] John W. Fisher, Jr., "Medium-sized Artiodactyl Butchering and Processing," *The Wyoming Archaeologist,* (Wyoming Archaeology Society, Inc., 27:1-2, Spring 1984), p. 63 - 82.

[8] Daniel H. Eakin, "Results of a Class III Cultural Resource Inventory of the Route 296 Chief Joseph Highway, Dead Indian Pass - Wyoming 120," *Wyoming Highway Project Paea -1507 (20), Park County, Wyoming.* Report prepared for the Wyoming Highway Department by the Office of the Wyoming State Archaeologist, 1990; "A Prehistoric Stone Line Complex from Northwestern Wyoming," *The Wyoming Archaeologist,* (Wyoming Archaeology Society, Inc., 41:1, Spring 1997), p. 1-13.

[9] Some of the early archaeological finds in the Clark documented in newspaper accounts include: "Jack Spicer Finds Human Skull on Pat O'Hara Slide," *Cody Enterprise,* August 23, 1923, p. 1; "Andy Marler Finds A Fine Indian Relic," *Cody Enterprise,* July 23, 1924, p. 5; "Ancient Indian ovens Unearthed by Cody Farmer," *Cody Enterprise,* July 17, 1929, p. 1; "Human Foot Print in Paint Creek Rock," *Cody Enterprise,* June 08, 1932, p. 4; "Historians Mystified by Aged Skeletons," *Cody Enterprise,* July 16, 1953, p. 1.

[10] Frederick E. Hoxie, *The Crow,* (New York and Philadelphia, Chelsea Home Publishers, 1989), p. 23-31; Paul H. Carlson, *The Plains Indians,* (College Station, Texas A & M University Press, 1998), p. 33; Joseph Medicine Crow, *From the Heart of the Crow Country - The Crow Indians' Own Stories,* (New York, Orion Books, Crown Publishers, Inc., 1992), p. 2 and .David J. Wishart, *The Fur Trade of the American West 1807 - 1840,* (Lincoln and London, University of Nebraska Press, Bison Book Edition, 1992), p. 35-37.

[11] Ibid.

[12] Ibid.

[13] Ibid.

[14] Burton Harris, *John Colter - His Life in the Rockies,* (Lincoln and London, University of Nebraska

Press, Bison Book edition, 1993), p. 37.

[15] John Rollinson stated that in 1902 he had become acquainted with Dave Fleming, a man then in his late seventies. Fleming told Rollinson that he was the stepson of Hancock and that when he was 10 years old his stepfather had taken him to the mouth of the Clarks Fork Canyon on a camping trip and pointed out the exact spot where he, Colter, and Dixon had spent the winter. (Harris, p. 54 – 55).

[16] Harris, p. 55.

[17] Phil Roberts, "Lessons from the Fur Trade: Colonialism, 'Boom-and-Bust,' "and "A Trail to Somewhere Else," in Phil Roberts, editor, *Readings in Wyoming History*, (Laramie, Skyline West Press, 2000), p. 5- 6.

[18] Harris, p. 79-81.

[19] Harris, p. 87-89.

[20] David J. Wishart, *The Fur Trade of the American West 1807 – 1840,* (Lincoln and London, University of Nebraska Press, Bison Book Edition, 1992), p. 35-37. For other details accounts of this era, see: LeRoy R. Hafen, Editor, *Fur Traders, Trappers and Mountain Men of the Upper Missouri,* (Lincoln and London, University of Nebraska Press, Bison Book edition, 1995); LeRoy R. Hafen, Editor, Mountain *Men and Fur Traders of the Far West.* (Lincoln and London, University of Nebraska Press, Bison Book edition, 1982); and James H. Maguire, Peter Wild and Donald A. Barclay, editors, *A Rendezvous Reader – Tall, Tangled, and True Tales of the Mountain Men 1805 – 1850,* (Salt Lake City, University of Utah Press, 1997).

[21] John Rollinson, *Wyoming Cattle Trails*, (Caldwell, Idaho, Caxton Printers, Ltd., 1948), p. 152)

[22] "Old Timer Traps for Government," *Park County Enterprise,* December 24, 1913, p. 1.

[23] "O'Hara told the Hoffmans he had lived in a cave on Pat O'Hara Creek just above where the George Heald ranch buildings were located. Mrs. Hoffman had noticed the cave and wondered about its occupant.

"Even though sage brush six feet high concealed the entrance, some one discovered it. He had accumulated a nice assortment of pelts and was going to take them out one morning but as he moved the buffalo hide that served as his door, several arrows pierced the hide. He remained in the cave until dark and then crept away minus the pelts.

"Another time he and two other trappers stopped to camp on Bald Ridge. Noticing the deer were running - an indication that the Indians were on the move - O'Hara advised the others to leave their saddle cinched. They failed to heed his advice.

"The Indians appeared just as the trappers were ready to eat. One man's saddle came loose as he tried to flee, and he was killed.

"As O'Hara looked back, the second man's saddle turned because of the loose cinch, and he was killed also. Only O'Hara escaped.

"Once he became quite ill while escaping Indians with his partner. Knowing he could not continue, he lad down to die. His partner shot a deer and left it beside O'Hara as the last kindness he could show.

"The weather was hot, and the meat soured. When he finally felt hungry, he ate some of the tainted meat, which had a purgative effect. This, he felt, saved his life." *(Cody Enterprise,* June 22, 1961, p. 5).

[24] Ibid.

6
Nez Perce Evasion

In the late 1870's two major events in the Clark area ensured its mention in future Wyoming history books. Both involved the U. S. Army and fleeing Indian groups. The most famous incident involved Nez Perce tribesmen.

The Nez Perce Flee Idaho

In August 1877 Chief Joseph and members of the Nez Perce tribe fled from their reservation in western Idaho in an attempt to gain freedom in Canada. Pursued by U. S. Army troops, the Nez Perce crossed through Yellowstone Park, passing south of Cooke City, and then followed the Clarks Fork River down into the Sunlight Basin.

U. S. Army Colonel Samuel Sturgis [1] was ordered to bring two battalions under his command from Crow Agency to intercept the fleeing Nez Perce. With about 360 officers and troopers divided into six companies, he headed south with orders to stop the Indians, as they exited the Park by two possible routes – the Clarks Fork River or the North Fork of the Shoshone River. [2]

On September 5th, 1877 Sturgis reached the Clarks Fork Canyon and proceeded up river approximately two miles where his men camped and using grasshoppers as bait hooked many fine trout as a welcome food change.

Discovering that there was no trail through the canyon, Sturgis became impatient and worried that the Nez Perce were coming east by the other route. His Crow scouts related that the country to the north of their location was impassable, and there was no way that the Nez Perce could descend that way into the canyon. Hearing this and against the advice of some of his senior officers, Sturgis made the decision to head south to the Shoshone or "Stinking Water," as it was known, to intercept the advancing Indians. [3]

After sending some of his wagons and men back to Crow Agency for more provisions, Sturgis and his troops headed up Pat O'Hara Creek toward Skull Creek fifteen miles away where they camped on that night of September 8th.

The Escape Through Clark

In the meantime the Nez Perce passed into the Sunlight Basin seeking an avenue of escape down the Clarks Fork through the canyon to the valley floor beyond. Exactly how 700 people with about 2000 horses accomplished this tremendous feat is still not certain. The most widely postulated theory is that the Indians discovered the opening through the canyon rim known as Dead Indian Gulch, followed the narrow trail down to the canyon floor, forded the Clarks Fork River to its northern side, and continued down the canyon passing the Army's former camp. [4]

Col. Sturgis in the interim headed up the Stinking Water or North Fork of the Shoshone in hopes of encountering the large Nez Perce group. When this didn't occur, he decided to head back toward the Clarks Fork by crossing the divide to Dead Indian Creek where it was discovered that the Indians had passed ahead of them. Here came the realization that the Nez Perce had escaped his trap and were beyond the canyon heading down the Clarks Fork valley toward the Yellowstone River. [5]

The Army troops were amazed how the Indians had found an opening from the canyon rim and traveled through it with their baggage and horse herds. General Howard, Sturgis' commander in his notes about this event wrote, "The rocks on each side came so near together that two horses abreast could hardly pass." [6]

General Howard also added that Joseph and his followers "passed into a narrow and slippery canyon without exposing a man to the view of General (Col. then) Sturgis. The mouth of this canyon, which debouches into Clark's Valley, was not more than twenty feet across from high wall to high wall. And one may imagine the scene of cavalry, infantry, and pack mules crowding through it and admire the quick wit of an Indian who had the hardihood to try the experiment and break the almost impassable roadway." [7]

Other Possible Escape Routes

In more recent years three other possible routes have been advanced concerning the Nez Perce escape from the Sunlight Basin. One scenario is that they climbed to the top over Dead Indian Pass to Bald Ridge, moved north and then northwest down its slopes partially concealed from Sturgis' scouts. When they reached the valley floor near the upper end of Newmeyer Creek, they followed it northward to the Clarks Fork about two miles below the Canyon mouth.

Another route theorizes that the group crossed Bald Ridge heading southeast for a couple of miles then turned east and northeast reaching the head of Paint Creek, which they followed down to the Clarks Fork.

A third possible course for the Nez Perce was that they traveled south of Dead Indian Creek and crossed a divide leading to the drainage of Trail and Pat O'Hara Creeks. Here they would have headed east and north around the east side of Pat O'Hara Mountain before heading north to the Clarks Fork. [8]

The Flight Across Montana

Their determination to reach sanctuary in Canada took them north through the Clarks Fork valley through or near the present towns of Belfry, Bridger, Fromberg, Edgar, and Silesia. [9]

South of the present town of Laurel, they crossed the Yellowstone River and continued up into northern Montana to the Bear Paw Mountains where they had their climatic six-day battle with the Army. The confrontation ended with the surrender on October 5th of Chief Joseph and his people to Colonel Nelson A. Miles. Soon after the surrender approximately two hundred Nez Perce slipped away and escaped to Canada. [10]

Possible Nez Perce evasion route was through the Clarks Fork Canyon. 1915 photo of the Pearson family riding across Cyclone Bench in the Canyon, courtesy of Carol Briggs Joy and Dorothy Pearson Williams.

Chapter 6 Notes:

[1] Col. Samuel D. Sturgis (1822-1889) was a graduate of West Point with the class of 1846. He served in the War with Mexico and the Civil War, and as commander of the 7th Cavalry in 1869 where George A. Custer was in his command. Sturgis was on detached duty when his son, Lt. James G. Sturgis, a recent West Point graduate, was killed along with other members of the 7th Calvary at the Battle of Little Big Horn. Following this he assumed personal command of the regiment to participate with Col. Miles' closing operations against the Sioux and Northern Cheyenne and availed his troops to try and stop the fleeing Nez Perce. (Jerome A. Greene, *Nez Perce Summer, 1877,* Helena, Montana Historical Society Press, 2000, p. 206).

[2] David Lavender, *Let Me Be Free - The Nez Perce Tragedy,* (New York, Harper Collins Publishers, 1992), p. 301.

[3] Greene, p. 208.

[4] Lavender, p. 302.

[5] Greene, p. 208.

[6] Alvin Josephy, *The Nez Perce Indians and the Opening of the Northwest,* (Boston and New York, Houghton Mifflin Company, 1965), p. 607.

[7] General O. O. Howard, *In Pursuit of the Nez Perce, The Nez Perce War of 1877,* as reported by Gen. O.O. Howard, Duncan McDonald and Chief Joseph and compiled by Linwood Laughy, 3rd printing, (Kooskia, Idaho, Mountain Meadow Press, 2001), p. 196.

[8] "This assessment of the Nez Perce's course in reaching Clark's Fork is based on communication with Stuart Conner, Michael Bryant, and Kenneth J. Feyhl of Billings, Montana, who jointly over many years have worked to determine that route as precisely as possible..." Greene, p. 211 and p. 442, footnote 31.

[9] Greene, p. 443, footnote 43.

[10] Greene, p. 293-340.

7
Conflict on the Clarks Fork

New Indian Problems

The cessation of Indian problems after the defeat of the Nez Perce in the fall of 1877 was short-lived. Increasing frustrations by Bannock Indians confined to the Fort Hall Reservation in Idaho were coming to a head in the spring of 1878. Dissatisfaction with reservation life and the increasing encroachment on their lands by white settlers and ranchers were the sparks to start Indian hostilities again. The Bannocks were particularly incensed by the continued destruction of their camas root staple by the ranchers' hogs. [1]

A group of 200 young warriors under Buffalo Horn left the reservation on May 30, 1878 and raided across southern Idaho until he was killed a week later. His remaining followers rode on into Oregon where Paiutes joined them from a reservation there. Under the leadership of Chief Egan, the now combined group of about 450 fighting men engaged General Howard's troops in two battles in which they were defeated. Most of the Bannocks returned to Fort Hall, but a group of about 80 decided to flee eastward to join Sitting Bull in Canada. [2]

Colonel Nelson Miles

During that summer Colonel Nelson Miles had organized an expedition to establish a wagon route and telegraph line west of Fort Keogh and to visit Yellowstone Park. On August 15th his party left Fort Keogh and consisted of "ten officers, four civilians, five ladies, three children, including my family, and one hundred soldiers." [3]

As the group neared the Park, Miles received word that the Bannock group was moving through Yellowstone Park. [4] They were following the same route that the Nez Perce had the previous summer.

He immediately divided his command sending about thirty troops to accompany the women and children to Fort Ellis, the nearest military post, located just east of present-day Bozeman. With the remainder he headed out in an attempt to intercept the fleeing Indians anticipating that they would attempt to leave the Yellowstone area through Boulder Pass or the Clark's Fork Pass. [5]

On reaching Crow Agency he sent forty men under Lt. Bailey up Boulder Creek. With his remaining troops along with 35 Crow Indians [6] that he had recruited at the Agency, he headed south on a forced march toward the Clarks Fork Pass [7] arriving on September 2nd. Miles' scouts informed him that the Bannocks were about 35 to 40 miles away. [8]

Watching the Bannocks

The Army detachment set up camp and watched hidden under tree cover from the northwestern slopes of Heart Mountain. Here they had a perfect view of Bald Ridge to their west and they waited for any sign of the approaching Bannock group. [9]

About 11 a.m. the following day, the troopers spotted a group of about 80 Indians with a large herd of horses about ten or twelve miles away beginning to cross over the summit from the west. They watched as the group slowly wound its way down a rocky trail to the valley floor and then disappeared along the Clarks Fork River. About six miles from Miles' position, the Indians made camp, unsaddled and turned out their horses, and posted lookouts on the bluffs overlooking their location. Here they "built their camp fires and settled down apparently confident of their safety, and utterly unconscious of the strong command concealed in their vicinity." [10]

Miles kept his troops in their position the remainder of the day waiting for darkness before moving to within two miles of the Bannock camp. Prior to leaving Miles issued orders that "all bits, picket-pins, carbine-snaps or other jingling appurtenances" were to be "carefully wrapped to deaden or obviate the sound." [11]

A blinding rainstorm that evening help conceal the troopers' movement across the valley, as well as the Crow scouts that Miles sent to pinpoint the camp's location. When the scouts returned between midnight and 1 a.m. on the morning of September 4th, they reported that "the Bannock camp was in a very strong position, difficult to approach, with the sage brush as high as a horse's back, and that if we attempted to take it we would get whipped. The rain had been pouring down in torrents for several hours and the conditions were anything but cheerful." [12]

Col. Miles' Battle Plan

Miles and his officers began formulating a plan for their attack and moved their troops to a place they believed would place them near the Bannocks. Here they waited until 4 a.m. when suddenly a light appeared about five hundred yards away. A Bannock had started a morning campfire which pinpointed the camp's exact location. [13]

As dawn approached, the troopers could see the Bannocks were located on the west bank and on a small exposed gravel island in the shallow Clarks Fork River. [14]

The size of the Bannock camp, which outnumbered his own troops, and the perceived undependability of his Crow allies in a battle situation, gave Miles some concerns. As part of his battle plan, he decided on subterfuge to give the appearance of large numbers when they attacked. He directed his bugler, when the order to fire was given, to "blow his bugle vigorously and to rapidly change his musical coign of vantage, so that many buglers would appear to be 'splitting the ear' of day with their melody, and thus the Bannock might assume that there were several attacking parties." [15]

When the bugler asked his commanding officer if he had a preference for a particular call, Miles answered, "Blow like hell." [16]

He ordered skirmish lines formed under the direction of Captain Andrew Saydam Bennett, a 48-year-old veteran of the Civil War, who had the full confidence of his commanding officer to lead the attack. [17]

The Battle

The Crow Indians were told to take a position to the right of the line. As the troopers passed through the horse herd toward the camp, the Crows began to quietly move off some of the Bannock horses to the rear. Colonel Miles then gave the order to open fire on the sleeping Indians. [18] As 25 rifles exploded in the early morning air, "it sounded like the crack of doom." [19]

The camp was taken completely by surprise. Some of the Bannocks fired back while others jumped into the river and scattered in confusion on the other side. During the attack Captain Andrew S. Bennett was shot in the chest and died instantly. [20]

By 6 a.m. the skirmish was over having lasted about twenty minutes. [21] Eleven Bannock were dead, thirty-two were captured and the rest scattered. Army casualties included Captain Bennett, Little Rock, the commands interpreter, and another Crow Indian named Two Crows, who had been shot in the abdomen. The army surgeon, unable to repair Two Crows' wound, injected him with morphine so "that he might suffer as little as possible." He died later that day. [22]

Private Sanger wrapped Captain Bennett's body in a blanket and placed it on his horse for transport, [23] while the other troopers gathered the captives and returned to their former camp "beside the rapid, clear, trout stream that came down from the mountains. [24] Here the army surgeon "carefully attended to all unsurgical wounds, Indians and soldiers alike." [25]

Aftermath

That evening the troopers and the Crows built a very large campfire around which the captured Bannocks were instructed to sit guarded by their captors who walked around them. Through a Bannock interpreter, they were told that they would be shot if they rose from the circle without permission. [26]

Also that evening the two Crows were buried by their fellow tribesmen on a high butte near the camp. [27]

Miles' account of the day's activities does not mention when or where the Bannocks killed during the battle were buried. In fact he does not mention what happened to them at all. [28]

Having their names affixed to several Clark landmarks has memorialized two of the battle dead. Bennett Creek, the nearby Bennett Buttes and the Bennett Buttes Cemetery are named in Captain Bennett's honor, while Little Rocky Creek honors the Crow interpreter.

A command under Lt. Col. Buell arrived from Fort Custer, Montana to transport the captives to Ft. Keogh, as well as Captain Bennett's remains, which had been embalmed at the camp. After arrival at Ft. Keogh, Private Sanger and Lt. Woodruff escorted the remains back to Captain Bennett's hometown of Waukesha, Wisconsin where he was buried in the family plot on October 9th, 1878. [29]

After Lt. Col. Buell's arrival, Colonel Miles prepared to resume his trip to Yellowstone Park. He sent couriers ahead to his party at Ft. Ellis requesting them to await his arrival in the Park. [30]

When he and his troopers departed, they were joined by John William Chapman who was in the area from Oregon searching for a location to establish a cattle ranch. More on Mr. Chapman will be found in the following chapter.

Captain Andew S. Bennett's tombstone, Prairie Home Cemetery,
Waukesha, Wis. Photo taken by and courtesy of Jim Beauchamp.

Where Did the Battle Take Place?

Perhaps no other aspect of Clark's history has been so controversial as the location of the Miles-Bannock battle, which occurred along the Clarks Fork in 1878. Through the years researchers and residents interested in the conflict have made educated guesses based on folklore, legend and a plethora of archaeological evidence found scattered across the valley. [31]

Colonel Miles' description of the battle site with its overlooking bluffs and long island near the banks of the Clarks Fork has been attributed by some to a place called Myling Bend, named for an early resident whose homestead this part of the river passes.[32]

Gravel islands appear and disappear in the river throughout the year depending upon the amount of flow. In fall when runoff is normally small, the level of the river is often at its lowest revealing such islands along its course. It is possible that there was a gravel island at Myling Bend at the time of the battle on September 4th, 1878.

Recently Historian Kyle Walpole devoted several years to analyzing all of the available historical, archaeological, and geographical evidence related to the battle and its location. As a result of his in-depth study, he concluded that the battle site was not at Myling Bend but further downstream where Little Sand Coulee empties into the Clarks Fork. He believes that this location meets all of criteria for the site when Colonel Miles description of the battle site is taken into consideration. [33]

At the Buffalo Bill Historical Center he also located an 1865 Remington New Model Army revolver (.44 caliber) donated by early Clark resident Ralph Fouse. Information with the donation indicated that it had been found "in a gravel bar at the mouth of Little Sand Coulee." [34]

While Walpole's detailed analysis provides a convincing argument for the Sand Coulee site, the area has long been used as a cultivated field and bears no resemblance to its former condition of 125 years ago. As a result, it may be impossible to ultimately settle the question of the exact location of this famous conflict along the banks of the Clarks Fork.

Chapter 7 notes:

[1] Robert M. Utley and Wilcomb E. Washburn, *Indian Wars,* (Boston and New York, Houghton Mifflin Co., 1987), p. 267.

[2] Utley and Washburn, p. 267-70.

[3] Nelson A. Miles, *Personal Recollections and Observations of General Nelson A. Miles,* Vol. 1, (Lincoln and London, University of Nebraska Press, Bison Book edition, 1992), p. 294-295; "Funeral of Captain Bennett," *Waukesha Freeman,* October 10, 1878.

[4] Miles, p. 295.

[5] Miles, p. 295-296.

[6] Miles in his recollections said there were "75 Crows warriors. It then appeared more like an Indian expedition than a march of white soldiers." Miles, p. 296; A newspaper account a month later reported that the number of Crows as 35. "Funeral of Captain Bennett, *Waukesha Freeman,* 10 October 1878.

[7] The long, open slopes of Bald Ridge located to the south of the Clarks Fork Canyon.

[8] Miles, p. 295-296; "Funeral of Captain Bennett, *Waukesha Freeman,* October 10, 1878.

[9] "Discovering that up to that time there had been no sign of their presence or approach, the command was concealed in a pocket in the mountains, a name given by hunters and trappers to a very small park surrounded by high buttes and steep cliffs. The soldiers, Indians, horses, pack-mules, all were kept concealed, and a few scouts only were sent out to occupy the crests of the high buttes and to use their field glasses or telescopes under the cover of some cedar or pine bush, to discover the first sign of the approach of the hostile Indians. Occasionally an officer would be detailed to crawl up the heights and examine the country, especially Clark's Fork Pass, with his glass. But he was instructed never to reveal as much as the top of his head over the crest unless it was covered by some bush or tall grass." (Miles, p. 296-297).

[10] Miles, p. 297.

[11] Fred A. Hunt, "A Purposeful Picnic," Part III, *Pacific Monthly,* Vol. XIX, No. 5, May 1908, p. 523.

[12] Miles, p. 297.

[13] Miles, p. 298.

[14] Col. Miles in a newspaper account three years later gave a description of the battle site: "The battlefield proper is on the left bank of the Clark's Fork. To the west at a distance of eight hundred yards, a line of low hills run at a small angle to the river, sloping gently toward it and carried with a loose drift where the grass grows sparsely. On these low hills was formed the first skirmish line. The bottom land is covered with a heavy growth of sage brush (artemisa) towering above the head of a horse. It affords good protection to the wily foe, and was chosen perhaps for that purpose. A few cottonwood trees are scattered at intervals over the battlefield and beyond the sage brush and between it and the river is an island three hundred yards long and half as wide. Opposite the island and on the convex side of the river, the bluffs about thirty feet in height and inaccessible present themselves. However, at the lower end of the island where the river bends, there is a ford where it may be crossed and the top of the bluffs reached. On the island among the thick sage brush the teepees of the Bannock were placed." ("Letter from Maj. Gen. N.A. Miles,

U.S.A., Headquarters, Fort Keogh, Montana Territory to Mr. Chas. W. Bennett, Waukesha, Wisconsin dated Jan. 10, 1880. In *Waukesha Freeman,* February 19, 1880)

[15] Hunt, *Pacific Monthly,* p. 523.

[16] Ibid.

[17] In writing about this officer two years later, Colonel Miles said, "Capt. Andrew S. Bennett, Fifth U.S. Infantry, has been an officer of my regiment for years. During the great civil war he served his country with distinction, and enduring all the hardships incident to that long and desperate struggle for human rights, and the maintenance of a just and liberal government. After the war, the fortunes of service placed him on the western frontier where his services have been valuable to the government and to the frontier settlements. He has served in most of the western territories east of the Rocky Mountains, maintaining an honorable record of devotion to his profession, and faithfulness in the discharge of every duty; he was engaged in numerous campaigns and several battles. His conduct always was such as to inspire confidence in his soldiers and respect in his companions." ("Letter from Maj. Gen. N.A. Miles, U.S.A. to Mr. Charles W. Bennett," *Waukesha Freeman,* 19 February 1880)

[18] Miles, p. 299.

[19] Hunt, p. 523-24.

[20] Miles, p. 299.

[21] "Funeral of Captain Bennett," *Waukesha Freeman,* October 10, 1878.

[22] Miles, *Personal Recollections*, p. 300; In his description of the battle, Hunt indicated that Little Rock's real name was Rocque Barcoume. (Hunt, *Pacific Monthly,* p. 524.) His name suggests that he was possibly of French, as well as Crow descent.

[23] "Funeral of Captain Bennett," *Waukesha Freeman,* October 10, 1878.

[24] Miles, p. 299.

[25] Hunt, p. 525.

[26] Ibid.

[27] "The Crows had made a shallow grave on the summit of an adjacent hill for the interpreter and the Crow. There they were entombed by the superposition of rocks and small boulders, so that a coyote-proof mausoleum was produced." The lid of a hardtack cracker box was utilized for a headstone, and "thereon the writer recorded the names of Rocque Barcoume and Two Crows with the date of their death" and Rest in Peace. (Hunt, p. 526).

[28] Miles, p. 300.

[29] "The remains of our fellow townsman, Captain Andrew S. Bennett, of the 5th U.S. Infantry, arrived at Waukesha on Monday afternoon in charge of Lieut. Woodruff and Private Sanger of the Captain's company. A hearse and a large delegation of citizens received the body at the depot whence it was taken to the residence of Mr. C. Bennett and remained there until the time of the funeral yesterday. Many of the old acquaintances of the deceased took the opportunity afforded by the transfer of the remains from the temporary coffin in which they were brought, to the beautiful metallic casket provided by the Masonic lodge of which he was a member, to take a last look at the familiar features of their friend. The body was found to be in a very good state of preservation, considering the length of time during which it has been exposed to the action of the atmosphere – more than a month."("Funeral of Captain Bennett," *Waukesha Freeman,* October 10, 1878).

[30] Miles, p. 300.

[31] "Jack Spicer Finds Human Skull on Pat O'Hara Slide," *Cody Enterprise,* August 22, 1923, p. 1); "Andy Marler Finds a Fine Indian Relic," *Cody Enterprise,* July 23, 1924, p. 5; "Ancient Indian Ovens

Unearthed by Cody Farmer," *Cody Enterprise,* July 17, 1929, p. 1; "Human Foot Print in Paint Creek Rock," *Cody Enterprise,* June 08, 1932, p. 4; "Historians Mystified by Aged Skeletons," *Cody Enterprise,* July 16, 1953, p. 1; Conversation with Clara Sirrine Brown, conversation with author, in May 1999 concerning bones found by her father while digging an irrigation ditch.

[32] Bronson Tolman, "How Bennett Creek Got Its Name." Manuscript, no date; Kenneth J. Feyhl, "Miles-Bannock Battle Site Examination" from *Archaeological Site Survey Form*, "Bannock Battlefield," 48PA315, September 10, 1978.

[33] Kyle V. Walpole, *Bennett Butte, Bivouac of the Dead – A Narrative of Miles' Fight on the Clarks Fork and Analysis of a Monumental Historical Mystery,* Rough Draft, Preliminary Conclusions, (Cody, Wyoming, Buffalo Bill Historical Center, 1997) and Kyle V. Wapole, "Bivouac of the Dead, The Battle of Bennett Butte (Miles' Fight on the Clark's Fork Reexamined)," *Annals of Wyoming, The Wyoming History Journal,* (Winter 1999, Vol. 71, No. 1), p. 17-40.

[34] Walpole, *Annals of Wyoming,* p. 32.

Bald Ridge looms above the Clarks Fork River

John Chapman
Photo courtesy of Jane Riddle Thompson

The main house on the Chapman Ranch about 1905. At this time the
ranch was owned by Allison and Bent. Photo courtesy of Elmer Bunn.

8
John William Chapman

John William Chapman was the first rancher and cattleman in the Clark area. His arrival here in the autumn of 1878 came by a circuitous route.

From Illinois to Oregon

He was born June 15, 1850 on a farm on the Sangamon River, about ten miles from Springfield, Illinois, the only child of James P. and Artinecia [1] Riddle Chapman.[2] James Chapman was a farmer and a Springfield area native, and six months after his son's birth, he died leaving his 20-year-old wife with a baby to raise by herself.[3] Luckily, the young widow had family nearby, but they were planning to move.

After a neighbor returned from the Oregon Territory with descriptions of its fertile valleys, clear running streams, bountiful forests and mountains, Artinecia's parents decided to move their family to this newly created territory. Newly organized in 1848, the Oregon Territorial Legislature was offering land incentives for new residents.[4]

The Riddle family worked all winter preparing for their long trip across the plains. Cattle and oxen were purchased, supplies were acquired and clothing packed. The family farm was sold and in April 1851, John Chapman, less than a year old, joined his mother, grandparents, aunts and uncles as they prepared to embark for Oregon. The group consisted of 13 members of the Riddle family plus two neighboring families, and three young men hired to drive the oxen teams. They traveled in three wagons, each drawn by three yolk of oxen; one large carriage for the family to be drawn by four horses and about forty head of cattle and heifers. One of the wagons and teams was the personal property of Artinecia Chapman.[5]

The seven-month trip on the Oregon and California Trails was not without its hazards. Indian parties attempted to steal their cattle and oxen on several occasions. One of the last incidents happened near the Humboldt River in northern California. Here John's mother was called upon to help with a medical emergency after raiding Indians shot and wounded a member of their party.[6]

The wagon train arrived in Cow Creek Valley, now in Douglas County, Oregon during the first week of November. Here they settled founding the later towns of Riddle and Weaver, named for the two leaders of the emigrant train.[7]

On February 10, 1853 Artinecia Chapman married William Harrison Merriman, a widower with a young daughter also from Sangamon County, Illinois. Their first two children were born in Cow Creek Valley before the family moved south to Jackson County in 1857 where they bought a ranch and 13 more children were born to the couple.[8]

Early Years

John Chapman grew up in the growing Merriman family and developed skill in working with horses and cattle on the family ranch. When he was sixteen he hired out as a cowboy

Artinecia Riddle Chapman Merriam and children from her second marriage

and ranged stock in eastern Oregon before heading to the vicinity of Nevada City where he hired out with some of the first cattle outfits ranging stock there. A freighting job took him to Virginia City, Nevada, for a while and then on through Bozeman to the Tongue River area near Miles City, Montana. One biography states that his travels even included a trip into the Indian Territory, now Oklahoma. All accounts agreed that he was searching for a location to start his own cattle ranch.[9]

First Visit to the Clark area

In 1878 on his return to Oregon, he made a side trip off the Yellowstone River traveling up the Clarks Fork of the Yellowstone. Arriving in early September he was impressed with a site that he found on Pat O'Hara Creek, a tributary of the Clarks Fork. Here he met Pat O'Hara, a former fur trapper with the American Fur Company, who had a dwelling on the creek, which was later named for him.[10]

As he headed back down the Clarks Fork, he met soldiers under the command of Colonel Nelson A. Miles, from whom he learned that the previous day, they had engaged in a skirmish with a band of Bannock Indians.

John Chapman requested permission to accompany the soldiers, as they headed west up the Clarks Fork, past Cooke City into Yellowstone National Park after some of the retreating Bannocks. Traveling with the military provided him some protection in case other marauding Indians were encountered. Chapman left the Park on the west side traveling along the Madison River and on to Henrys Lake, Idaho Territory and westward arriving back home at Riddle, Douglas County, Oregon in mid-November.[11]

The Beginnings of the Chapman Ranch

The following year in late fall, Chapman accompanied by Andrew and Henry Chapman (no relation), Jim and John Weaver, J.A. Bradley and Charley Morrison, made plans to return to Wyoming. Purchasing cattle in eastern Oregon, he made up a trail herd with his own stock and that of two men from the Tongue River country in Montana who also wanted to take them east.

Chapman and his men left before winter to cross the Snake River when the water was low. They pushed their stock across Idaho into Montana then followed the Yellowstone to the Clarks Fork, where the Tongue River herd was separated from Chapman's. A few days later they reached the Pat O'Hara range with 1200 cows, a number of new calves and 80 fine Oregon horses. [12]

With his herd out to pasture, Chapman and his crew turned their attention to construction work for his ranch. In the mountain forests above, logs were cut for fence posts, and to build a cabin and barn. Building activity continued through the summer. [13]

More Stock and Marriage

The following fall John Chapman returned to Oregon to purchase more horses for his ranch, as well as to sell to the new settlers for use as plow horses and freight teams. In Oregon horses were plentiful and relatively cheap but the market there had few buyers. By spring he had gathered a large herd and hired men for the return trip over the same trail to Wyoming. [14]

Just prior to leaving in April 1881, John Chapman married Alphia Chapman, sister of his friends, Andrew and Henry, in Canyonville, Oregon. [15] Immediately after their wedding, they left for Wyoming with their horses. Their six-month honeymoon was spent on the trail with Affie "lending a hand to the cook when he needed it." Looking back years later she said, "Cooking was nothing to me. I'd been a biscuit shooter in my mother's hotel in Grant County. I was a darn good one too. It isn't so much what your job is. It's how you do it." [16]

To help herd the stock, Chapman had hired professional horse breakers and bronco riders, who took turns riding and breaking each of the horses during the thousand-mile journey. By the time they reached Wyoming the stock would be easier to handle and thus easier to sell [17]

Bad weather, insect pests, encounters with Indians and high water were all hardships of the trip. When they reached the Snake River they had to wait ten days for the waters to recede so they could cross. [18]

Finally the trip was over and the Chapmans and their wranglers delivered the stock to their Pat O'Hara ranch. A three-room log house with handcrafted floors, cupboards and shelves became Mrs. Chapman's first home here. Some of its furniture had been made, while other pieces had been ordered from St. Louis the summer before and freighted down from Fort Benton, Montana. [19]

Expansion of the Chapman Enterprises

The Chapmans ranged their stock from today's Cody area north into Montana. Their cattle were of the best quality and their bulls were sought after by other cattlemen to use as breeding stock in the development of their own herds. By 1889 it was estimated that the Chapman operation included 700 to 800 horses and 3,000 cattle. [20]

Their stock enterprise continued to grow and to prosper, and they had under ownership or lease large tracts of land not only in Wyoming but also in Montana. The U. S. Government conveyed title to 634.82 acres of land to John Chapman on May 28, 1890 under the authority of the Desert Land Act of March 3, 1877. The following year records show that he purchased by cash sale an additional 158.23 acres on March 9th, 1891.[21] Andrew and Henry Chapman, John's brothers-in-law, had also filed on and received title to nearby acreage. [22]

With the beginnings of the Red Lodge community in 1889 and the coming of the railroad there, the Chapmans' business transactions and trade were carried on almost entirely there. John and Alphia Chapman, their Heart Mountain ranch, its visitors and their activities were documented extensively in the Red Lodge newspapers beginning in October 1891 through the remainder of their lives.[23] When John Chapman came to Red Lodge to transact business, he was often interviewed concerning weather, range conditions, and even law enforcement problems in his area of northern Wyoming.[24] Amounts and destinations of Chapman horse and cattle shipments by railroad from the Red Lodge could be found in the local newspaper.[25]

Horse Rustlers

In the late 1880's horse rustling grew in epic proportions in southwestern Montana and into Wyoming. The Chapman ranch lost about 200 head while his brothers-in-laws about 150. Other area ranches were also losing stock, so they organized and declared war on the thieves. $20,000 was raised for rewards and to hire stock detectives to track down the culprits. [26]

When word was received that a group of rustlers was holed up for winter in the Jackson Hole with about 1,000 horses, two groups of men headed south in the spring to apprehend them. One party left from Big Timber, Montana while the second group, led by the John and Henry Chapman, was to meet up with them about the same time south of Yellowstone Park. Gott Spencer and Jack Burnett, two well-known horse thieves were confronted on the Cunningham ranch and in the shoot-out there, were killed. Fifty-four horses reportedly belonging to Wyoming stockmen were in their possession.[27] Otto Franc tells of John Chapman's return from this successful horse hunt in a diary notation on December 26, 1892. [28]

Expansion into Banking

John Chapman's financial fortunes continued to escalate through the 1890's. While his ranch continued to be profitable, he also found it profitable to loan money at 2% interest.[29]

In June of 1895 he went into the banking business in Red Lodge with Montana Senator W. F. Meyer, and Paul Breteche.[30] That same year, Breteche sold out his extensive cattle interests on Trail Creek (north from present-day Cody) and moved to Nantes, France where he died in January 1898.[31] With the death of their partner, Meyer and Chapman became the sole proprietors of their joint banking interests.

Mrs. Alphia Chapman in Red Lodge in 1940's.
Photo courtesy of Jane Riddle Thompson.

While John Chapman was reorganizing the Meyer and Chapman Bank, his wife went to California for a two-month's vacation.[32] .

In July they had plans ready to build a fine stone residence on their Heart Mountain ranch that was supposed to be completed by the end of the summer. [33] Historian David Wasden believed that the three-story rock structure was actually started in 1896 and completed before March 1900. He said that as many as seven workmen worked at various times to complete the structure utilizing sandstone that was quarried on the hill back of the house. Finished lumber and other materials were hauled from Red Lodge. [34] In any case construction on the house was still on going in 1899. [35]

Chapman Ranch Sold

By the turn of the century, the work on the Chapman ranch had diminished. Most of their cattle and horses had been previously sold to F. C. Valentine of Aurora, Nebraska in 1897.[36] In June 1900 there were only three cowboys working at the ranch: William Miller, Albert Unley, and Osborne Williams. [37]

The Chapmans sold their ranch to John Perry Allison, a Sioux City, Iowa banker in January 1902 and left for the California coast to vacation and to search for a place to live all year round. Unable to find a location that suited their needs, they returned in April and by July had decided to make their permanent home in Red Lodge. [38]

Alphia Chapman made the decisions for their house including the purchase of four lots on Hauser Avenue north of the Meyer mansion. [39] Her husband was only in the house twice during its construction,[40] which took over a year. They moved into their new residence in October 1903. [41]

John Chapman continued to manage his extensive property interests in Wyoming and

Montana traveling throughout both states. In 1905 he went into a partnership with the Yegan Brothers as co-proprietors of a summer mountain resort known as Rose Bud Lake and hoped to eventually provide hotel accommodations there for eastern tourists.[42] This and other property and stock interests in both Wyoming and Montana along with his banking operation in Red Lodge consumed most of his time.

John Allison died suddenly in July 1910 at his home in Sioux Falls. In September 1912 Chapman and Martin A. Jobe, Allison's former range manager and partner, became the owners of the stock in the Hart Mountain Livestock Company. The property included the old Chapman ranch house and livestock sold to the corporation years earlier. Jobe and his wife continued to live at the Heart Mountain ranch to oversee operations there. [43]

In 1912 the Meyer and Chapman bank was reorganized under state laws as the Meyer and Chapman State Bank. After his banking partner, William F. Meyer, died in late October, John Chapman became president. [44]

In March 1916 the partnership of John Chapman and Martin Jobe sold their Heart Mountain ranch to August H. Barth and Joseph Ganguet for a sum ranging from $150,000 and $200,000. The property consisted of 4,000 acres of deeded lands and about 7,000 acres of leased and script lands. The sale also included some 11,000 head of sheep. [45] The ranch's name eventually became the Two-Dot because of the two-dot brand Joseph Ganguet, a Frenchman, had used there with his sheep.[46]

John Chapman's Last Years

During the remainder of his life, John Chapman continued to manage his extensive ranch properties in Wyoming and in Montana, as well as his banking operation in Red Lodge. With a deflation in the cattle market in the 1920s, many ranchers who had borrowed money from the Meyer and Chapman State Bank suddenly found themselves unable to make payments on their loans. One of these was the Harry Simpson family in the Pioneer area of Clark, and in January 1925 Chapman instituted foreclosure proceedings against the family holdings for their $30,000 loan. After the suit went to court in Park County, John Chapman was awarded a judgment of $28,000. [47]

Beginning in 1932 John Chapman's health began to decline, and in January 1933 word came from Red Lodge that his condition was serious. [48] He died at his home in Red Lodge on December 18, 1933 and was buried in the mausoleum at the Red Lodge Cemetery. [49]

The will of John Chapman provided that his wife, Alphia Chapman, who was virtually his sole beneficiary, be appointed as executrix with full power to conduct business for the estate. She became active in the management of the Meyer and Chapman State Bank and on August 26, 1940 became its president, a position she held until her death. On February 14, 1950 Alphia Chapman died in Billings at the Deaconess Hospital where she was being treated for a broken hip that she had suffered a week earlier in her Red Lodge home. She was buried beside her husband and near her brother, Andrew Blair Chapman in the mausoleum at the Red Lodge Cemetery. [50]

Main house at the headquarters of the Two-Dot Ranch after snowfall in April 2004

Chapter 8 notes:

[1] There are a variety of spellings for the first name of John Chapman's mother in newspaper and other biographical sources. These include: Artencia, Artenicia, Artinecia, and Artamesia. Her brother, George Riddle, in his account of the family's history mentioned below, spells it as Artinesia, which is what I have chosen to use.

[2] Artinesia Riddle was the second child of William and Maxmillia Bousman Riddle. She was born on October 11, 1830 in Sangamon County, Illinois. Her father was a blacksmith and had a shop on his farm where he plied his trade for other neighboring farmers. Artinesia was married to James P. Chapman there in February 1849. See John Carroll Powell, *Early Settlers of Sangamon County, 1876*, extracted in rootsweb.com/~ilsangam/1876/riddlew.htm; George W. Riddle, *Early Days in Oregon, A History of the Riddle Valley*, (Myrtle Creek Mail, February 1953), p. 9-10.

[3] Tom Stout, *Montana, Its Story and Biography*, (Chicago and New York, American Historical Society, 1921), II, p. 60; "John W. Chapman, Pioneer, Dies at Red Lodge Home," *Cody Enterprise*, December 20, 1933, p. 1; "John Chapman Succumbs Here Monday Night," *Carbon County News*, December 20, 1933, p. 1.

[4] The Donation Land Act of 1850 gave 320 acres to every male over 18 years of age living there, and 160 acres to those settling in the Territory by the end of 1853. If he was married, his wife could receive an additional 160 acres. *The Handbook for Genealogists*, 8th ed., (Logan, Utah, Everton Publishers, 1991), p. 207; "By 1848, thanks to the trail, Congress made Oregon a territory. The Oregon migration, well developed by 1843, is an example of how a frontier can quickly jump nearly 2000 miles over an unoccupied country. There has been no other phenomenon like this in American history..." [Bill Yenne, *The Opening of the American West*," (Secaucus, New Jersey, Chartwell Books, Inc., 1993), p. 57].

[5] Riddle, p. 10-12.

[6] "John Welch and his two wagons were ahead of the train approximately a half mile and was fired upon by Indians. One of their shots shattered the bone of his left arm above the elbow. They shot one of the oxen and looted one of the wagons as he made his escape with his wagon back to the train. Mr. Welch had a great hole through his arm and the bone badly shattered. No one with the train having any surgical skill, my oldest sister, was called on to dress the wound. Her fingers being slender, she could feel for and extract the shattered bones. I witnessed the operation and it made such an impression upon my mind that at times I can visualize the operation. My sister, Artinecia, was a brave girl. Mr. Welch made a good recovery." (Riddle, p. 26).

[7] Riddle, p. 51; *Cody Enterprise,* December 20, 1933, p. 1.

[8] William Merriman died at the family's farm between Medford and Central Point, Oregon in September 1877. His wife Artinecia died in 1917. Both are buried in Jacksonville Cemetery, Jacksonville, Oregon. ("10th Generation, William Harrison," *Merriman Surname* angelfire.com/wa2/wadleigh/Merriman.html).

[9] *Cody Enterprise,* December 20, 1933, p. 1; *Billings Gazette,* Illustrated Historical Edition, October 06, 1899, p. 49; Stout, *Montana, Its Story and Biography* p. 60; *Carbon County News,* December 20, 1933, p. 1.

[10] John K. Rollinson, *Wyoming Cattle Trails,* Caldwell, (Idaho, Caxton Printers, Ltd., 1948), p. 184; Lawrence M. Woods, *Wyoming's Big Horn Basin to 1901, A Late Frontier,* (Spokane Washington, The Arthur H. Clark Company, 1997), p. 72; Lucille Nichols Patrick, *The Best Little Town By A Dam Site,* 3rd ed., (Cody, Wyoming, May, 1984), p. 6.

[11] Rollinson, p. 184.

[12] Rollinson, p. 185-186.

[13] Ibid.

[14] Ibid.

[15] Alphia Chapman, daughter of Addison and Susan (Shuey) Chapman, was born September 21, 1860 in Canyonville, Douglas County, Oregon. She had four brothers: Andrew Blair Chapman (1850-1923), Henry Chapman 1856-1915), and Lewis P. Chapman 1861-1932), and John Luke Chapman (1863-1944). Her father, Addison was born in Illinois and her mother, Susan was a native of Pennsylvania. Complete obituaries of Alphia and her brothers can be found in the following Red Lodge newspapers: *Carbon County News,* February 21, 1951, p. 1; *The Picket Journal,* December 20, 1923, p. 1; *Red Lodge Picket,* August 20, 1915, p. 1; *Carbon County News,* November 23, 1932, p. 1 & 8; *Carbon County News,* October 12, 1944, p. 1.

[16] "Long-Time Red Lodge Resident Recalls Overland Trip as Bride in 1881," *Billings Gazette,* October 01, 1944.

[17] Rollinson, p. 189; Tobias Riddle, John Chapman's uncle came out to Wyoming with him on several trips. (Oscar and Jane Riddle Thompson. Interview with author, Clark, Wyoming, November 29, 1999).

[18] In this same newspaper article Mrs. Chapman described an impatient man who tried to cross the Snake River while they were waiting. Against his better judgment, the ferryman loaded the man and his wagon team. When they reached the middle of the raging river, the wagon jerked loose from its fastenings and slid to the edge of the ferry before going off end over end taking horses and driver with it. (*Billings Gazette,* October 01, 1944).

[19] Rollinson, p. 189.

[20] David J. Wasden, "*From Beaver to Oil,* (Cheyenne, Wyoming, Pioneer Printing & Stationary Co,

[21] BLM Accession and Serial No. WYWYAA020524, Doc. No. 154 and WYWYAA020527, Doc. No. 85.

[22] BLM Accession and Serial Nos. WYWYAA020528, Doc. 86 (157 acres) and WYWYAA020505, Doc. 156 (400.26 acres). They would increase their individual holdings in the next fifteen years by 239 acres.

[23] Between 1891 and 1899 alone I counted 48 mentions of the Chapman activities in *the Red Lodge Picket.*

[24] "NEWS FROM THE RANGES - John Chapman, the extensive-stockman, came into camp Tuesday from his range on Pat O'Hare creek and Heart mountain. THE PICKET man had a talk with Mr. Chapman, during the course of which he informed us that the roads were in fair condition with the exception of that portion passing. through the bad lands. He reports no snow in his locality and the range almost barren of feed for cattle and horse and consequently both are in bad condition, but a decided improvement is looked for in the condition of the range within the next end days or two weeks. There have been no losses of stock from exposure. What few sheep there are in that locality are doing fairly well, with better pasturage expected soon. Mr. Chapman had no information to impart regarding the cattle rustlers." (*Red Lodge Picket,* Saturday, April 30, 1892, p. 3).

[25] Some of John Chapman's stock shipments are documented in the following *Red Lodge Picket issues:* June 03, 1893, p. 3; November 25, 1893, p. 3; September 08, 1894; November 03, 1894, p. 3; December 01, 1894, p. 3; June 22, 1895, p. 3; July 06, 1895, p. 3; October 26, 1895, p. 3; November 16, 1895, p. 3; and December 05, 1896, p. 3.

[26] *Helena Independent,* August 11, 1889 and August 05, 1890; Letters from John N. Tolman, Manager, Dilworth Cattle Company, September 26, 1891, September 28, 1891, October 03 and 04, 1891; *Red Lodge Picket,* January 30, 1892; *Livingston Enterprise,* February 06, 1892.

[27] For a full and thorough discussion of the shoot-out and related history see *Doris* B. Platts, *The Cunningham Ranch Incident of 1892,* (Wilson, Wyoming, 1992).

[28] David J. Wasden, *Two-Dot Ranch,* (Manuscript prepared for the Wyoming State Historical Society Trek, 17 July 1977), p. 2.

[29] David J. Wasden, *From Beaver to Oil,* p. 105.

[30] Shirley Zupan and Harry J. Owens, *Red Lodge, Saga of a Western Area,* 2nd printing, (Red Lodge, Montana, Carbon County Historical Society), June 2000, p. 361; *Billings Gazette, Illustrated Historical Edition,* 06 October 1899, p. 49.

[31] *Red Lodge Picket,* January 22, 1898, p. 3.

[32] *Red Lodge Picket,* February 19, 1898, p. 3 and April 30, 1898, p. 3.

[33] *Red Lodge Picket,* July 02, 1898, p. 3.

[34] Wasden, *Two-Dot Ranch,* 1977, p. 2.

[35] *Billings Gazette,* 06 October 1899, p. 49.

[36] John K. Rollinson, "Brands of the Eighties and Nineties Used in Big Horn Basin, Wyoming Territory," *Annals of Wyoming,* XIX, No. 2, p. 65-66.

[37] William Miller was single, 23 yrs. old and born in Illinois; Albert Unley was single, 26 years old, and born in Minnesota; Osborne Williams was single, 16 years old, and born in Illinois. Occupation of all was listed as "cowboy." (*Twelfth Census of the United States, Schedule No. 1 - Population,* Clark Precinct, Big Horn County, Wyoming, Enumerated on June 17 and 18, 1900, p. 190-B, Lines: 53 – 55).

[38] *Carbon County Chronicle,* April 15, 1902, p. 5; *Red Lodge Picket,* July 11, 1902, p. 5.

[39] *Red Lodge Picket,* July 02, 1898, p. 3.

[40] *Billings Gazette,* October 01, 1944.

[41] *Carbon County Chronicle,* October 13, 1903, p. 3.

[42] *Carbon County Gazette,* August 31, 1905, p. 1.

[43] *The Picket-Journal,* September 05, 1912, p. 4. Martin A. Jobe was born in 1872 in Missouri and started out as a telegraph operator there before he came to the Big Horn Basin. For many years he worked as a cowboy, ranch hand, and ranch foreman before John Chapman put him in charge of his immense ranching interests. For a time he went to Greybull and developed one of the finest ranches on the Big Horn River. Then John Allison selected Jobe to manage his ranch, later taking him on as a full partner. After his death, Jobe was selected as the administrator of his estate and stayed on to manage the ranch. He continued as manager of the ranch after he and John Chapman formed their own partnership. For more on Martin Jobe see: *Park County Enterprise,* October 29, 1910, p. 8; November 02, 1910, p. 6; November 05, 1910, p. 1; November 19, 1910, p. 8; April 15, 1911, p. 1 & 5; November 16, 1912, p. 1; and September 22, 1915, p. 1.

[44] Zupan and Owens, p. 302.

[45] *Park County Enterprise,* March 29, 1916, p. 1. Area newspaper issues claim that after the sale, Mr. and Mrs. Martin Jobe moved to Cody for a time while still looking after their ranch near Greybull. It is further reported that in February 1917 they bought a house one mile east of Cody and lived there for a while. (*Park County Enterprise,* April 05, 1916, p. 5; January 10, 1917, p. 5; February 14, 1917, p. 5). David Wasden claims "the Jobe brothers continued their association with the ranch while Barth and Ganguet owned it after Allison's death."("Two-Dot Ranch," *Annals of Wyoming,* 49:2: 278). Cody newspapers continue to report on Martin Jobe. In 1923 he was a resident of Livingston, Montana, and in January 1928 he came back to visit friends in Cody hoping to get work in the area's oil fields. After that he could not be found in area newspapers. (*Park County Enterprise,* April 27, 1921, p. 8; *Cody Enterprise,* December 06, 1922, p. 8; April 11, 1923, p. 8; November 21, 1923, p. 4; January 11, 1928, p. 8).

[46] Wasden, "Two-Dot Ranch," 1977, p. 6.

[47] *Cody Enterprise,* January 14, 1925, p. 1 and February 11, 1925, p. 1.

[48] *Cody Enterprise,* January 04, 1933, p. 5.

[49] For long obituaries on John Chapman, see *Cody Enterprise,* December 20, 1933, p. 1 and 2 & *The Picket-Journal,* December 21, 1933, p. 1.

[50] "Will of John W. Chapman Is Probated in District Court," *The Picket-Journal,* March 01, 1934, p. 4; "Mrs. John Chapman Dies This Morning," *Carbon County News,* February 14, 1950; "Chapman Rites Set For Friday At Cemetery," *Carbon County News,* February 16, 1950, p. 1; "Former Owner of Two-Dot Ranch Dies in Billings," *Cody Enterprise,* February 17, 1950, p. 1; "Mrs. Chapman Buried At Rites Friday Afternoon," *Carbon County News,* February 21, 1950, p. 1.

9
Homesteaders Arrive

"Over on the Clarks Fork one will find some of the finest ranches in the West. The fortunate settlers there have more water than they know what to do with."

"Matthew Connell has filed a homestead over near Clark's Fork."

"Miles Decker came in from Paint creek last Saturday and filed on a homestead."

"George Schnitker offered final proof on his Paint creek desert land last Saturday at this office, and Mrs. S. filed a desert claim." [1]

*   *   *

Wyoming was one of the thirty western states that were formed from "public domain" land. In the 1880's the lure of free land, the dream of owning and building a ranch, and hopefully a new and exciting life, brought to the Clark area its first residents. Most traveled by wagon from great distances to settle here in the shadow of the Beartooth.

Getting Title to the Land

How title to public domain land was transferred from the federal government to individual ownership was dictated by Congressional legislation. While there were different ways for land transfer to take place, early Clark residents acquired title to their property under the provisions of three major legislations - the Pre-emption Act of 1841, the Homestead Act of 1862 and the Desert Land Act of 1877.

The Pre-emption Act of 1841

This act and its later amendments allowed individuals who had established themselves illegally on unsurveyed public lands before they were put up for public sale. It allowed a "squatter," after fourteen months of residency, the right to purchase up to 160 acres for $1.25 per acre. The patent to the land was issued under the Land Purchase Act of April 24, 1820 as Sale - Cash entry. [2]

The Homestead Act

The Homestead Act of 1862 allowed any person who was a native born or naturalized U. S. citizen, or who had declared his intention to become a citizen, to file for no more than 160 acres of unoccupied government land. The individual had to be at least twenty-one years of age and the head of a household, which could also be an unmarried woman, a widow or a deserted wife. In filing the original papers, an affidavit was required stating that the land requested for the purpose of actual settlement and was not directly or indirectly for the use or benefit of anyone else.

Within six months of filing, the individual had to make his or her home on this land for a continuous period of five years. If the individual had a family, it must reside there too. A leave of absence for six months could be secured from the local land office. If this was not secured, the land claim was subject to cancellation. At the end of five years and within seven years of filing, the individual must offer final proof of compliance with the requirements of the law, bringing at least two witnesses to the hearing.

The initial fee for filing for a 160-acre homestead was $16 for the land office fee. At the time of final proof the fees were $7.57 at the land office, $10 for the newspaper notice and a fee to the officer before whom the proof was taken. This made the cost of a homestead of 160 acres to be less than $45.

Those individuals not wishing to fulfill the five-year requirement, could after a residency of 14 months, acquire title to their land by paying the government $1.25 for each acre and offering final proof. [3] This sale was by cash entry.

In 1909 the General Land Office tightened up the requirements to commute the full five-year term after only a 14-month residency. The new law stipulated that it could only be exercised due to sickness, crop failure, or some other urgent reason which prevented the settler from living on the land for the full five years. It further decreed that "where it appears that claimant entered his homestead with the intention of commuting, his claim will be cancelled. [4]

Three years later in June 1912 the five-year residency requirement to secure title to land under the Homestead Act was reduced to three years, but the proof had to be filed within five years. The settler was also permitted to be away from his claim for five months out of the year. The new law applied to homesteads of 320 acres, as well as those 160 acres. It also included not only new filings but those already made. [5]

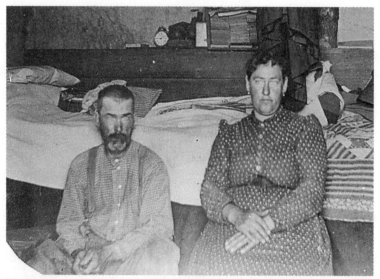

Mr. and Mrs. Davis in their Paint Creek area homestead cabin, 1896.
Photo fromTolman Collection, Carbon County Historical Soc. Archives

An editorial in the same issue of the *Park County Enterprise* supported this change stating:

> "The bill just passed will encourage settlement. It may also appeal to persons who have neither the energy, ability or means to grapple with the problems of homesteading. A homestead is not really a poor man's opportunity, unless he has the qualities that would win in any undertaking. There are long periods of struggle before things get going on a self-supporting basis, and he must have the means to tide him over that period, and he must be so adaptable that he can solve the problems of his particular locality. But if he does so, after perseverance and hard labor, the rewards are ample to repay him." [6]

The Desert Land Act

Another act under which early Clark residents could acquire title to land was the Desert Land Act of 1877. Under its provisions, an individual could buy up to 640 acres of desert land, which could not be cultivated without artificial irrigation. Married women were also allowed to file desert claims. When filing an individual had to substantiate the character of the land by his own affidavit corroborated by those of two disinterested witnesses. The payment of 25 cents an acre at the time of filing was required, as well as an additional $1.00 an acre at the time of final proof.

During the three-year requirement, the individual must spend at least $1.00 an acre each year in its reclamation or $3.00 total the first year. Residency was not a requirement. Within four years of filing, he or she must offer final proof, show that at least $3.00 an acre was spend in the reclamation of the land, that water was delivered to the land and he has irrigated and reclaimed all the land that was naturally susceptible. It was also required that the individual had secured a perpetual water right from the state engineer or from some person or corporation who had a clear water right for this land. The filer also had to have produced a paying crop on this land as a result of irrigation. After all of these provisions were met, title to the land was secured. [7]

The Timber and Stone Act

This 1873 act allowed for acquisition and payment for land that was non-mineral in character, that was unfit for cultivation and chiefly valuable for its timber or stone. These claims were limited to 160 acres to any one person or association of persons. A married woman could file on one of these claims if she paid for it with her own money, and she was taking it for her own personal use or benefit. Residence and improvements were not necessary requirements. The claimant paid the required fees and $2.50 an acre for the land. [8]

A review of newspaper entries from 1900 to 1960 for notice of intent to purchase land in Clark under this act resulted in only one entry. [9]

This scarcity of entries in Clark was not unusual but common for the entire state of Wyoming. Of the 3,123 original filings under this act, only 333 led to final entry under the

Wilbur and Ethel Bunn and their children, Mrs. Lucy Bunn and her children, and Mrs. Josephine Bunn collecting berries in 1920. Photo courtesy of Elmer Bunn.

law and 125 of these were commuted or exchanged. "A common practice was to file on a homestead and a timber claim side by side. Sometimes the homestead was later commuted for cash and the timber claim converted to a homestead." [10]

Thus an individual could obtain title to as much as 800 acres by combining the provisions of the Pre-emption Act (Cash entry), the Homestead Act, the Desert Land Act, and Timber and Stone Act.

Relinquishments

When a homesteader did not fulfill all the requirements to secure title to the land, he or she could lose it. A number of early Clark families who had filed on public land with great expectations, soon lost interest in the hard work and lifestyle required to complete their requirements. Others ran out of money or other resources and decided to move elsewhere. Some sold the property for a token payment, and its new owners completed the requirements to get final title from the government. [11]

Others lost their property through outright default. This included not living on the land or by not making the necessary required improvements. As a result, the filer "relinquished the property," and it was returned to the government who could then offer it to someone else.

If someone was aware that the requirements for property transfer were not being met, they could challenge or contest the homesteader who had filed on that parcel or parcels. If the charges were proven and the property was relinquished back to the government control, the challenger might then file on it and after completing the requirements, gain title to it.

The following June 1905 newspaper announcement in the *Wyoming Stockgrower and Farmer* illustrates how this challenge on a Clark homestead entry was accomplished:

"CONTEST NOTICE – Department of the Interior, United States Land Office, Lander, Wyoming, May 31, 1905.

"A sufficient contest affidavit having been filed in this office by **Henry A. Luce**, contestant, against homestead entry No. 1172, made February 13th, 1902 for lots 2, 3, 4, Sec. 2, Twp. 55 N., R 103 W., and SE $\frac{1}{4}$ SW $\frac{1}{4}$, Section 35, Township 56 N., Range 103 W., by **Melissa J. Davis** has wholly abandoned said tract, that she has changed her residence there for more than six months since making said entry; that said tract is not settled upon and cultivated by said party as required by law; that there is no house or other buildings on said land; that no one is living on or improving said land according to law. Said parties are hereby notified to appear, respond and offer evidence touching said allegation at 10 o'clock a.m. on July 24th, 1905, before J. K. Calkins, a U.S. Commissioner, at his office Cody, Wyoming, and that final hearing will be held at 10 o'clock a.m. on July 31st, 1905 before the Register and Receiver at the United States Land Office in Lander, Wyoming. William T. Adams, Register, J. A. Swenson, Receiver. First publication June 14." [12]

At the hearing the challenge against the Davis land was successful, and it was returned to government control. Maude Luce, Henry's wife, then filed on the relinquishment and began completing the requirements to secure its title. Four years later she filed her own intention to make final proof on the property:

"NOTICE FOR PUBLICATION – Department of the Interior, U. S. Land Office at Lander, Wyoming, September 10, 1909. Notice is hereby given **Maud G. Luce**, of Cody, Wyoming, who on August 14, 1905, made desert land entry No. 1036 serial No. 02386, for lots 2, 3, 4, Sec. 2, T. 55 N., R. 103 W., SE $\frac{1}{4}$ SW $\frac{1}{4}$, N $\frac{1}{2}$ SW $\frac{1}{4}$, NW $\frac{1}{4}$ SE $\frac{1}{4}$, SW $\frac{1}{4}$ SW $\frac{1}{4}$, Section 35, Township 56 N. Range 103 W., 6th Principal Meridian, has filed notice of intention to Final desert land Proof, to establish claim to the land above described, before John K. Calkins, U. S. Commissioner, at Cody, Wyoming, on the 23rd day of October, 1909.

"Claimant names as witnesses: Owen C. Bevelhymer, Frank A. Waples, Henry A. Luce, all of Cody, Wyoming." [13]

There was often a delay between the time of the hearing to make final proof and the actual transfer of the land patent to its new owner. For Maud Luce this process took over four years. Her patent for the 202.19 acres was issued under the authority of Land Purchase Act of 1820 – Sale Cash Entry on May 21, 1915. [14]

Land disputes not only involved the homesteader and challenger, but could also involve neighbors and others as witnesses. These contests often were reported in local newspapers, as in this example from 1911:

"A hard fought land contest case was held at the city hall before U. S. Commissioner John K. Calkins Monday and Tuesday, the parties to the matter being Frank A. Huggins vs. Aurelia Callahan, the land in dispute being a desert land entry in the Clarks fork vicinity. A large number of people from that community were in town to testify, among the number being P. O. Simpson, Ben Eckloe, Ira Toothaker, Henry Schmidt, Mr. and Mrs. Emerson Bunn, Sim C. Kimball, John Brough, Frank Brough, Julius King, Henry Wogoman, H. C Henry, S. Ramsey, William Green, D. M. Simpson, and Mr. and Mrs. Hubbard."[15].

A few homesteaders sold their properties outright after completing all of the requirements, while others took out mortgages to get needed funds for further development. Cody newspapers, as well as Big Horn and Park County mortgage records document numerous examples of both activities. [16]

A review of Bureau of Land Management, as well as county land records indicate the following individuals had completed the requirements to acquire public land in the Clark area and had been issued patents through 1930. When the title was transferred, the number of acres involved and the authority for the transfer are included below in date order:

Owner	Title Transfer	Acres	Authority
Henry Chapman	January 28, 1890	400.26	Desert Land Act
John Chapman	May 28, 1890	634.82	Desert Land Act
Affie Chapman	December 31, 1890	600	Sale – Cash Entry
Andrew B. Chapman	March 09, 1891	157	Sale-Cash Entry
John Chapman	March 09, 1891	158.23	Sale – Cash Entry
William O. Pound	November 16, 1891	160	Sale-Cash Entry
Zachariah T. Brown	November 16, 1891	160	Sale – Cash Entry
William B. Nutting	October 23, 1894	160	Desert Land Act
William B. Nutting	November 12, 1894	160	Sale-Cash Entry
Robert L. Davis	December 11, 1896	280	Desert Land Act
Emerson Bunn	April 23, 1898	80	Desert Land Act
Emerson Bunn	December 01, 1898	160	Homestead Entry
Warren O. Sirrine	December 01, 1898	320	Desert Land Act
Clarence Sirrine	February 06, 1899	320	Desert Land Act
Zachariah T. Brown	September 30, 1899	160	Homestead Entry
Charles F. Curtice	November 8, 1901	160	Homestead Entry
Warren O. Sirrine	November 8, 1901	160	Homestead Entry
Andrew B. Chapman/ William L. Clason	December 4, 1901	80	Homestead Entry
John W. Chapman/ David W. Roberts	December 12, 1901	320	Desert Land Act
Mary E. Sirrine	December 12, 1901	320	Desert Land Act
Henry Chapman/ Alfred J. Hamilton	January 17, 1902	80	Homestead Entry
David M. Simpson	August 25, 1902	160	Desert Land Act

Henry M. Simpson	August 25, 1902	240	Desert Land Act
William Watson	August 25, 1902	160	Sale – Cash Entry
Russell Kimball/ Samuel Kimball	September 6, 1902	80	Homestead Entry
Elisha M. Clark/ James S. Clark	October 20, 1902	80	Homestead Entry
William Conger/ Russell Kimball	October 20, 1902	40	Homestead Entry
Elisha M. Clark/ Moses Plotts	December 30, 1902	79.47	Homestead Entry
William H. Fouse	February 12, 1903	160	Homestead Entry
Henry Chapman/ Richard H. Dilley	May 19, 1903	79.62	Homestead Entry
James Dwyer	July 11, 1903	120	Exchange – Nat. Forest
Peter M. Collins	August 24, 1903	40	Exchange – Nat. Forest
August A. Myling	October 12, 1903	40	Sale – Cash Entry
August A. Myling	October 12, 1903	159.24	Sale – Cash Entry
Orton Sirrine	November 2, 1903	40	Sale – Cash Entry
Orton Sirrine	November 10, 1903	160	Homestead Entry
Orin H. Woods	December 17, 1903	80	Homestead Entry
Sidney B. Henry	December 17, 1903	160	Homestead Entry
Frank C. Reid	January 22, 1904	40.84	Exchange – Nat. Forest
David L. Berry	February 25, 1904	160	Sale – Cash Entry
Peter M. Collins	March 9, 1904	273.38	Exchange – Nat. Forest
Zachariah T. Brown	March 14, 1904	120	Desert Land Act
Walter S. McCorkle	August 10, 1904	147.44	Homestead Entry
David M. Simpson	August 10, 1904	160	Homestead Entry
Frank W. Brown	January 30, 1905	162.72	Homestead Entry
Edgar Simpson	January 30, 1905	160	Homestead Entry
Harry G. Simpson	January 30, 1905	160	Homestead Entry
Eli A. Vickery	January 30, 1905	153.53	Homestead Entry
Lindley M. Clark	June 26, 1905	160	Sale – Cash Entry
S. Judson Hubbard	August 31, 1905	160	Homestead Entry
Bishop B. Kelly	March 05, 1906	320	Sale – Cash Entry
Peter P. Dickinson	September 6, 1905	40	Sale – Cash Entry
John Fry	September 11, 1905	160	Sale – Cash Entry
Frank Sparhawk	September 11, 1905	160	Homestead Entry
Aztec Land and Cattle Co.	October 2, 1905	40	Exchange – Nat. Forest
William Green	December 30, 1905	160	Homestead Entry
William H. Woods	December 30, 1905	320	Sale – Cash Entry
Eli A. Vickery	May 1, 1906	160	Desert Land Act
William Brown	June 30, 1906	160	Sale – Cash Entry
Clifford D. Markham	June 30, 1906	160	Sale – Cash Entry
Joseph B. Hundley	September 5, 1906	159.86	Homestead Entry
William L. Barber	December 6, 1906	160	Homestead Entry
Harry M. Spry	December 6, 1906	160	Homestead Entry
John Smith	July 31, 1907	160	Sale – Cash Entry

Archy Beaton	August 07, 1907	160	Homestead Entry
Peter P. Dickinson	August 27, 1907	40	Sale – Cash Entry
Orton N. Sirrine	March 16, 1908	160	Desert Land Act
William G. Brough	March 19, 1908	144.41	Homestead Entry
George T. Browne	March 19, 1908	119.31	Homestead Entry
Oscar F. Hardee	March 19, 1908	160	Homestead Entry
David W. Owen	March 19, 1908	159.58	Sale – Cash Entry
Walter D. Browne	April 13, 1908	160	Homestead Entry
Robert Holmes	April 13, 1908	160	Homestead Entry
William L. Barber	April 23, 1908	40	Desert Land Act
Emerson Bunn	April 23, 1908	160	Sale – Cash Entry
Edward J. Boudon	April 23, 1908	80.46	Sale – Cash Entry
Matt Wagner	April 23, 1908	146.91	Sale – Cash Entry
George Schnitker	May 18, 1908	151.6	Desert Land Act
Irwin H. Will	May 25, 1908	152.81	Desert Land Act
Enoch McH. Brown	June 18, 1908	160	Desert Land Act
Sidney B. Henry	June 18, 1908	40	Desert Land Act
Joseph B. Hundley	June 18, 1908	158.81	Desert Land Act
John Green	July 6, 1908	80	Homestead Entry
James N. Hunter	July 23, 1908	160	Sale – Cash Entry
Enoch McH. Brown	August 13, 1908	151.96	Homestead Entry
Marcus T. L. Davenport	August 13, 1908	160	Homestead Entry
Ellen J. Cunningham/ Camilla F. Osborn	August 27, 1908	200	Sale – Cash Entry
James N. Hunter	October 1, 1908	160	Homestead Entry
Archy Beaton	October 5, 1908	80	Desert Land Act
Alvin A. Dix	October 5, 1908	120	Desert Land Act
William H. Fouse	October 5, 1908	78.6	Sale – Cash Entry
Samuel Rickard	October 5, 1908	160	Homestead Entry
George G. Thompson	October 5, 1908	200	Sale – Cash Entry
Solomon F. Weathermon	October 5, 1908	320	Desert Land Act
John Bush	November 12, 1908	160	Homestead Entry
Mattie D. Johnson/ Mattie D. Simpson	November 12, 1908	155.49	Homestead Entry
John McKever	December 1, 1908	80	Desert Land Act
Abraham L. Carter	January 25, 1909	161.29	Desert Land Act
Samuel Rickard	March 19, 1909	160	Homestead Entry
Thomas E. Frasure	April 8, 1909	158.34	Sale – Cash Entry
Mary J. Palmer	May 4, 1909	160	Homestead Entry
Milton Gorsuch	July 15, 1909	158.4	Sale – Cash Entry
Henry A. Luce	August 26, 1909	160	Sale – Cash Entry
Owen S. Hall	November 1, 1909	160	Sale – Cash Entry
James D. Owens	December 13, 1909	160	Sale – Cash Entry
Carl A. Busch	February 17, 1910	160	Homestead Entry
Thomas W. Bentley	April 28, 1910	160	Homestead Entry
Peter Johnson	April 28, 1910	160	Homestead Entry
Frank W. Brown	May 17, 1910	40	Sale – Cash Entry

George T. Browne	May 17, 1910	39.05	Sale – Cash Entry
Walter D. Browne	May 17, 1910	81.68	Sale – Cash Entry
William Green	May 17, 1910	160	Sale – Cash Entry
Farley Kimball	July 7, 1910	159.3	Homestead Entry
Joseph C. Brown	July 14, 1910	150	Homestead Entry
Peter M. Collins	July 29, 1910	80	Exchange – Nat Forest
Farley Kimball	October 6, 1910	160	Sale – Cash Entry
James P. Kimball	October 9, 1910	153.2	Desert Land Act
Peter M. Collins	October 20, 1910	160	Forest Lieu Selection
Benjamin Eckloe	October 20, 1910	136.60	Sale – Cash Entry
Oscar F. Lindquist	November 9, 1910	320	Sale – Cash Entry
Clarence Sirrine	January 12, 1911	40	Sale – Cash Entry
Daniel D. Wildman	January 16, 1911	134.35	Homestead Entry
Benjamin Eckloe	January 19, 1911	148.33	Homestead Entry
Frieda L. Wesenberg	January 19, 1911	133.47	Sale – Cash Entry
Peter M. Collins	January 23, 1911	40	Exchange – Nat Forest
Ella J. Sirrine	February 13, 1911	58.97	Sale – Cash Entry
Hugh C. Henry	February 16, 1911	160	Sale – Cash Entry
Frank A. Huggins	March 27, 1911	40	Sale – Cash Entry
Granville L. Berry	April 5, 1911	160	Homestead Entry
Charles E. Lindquist Heirs	April 27, 1911	320	Sale – Cash Entry
Peter Johnson	April 28, 1911	160	Homestead Entry
Elisha M. Clark	May 26, 1911	40	Homestead Entry
Russell Kimball	June 8, 1911	314.35	Sale – Cash Entry
Granville L. Berry	June 19, 1911	152.11	Sale – Cash Entry
Thomas W. Bentley/ Clifford D. Markham	June 19, 1911	160	Sale – Cash Entry
Peter Johnson	June 22, 1911	87.35	Sale – Cash Entry
Elisha M. Clark/ Julius H. Laughlin	June 26, 1911	40	Homestead Entry
Alfred Olson	June 26, 1911	80	Sale – Cash Entry
Fred Olson	June 26, 1911	160	Sale – Cash Entry
Peter O. Simpson	July 24, 1911	160	Homestead Entry
Mina Kimball	October 30, 1911	320	Sale – Cash Entry
James McWilliams	November 12, 1911	160	Homestead Entry
James P. Kimball	March 28, 1912	153.2	Desert Land Act
Ida M. Forrest	June 1, 1912	40	Sale – Cash Entry
William H. Schmidt	September 9, 1912	160	Homestead Entry
Albert W. Connell	October 7, 1912	160	Homestead Entry
John E. Ricketts	October 7, 1912	160	Homestead Entry
Lulu E. Johnston	October 25, 1912	160	Homestead Entry
Charles E. Smith	January 28, 1913	160	Sale – Cash Entry
Mountain View Ranch Co./ Herbert L. Sweet	February 28, 1913	268.1	Sale – Cash Entry
William F. Davis	May 31, 1913	160	Homestead Entry

John E. Ricketts	September 12, 1913	160	Sale – Cash Entry
Elizabeth Denney	May 21, 1914	40	Sale – Cash Entry
Peter M. Collins	April 9, 1915	120	Forest Lieu Selection
Maud G. Luce	May 21, 1915	202.19	Sale – Cash Entry
Carl M. Johnson	June 1, 1915	320	Sale – Cash Entry
Charles E. Taylor	June 4, 1915	160.56	Homestead Entry
Annie E. Hogan	June 17, 1915	162.27	Sale – Cash Entry
Joseph A. Crum	August 23, 1915	256.27	Sale – Cash Entry
Matt Wagner	August 26, 1915	82.36	Homestead Entry
Charles S. Frazier	August 31, 1915	40	Sale – Cash Entry
Jacob Gloeckner	September 21, 1915	160	Homestead Entry
Frank G. Hopkins	September 21, 1915	80.65	Homestead Entry
George T. Hopkins	October 2, 1915	161.85	Homestead Entry
Caroline A. Johnston	October 2, 1915	41.36	Sale – Cash Entry
Julia Leonhard	October 19, 1915	162	Sale – Cash Entry
Owen C. Bevelhymer	November 8, 1915	162.21	Homestead Entry
Edwin Manning	November 8, 1915	161.84	Homestead Entry
Edward S. Ramsey/ Edgar Simpson	December 9, 1915	160	Sale – Cash Entry
Joseph C. Brown	February 24, 1916	122.04	Sale – Cash Entry
Josephine Brown	February 24, 1916	284.39	Sale – Cash Entry
Everetta E. Ricketts	March 1, 1916	159.15	Sale – Cash Entry
Edwin Manning	March 15, 1916	121.32	Sale – Cash Entry
Augusta W. Brough	April 1, 1916	40.76	Sale – Cash Entry
W. O. Percy Fullerton	April 24, 1916	165.82	Sale – Cash Entry
Harry Temple	July 17, 1916	160	Sale – Cash Entry
Albert A. Owens	September 5, 1916	101	Homestead Entry
Jocob Bevelhymer	January 30, 1917	158.94	Homestead Entry
Ole Johnson/ Sophia Johnson	February 14, 1917	160	Homestead Entry
Elisha M. Clark	April 4, 1917	158.99	Sale – Cash Sale
Emily M. Johnson	May 17, 1917	117.88	Desert Land Act
Martin G. Gloeckner	July 25, 1917	40	Sale – Cash Entry
Mayme Temple	August 6, 1917	160	Desert Land Act
Albert A. Owens	July 18, 1918	160	Desert Land Act
Chauncey C. Bever	13 Aug 1918	160	Homestead Entry
Henry McDade	October 11, 1918	27.31	Homestead Entry
Grace M. Hooker	January 1, 1919	160	Desert Land Act
Emma H. Wilson	January 29, 1919	72.14	Homestead Entry
Andrew J. McCleary	February 18, 1919	160	Homestead Entry
Henry A. Luce	April 14, 1919	164.54	Homestead Entry
Oscar Olson	August 1, 1919	120	Homestead Entry
Mary M. Cravens	February 9, 1920	160	Homestead Entry
John E. Brown	February 24, 1920	162.21	Desert Land Act
Edith M. Schmidt	July 22, 1920	203.91	Desert Land Act
Henry H. Sirrine	September 20, 1920	149.23	Homestead Entry
Clarence Sirrine	September 24, 1920	91.58	Homestead Entry

Andrew B. Chapman/ William L. Clason	October 15, 1920	80	Homestead Entry
Anna Akin/Elda B. Martin	October 22, 1920	198.17	Desert Land Act
Charles Bradsky	April 11, 1921	40	Desert Land Act
Eliza J. Johnston	June 29, 1921	162.94	Homestead Entry
Fred A. Bunn	October 6, 1921	200	Homestead Entry
Fred A. Bunn	October 6, 1921	120	Homestead Entry
Frank L. Clark	June 22, 1922	360	Homestead Entry
Jesse E. Bunn	March 31, 1923	220.38	Homestead Entry
William H. Schmidt	January 1, 1924	157.33	Homestead Entry
Samuel S. Lightner	June 11, 1925	160	Homestead Entry
Frank L. Clark/ Jonathan E. Johnson	August 28, 1925	28.29	Homestead Entry
John D. Robertson	November 24, 1925	80	Homestead Entry
Fred Schmidt	November 18, 1925	164.61	Desert Land Act
Charles A. C. Snow	January 6, 1926	41.23	Desert Land Act
George B. Ogden	April 13, 1927	160	Homestead Entry
Ruth Wilkinson	April 14, 1927	200	Desert Land Act
Frank Sparhawk	April 28, 1930	480.54	S. R. Homestead Entry

Chapter 9 notes:

[1] *Wyoming Stockgrower and Farmer*, June 09, 1903, p. 4; May 03, 1905, p. 1; November 01, 1905, p. 4; November 22, 1905, p. 4.

[2] T. A. Larson, *History of Wyoming*, 2nd. ed. (Lincoln and London, University of Nebraska Press, 1990), p. 174.

[3] The rules for this and other types of land acquisition are detailed in *The Wyoming Stockgrower and Farmer*, December 06, 1906, p. 1.

[4] "New Land Rulings," *The Wyoming Stockgrower and Farmer*, January 07, 1909, p. 4.

[5] *Park County Enterprise*, June 05, 1912, p. 2.

[6] Ibid.

[7] *The Wyoming Stockgrower and Farmer*, December 06, 1906, p. 1.

[8] Ibid.

[9] "TIMBER LAND, ACT JUNE 3, 1878 - **NOTICE FOR PUBLICATION** - United States Land Office, Lander, Wyoming, May 7, 1906.

"Notice is hereby given that in compliance with the provisions of the act of Congress of June 3, 1878, entitled 'An act for the sale of timber lands in the States of California, Oregon, Nevada, and Washington Territory,' as extended to all the public Land States by act of August 4, 1892, **James Hogan**, of Clark, county of Big Horn, State of Wyoming, has this day filed in this office his sworn statement No. 138, for the purchase of the Lots 3 and 4, of section No. 4, in Township No. 55 N., Range No. 103 W., and will offer proof to show that the land sought is more valuable for its timber or stone than for agricultural purposes, and to establish his claim to said land before Victor G. Lantry, U. S. Commissioner, at his office, Cody, Wyoming, on Tuesday, the 2nd day of October, 1906.

"He names as witnesses: Matt Wagner, William G. Brough, William Goodfellow, Ernest Walters, all of Clark, Wyoming.

"Any and all persons claiming adversely the above-described lands are requested to file their claims in this office on or before said 28th day of July, 1906.

"William T. Adams, Register." (*Wyoming Stockgrower and Farmer*, August 09, 1906, p. 2).

[10] T. A. Larson, p. 174 -75.

[11] One example was "James R. Owens of Joliet, Mont., has purchased the old A. A. Owens Desert Claim and will take possession in the near future." (*Park County Enterprise*, March 04, 1911, p. 2).

[12] *Wyoming Stockgrower and Farmer*, June 14, 1905, p. 2. Other Clark land challenges announced in the *Wyoming Stockgrower and Farmer* include: **George Schnitker**, contestant, against homestead entry No. 1314, made September 4, 1902 for NW ¼ Section 25, Township 56 N., Range 103 W., by **Keas L. Gilland**, contestee. (August 23, 1905, p. 2); **John E. Ricketts**, contestant, against homestead entry No. 1791, made May 1, 1905, for E ½ NE ¼, SW ¼ NE ¼, NW ¼ SE ¼ Section 11, Township 57 N., Range 102 W, by **Fred Hodges**, contestee. (April 11, 1907, p. 2); and **Martin Gloeckner**, contestant, against homestead (serial number 0864) entry No. 1321, made Sept. 19, 1902, for lots 1, 2, 3, SE ¼ NW ¼, section 2, township 54 N, range 101 W., by **William P. McWilliams**, contestee. (January 21, 1909, p. 7). (Note: Names in bold added for ease in reading).

[13] *Wyoming Stockgrower and Farmer*, October 15, 1909, p. 7.

[14] BLM Land Patent Serial # WYL 0002386; Park County Records Book 16, page 167.

[15] *Park County Enterprise,* May 03, 1911, p. 1.

[16] Several examples of these land transactions include the following: Zachariah T. Brown received patent title to 156.56 acres on November 16, 1891 then sold the same to Thomas Hogan, John Hogan, and James Hogan for $2500 on January 22, 1892 (Big Horn County Record Bk. 1, p. 195; Warranty deed # 8895 dated Oct 05, 1892 from Henry Chapman to Andrew Chapman. Filed in Park County, Wyoming Records Book 1, p. 589 on January 02, 1903; Warranty deed # 2246 dated 14 March 1900 from Andrew B. Chapman to E. M. Clark et al. Filed in Park County courthouse in Book 1, p. 412 on July 03, 1900; Warranty deed #10252 from David T. Berry and his wife, Mahala Jane Berry to Granville L. Berry for the amount of $1025 for 160 acres. W2SW4 and SE4SW4, Section 13 and NW4NW4 of Section 24 in Township 57, Range 102W. Recorded in Big Horn County records on June 03, 1903; Warranty deed from David L. Berry to Granville L. Berry dated June 02, 1903. Deed # 10252. Filed in Park County, Wyoming Records Book 2, p. 20 on June 12, 1903; "George Brown has sold his ranch to Mr. Ballard." ("Clark's Fork Squibs," *Wyoming Stockgrower and Farmer,* August 06, 1909, p. 4; "Frank Brown has sold his ranch to E. Huntington and he and his brother, George, are starting for N.W. Canada, where they expect to make their future home. They will take in the sights in the park as they leave, going via the Cody entrance." ("Clark's Fork Squibs, " *Wyoming Stockgrower and Farmer,* August 27, 1909, p. 2; "Joe Hundley, having sold his ranch to the Mt. View Ranch people, will take his $10,000 and his family and hike it for the Florida coast." (*Park County Enterprise,* November 12, 1910, p. 8); Warranty deed from Granville L. Berry to Meyer and Chapman Bank dated 19 August 1911, filed in Park County Courthouse, Park County Records Book 4, p. 72. Filed on August 24, 1911; U.S. patent to Granville L. Berry dated June 19, 1901, filed in Park County Courthouse, County Records Book 16, page 36 on August 24, 1911; "A patent from the United States to Granville L. Berry has been recorded at the local court house, covering lots 2 and 3 in Sec. 11 and E ½ NE ¼ of Sec. 14 Twp. 57 N. R 152 W." (*Park County Enterprise*, August 26, 1911, p. 8); and "LATE DEALS IN PROPERTY - Granville L. Berry to J. W. Chapman. Consideration $7300. Property is described as lots 2 and 3 or the E ½ of SE ½ Sec. 11; the E ½ of the E ½ Sec. 14; W ½, SW ¼; SE ¼ SW ¼ of Sec. 13; NW ¼ NW ¼ Sec. 24; E ½ of NE ¼ Sec. 23 all of Twp. 57 N. of R 102, containing 472.11 acres. Also water rights from Bennett creek." (*Park County Enterprise,* November 18, 1911, p. 4).

10
Community Beginnings

"A trip to Clark reveals the fact that our friends in that section are making rapid progress in improvements. Land values are steadily advancing and few ranchmen desire to sell. W. L. Barber has a fine orchard growing and will soon have lots of fruit. The people in that section make a great success of melons, tomatoes and even corn." [1]

Livestock and Agriculture

As homesteaders and ranchers settled up and down the Clarks Fork Valley, many brought cattle with them or acquired them from others already here. During the winter of 1893 a number of them lost some of their stock due to the cold weather and scarcity of feed. They were to learn that "a large amount of hay is necessary for those men who expect to pull through the winter all right." [2]

This wisdom paid off because ten years later Clark area ranches were doing well. Spring rains were helping the alfalfa, timothy, oats, and other crops as well as the range. Early residents were planting orchards and ornamental and shade trees, which "added much to the value of their ranches. [3]

"The Paint creek ranchers have received their new threshing machine and are getting it put together ready for work." (*Wyoming Stockgrower and Farmer,* August 27, 1909, p. 2,) This threshing crew includes: Jesse Bunn, Ed Card, Bert Card, J. C. Brown, Charley Bevelhymer, Ed Brown, Clarence Brown, George Hopkins, Jack Carter, George Schnitker, and Joseph Skipper. Photo courtesy of Elmer Bunn.

J. K. Calkins, the owner and editor of the *Wyoming Stockgrower and Farmer* newspaper, as well as the Land Commissioner, made a visit to hear some annual desert land proofs from those completing the requirements for ownership. He was very impressed with many of the properties that he saw. He wrote that through the "application of intelligent effort and refreshing water, this has become a land flowing with milk and honey." [4]

One of the ranches he visited was that of Warren Sirrine, who had arrived 14 years earlier, and was now a wealthy man. He was lauded for having "640 acres of the finest land all under ditch, lots and sheep and other stock", as well as a two-story house, "its white paint contrasting beautifully with the dark alfalfa which covers hundreds of acres surrounding it." [5]

Calkins was also impressed with the apple trees and currant bushes that the Sirrines had planted, which at the time of his visit were full of young fruit. Calkins added that "the streams are alive with trout, and the Clark's Fork country is a most desirable location for a home." [6]

The first decade of this community was one filled with promise, hope and success. Area residents were busy plowing, planting and harvesting their crops. Enoch Brown was making regular trips to Cody to sell his vegetable produce. He had planted two acres of potatoes along with cabbage, radishes and celery, [7] and in May he brought in to Cody a four-horse load of potatoes, which he was able to sell for $1.25 per hundred pounds. [8]

His brother, Joseph Brown and his wife, Josephine, who had arrived in Paint Creek just three years earlier by wagon from Oklahoma, took six horses loaded with vegetables that they had grown into Cody to sell. [9] In June they took two wagons with butter, eggs, vegetables and other ranch produce to Cody and returned with two loads of machinery for their ranch. [10]

That same month Archy Beaton plowed 20 acres for alfalfa, 15 acres for corn and 5 acres for potatoes on his desert claim under the Paint Creek ditch. George Schnitker regularly made trips to Cody taking fresh ranch eggs and pure horseradish. [11]

Early Pioneer area residents enjoying fresh-picked watermelons, 1911.
Photo courtesy of Carol Briggs Joy and Dorothy Pearson Williams.

Accounts of the prosperity in the area during that first decade were rampant:

"Milt Benedict came in and took out a load of supplies. He reports everything is booming on Paint Creek." [12]

"John Bush of Clark's Fork was in town yesterday and reports the first crop of hay in that section is nearly all in the stack. Help is scarce this season and the farmers have been paying $2.25 a day and board." [13]

"This country is looking beautifully green and grain fields lend an air of prosperity. The gardens are flourishing, owing to an abundance of water and muscle applied to the hoe. Everyone is busy haying and cannot get enough help. The hay on the Schnitker ranch is so heavy it can not be cut in places." [14]

But not everything was idyllic in 1903. Just north of Clark in Montana, ranchers were losing horses and cattle to thieves. It was noted that "stockmen along the Clarke Fork seriously contemplate the holding of a neck-tie party for the benefit of the horse thieves who are getting too plentiful in that vicinity. It promises to be a swell affair and when started the entertainment will proceed at a break neck pace." [15]

The next summer in 1904 the problem had touched the Clark area, as Justice E. A. Vickery issued warrants for the arrest of several parties on the charge of horse stealing, and Constable Frank Brown headed off towards Cody to apprehend the accused and to return them to Clark for a hearing. Jack McCleary, a Line Creek rancher, alleged that five individuals "broke down his pasture fence, took an unbranded mare from the field and drove her off with a bunch of horses. The owner of the bunch claims that the mare followed the band." [16]

In December of 1906 Paint Creek area rancher, James Hogan, was willing to "pay $100 reward for the arrest and conviction of any person stealing, driving away or killing any stock branded 'quarter circle YT' on left side." [17]

Many of the ranchers and cattlemen decided to join together to protect their stock. In April 1907 the Upper Clark's Fork Stock Association was formed at the Bennett Creek schoolhouse with 21 members including: James Hunter, president, E. A. Vickery, vice president, and William Wood, secretary. The boundaries of the organization were from Bearcreek on the north to the Shoshone River on the south, and from Crandall Creek to the divide near Pryor Gap. By-laws were adopted and it was "decided to offer a reward of $500 for the conviction of any one stealing or killing stock belonging to members of the association." [18] By 1909 the association was paying a reward of $1,000 for "the arrest and conviction of any person or persons guilty of stealing, unlawfully killing or branding cattle or horses belonging to members of the association," and were running announcements to that effect in each week's newspaper. [19]

In 1909 with the introduction of sugar beets in the Clarks Fork valley, some land formerly dedicated exclusively to hay production, changed to beets. Henry Sirrine, who had put in beets along with other crops on his parent's stage station ranch, had a good yield.

Quince Chance hauling beets on a spring wagon to Belfry for shipment in 1911 or '12. Photo courtesy of Irma Chance McLuskie.

He wasn't the only one. "Anyone who is skeptical about beet growing in this valley don't have to go to Missouri to be showed." [20]

Successful beet production contributed to a decline in hay production. Some ranchers were unable to buy additional hay to supplement their own grown crop. Knowing that they would not have enough feed for their cattle during the upcoming winter, they decided to sell off some of their stock. There was "less hay fed cattle in the valley this winter than any winter before." [21]

One rancher, Clarence Sirrine, who had switched from hay to sugar beets to feed his stock, fattened 350 head of steers for a December first shipment to market. [22]

Some sheep men also reduced their holdings in anticipation of the winter feed shortage. In June William H. Woods sold some of his sheep to Frank Clark,[23] and in October he sold more of his sheep to John Allen in Chance with his old ewes going for $3.75 a head. [24]

The harsh winter of 1909-1910 compounded the food shortage. Extremely low temperatures and heavy snowfall beginning in December and continuing into January 1910, was described as "the worst it has been in eleven years." This caused problems for both cattlemen and sheep men. Mart Gloeckner, a Pioneer area flock master, had to abandon one band of sheep, which he offered for sale for less than a dollar a head. James Hunter on Line Creek had a problem getting feed to his flocks. Some of the cattlemen lost half of their stock before they could get them to hay.[25]

As a result of this bad experience, flock masters warned that the day of winter sheep range was over and that all sheep men must prepare to keep their flocks on feed throughout the winter. [26]

One of the benefits of the heavy snowfall that winter was that the range blossomed the following summer. Many area cattlemen sent their cattle up into the mountains to graze. In July the Simpson Brothers - David, Edgar, and Harry - who were "among the most progressive stock raisers of Park County," purchased between 1800 and 2000 yearling cattle from Nebraska which were described as "of good stock and will fatten well." [27] In September Edgar Simpson came down from the mountains and reported that his cattle were all on good feed and they were looking fine. [28]

That same summer Frank L. Clark, George M. Heald and Lindley M. Clark filed incorporation papers for their Clarks Fork Sheep Company, whose operation would be in the Clark area but whose offices would be in Red Lodge. With a capital stock of $100,000 the object of the company was to "buy, sell, lease and let, acquire, own, and operate farms, ranches and real estate, to appropriate, acquire, own and operate water rights, power sites, engage in farming, ranching, wool growing, and do all things necessary to conduct ranching and stock grazing." [29]

Vegetable and fruit produce during that next summer was excellent also due in part to the heavy snowfall the previous winter. H. L. Sweet put together an exhibit of some of the Clark produce for the Billings fair proving that "the Clark vicinity is not the barren waste it is maliciously claimed to be." [30]

Members of the Cody Club who were collecting an array of Big Horn Basin fruits and vegetables for exhibits back East, spent two days in Clark visiting area ranchers and farmers in search of excellent produce. Bennett Creek rancher, Bruno Becker and his partner, Herbert Sweet, gave five fine varieties of apples, some weighing as much as a pound each, as well as onions, and field corn. Frank Hopkins from Pat O'Hara Creek, furnished sugar beets and pumpkins; E. M. Clark gave cabbage; William H. Fouse contributed some of the finest potatoes found out here, which he gave along with alfalfa seed, Australian spring wheat, oats, rhubarb and squashes. Clarence Sirrine contributed macaroni wheat, and the Simpson Brothers gave white elephant and Hamilton potatoes. "The fine array of products in this region was a surprise even to those acquainted with its fertility and its previous reputation of good crops." [31]

Elections and Voting

On May 4th, 1909 Big Horn County voters went to the polls to decide whether or not a new Park County would be created out of part of their county. At the time of that election area residents of Sirrine, Clark, Bennett Creek, Line Creek, and Paint Creek were divided into two voting precincts. Clark Precinct # 1 used the Sirrine schoolhouse as the voting place, and that year had William Barber, Eli Vickery, and Joseph Hundley as precinct judges, while Clark Precinct #2 voted at the Paint Creek schoolhouse with James Hogan, Farley Kimball and Robert Hopkins as judges. [32] These precincts and judges were reaffirmed by the Big Horn County Board of Commissioners. [33]

As a result of that election, Park County was created with county-wide results of 1001 voting in favor and 274 voting against its establishment. [34] The voters in Clark Precinct # 1 voted 47 for and 2 against, while Precinct # 2 cast 36 votes in favor with none against. [35]

In April 1910 the editor of the *Park County Enterprise* called attention to a problem in the Clark area concerned with voting. He reported that some residents, including the area's newspaper correspondent were "righteously indignant because he and the people of his community are obliged to make a trip from twenty to twenty-five miles in order to vote," and "because of this distance, it is seldom that he or his neighbors get out to the polls on election day." [36]

Charlie Snow in his own column in that issue further discussed the problem writing:

"If we are to have a voting place at or near the Clark post office in time for the next election, it is about time there was a move being made to get it. How can people be blamed for not voting when they have to make a trip of 20 to 25 miles to and from their voting place, and that over a road of unbridged ditches that are almost impossible to cross." [37]

In June Mr. Snow again addressed the Big Horn County officials to do something about the Clark voting problem. "Remember we need a voting place here at Clark. Don't forget us until it is too late." [38]

On July 6, 1910 the County Commissioners proceeded to lay out the new county of Park into Election Districts, and District # 1, named Clark was established. It's boundaries were: "All that territory embraced within Township 57 and 58 North, Range 101 West, which is west of the Clarks Fork River, and that portion of Township 56 North, Ranges 102-103 West, which is north of the Clarks Fork River." The new polling place would be the Clark schoolhouse. [39]

Charles Snow and other area residents were ecstatic! "Hurrah for Clark! A voting place at last! Also the best wooden bridge on the river, that at the Dredge ford, and the Hopkins bridge isn't to be sneered at either." [40]

During the November 1910 election, a number of Clark area residents were running for offices in the newly-created Park County. Frank G. Hopkins of Paint Creek was running for County Assessor against Henry Fulkerson of Powell, while Pioneer area farmer and current Big Horn County Assessor, William H. Fouse was pitted against Pat O'Hara rancher, Martin A. Jobe for the 4-year term as county commissioner. In Election District # 1 (Clark) Bruno J. Becker was running against Charles A. C. Snow for Justice of the Peace. Benjamin Eckloe was running unopposed for constable, and Emerson Bunn was unopposed for road supervisor. [41]

Charles A. C. Snow, 1868 – 1930
Photo courtesy of Hazel Cochrane & Dorothy Cochrane Napier

Although only 39 Clark residents out of a possible 60 voted in the election,[42] there was a good turn out in the rest of the county. After the votes were counted, Clark area residents Fouse, Snow, Eckloe, and Bunn were successful in their bids for office. [43]

When the first Park County Board of Commissioners took their seats on January 3, 1911, Clark area residents were elated that one of their own, William H. Fouse, was among its three members ensuring that their needs and problems had a good chance of being heard and resolved. Knowing of the continued road problems in this area, the Commissioners appointed Jake Bevelhymer as the Road Supervisor for the Paint Creek area on May 1, 1911. [44]

Optimism for the Future

These first few decades of the community were a learning experience for early residents, many of whom were not at first prepared for the challenges that they were to face here. By the fall of 1911 Charles A. C. Snow, the Clark correspondent to the Cody newspaper, wrote with tongue-in-check his optimism about the future development of Clark:

CLARK PUTTING ON AIRS SINCE BECOMING A TOWN

"Clark, Wyoming, Oct. 25, 1911 – Lindquist Bros. will begin that store building in the new town of Clark just as soon as they can sell their lots. Bruno Becker says the only desirable location in the new town of Hyde-Clark, Wyo., would be on the Bennett Creek boulevard, but that is out of the question as the location is bound to be taken up by the manufacturing industries. Thomas Jones was the first to settle in the new town of Hyde-Clark, and he has his rooming house going too. Emerson Bunn is sleeping with one eye open these nights dreaming of the new addition he will lay off, which is to be called Rocky Point Heights, and of the adamantine roadway he will build to connect with the business thoroughfares of the new city. George Berry won't have a surveyor, but is stepping off his lots to the tune of 50 X 140. It is expected his addition will be named Swamp Alley, and will be chiefly valuable for raising bullfrogs and mushrooms." [45]

Chapter 10 notes:

[1] *The Wyoming Stockgrower and Farmer*, March 15, 1905, p. 4.

[2] *Red Lodge Pickett*, December 23, 1893, p. 3.

[3] "Bennett Creek Briefs," *The Wyoming Stockgrower and Farmer*, May 30, 1903, p. 1.

[4] J. K. Calkins, Editor and Proprietor, "Clarks Fork Valley," *The Wyoming Stockgrower and Farmer*, June 9, 1903.

[5] Ibid.

[6] Ibid.

[7] "Paint Creek Points," *The Wyoming Stockgrower and Farmer*, April 26, 1905, p. 3.

[8] "Paint Creek Points," *The Wyoming Stockgrower and Farmer*, May 10, 1905, p. 3 and 4.

[9] Ibid, p. 3)

[10] Ibid, June 7, 1905, p. 4.

[11] *The Wyoming Stockgrower and Farmer*, March 7, 1906, p. 4; and April 11, 1906, p. 4.

[12] *The Wyoming Stockgrower and Farmer*, May 17, 1906, p. 4.

[13] *The Wyoming Stockgrower and Farmer*, July 19, 1906, p. 4.

[14] "From Paint Creek," *The Wyoming Stockgrower and Farmer*, August 8, 1907, p. 2.

[15] *Carbon County Chronicle*, April 21, 1903, p. 3.

[16] *The Free Press*, August 19, 1904, p. 3.

[17] *The Wyoming Stockgrower and Farmer*, December 18, 1906, p. 4.

[18] *The Wyoming Stockgrower and Farmer*, April 11, 1907, p. 1.

[19] *The Wyoming Stockgrower and Farmer*, December 3, 1909, p. 8.

[20] "Clark Squibs," *The Wyoming Stockgrower and Farmer*, October 8, 1909, p. 8.

[21] "Clark Squibs," *The Wyoming Stockgrower and Farmer*, November 26, 1909, p. 8.

[22] "Clark Squibs," *The Wyoming Stockgrower and Farmer*, October 8, 1909, p. 8; and November 12, 1909, p. 5.

[23] Clark Fork Squibs," *The Wyoming Stockgrower and Farmer*, June 4, 1909, p. 7.

[24] "Clark Squibs," *The Wyoming Stockgrower and Farmer*, October 8, 1909, p. 8.

[25] "Clark Squibs," *The Wyoming Stockgrower and Farmer*, December 31, p. 2 and January 14, 1910, p. 5.

[26] "Clark Squibs," *The Wyoming Stockgrower and Farmer*, January 28, 1910, p. 8.

[27] *Park County Enterprise*, July 12, 1911, p. 1.

[28] *Park County Enterprise*, September 30, 1911, p. 5.

[29] *Park County Enterprise*, August 5, 1911, p. 1.

[30] *Park County Enterprise*, September 9, 1911, p. 4.

[31] "Products from Clarks Fork of Unusual Excellence," *Park County Enterprise*, September 27, 1911, p. 1.

[32] *The Wyoming Stockgrower and Farmer*, April 8, 1909, p. 7.

[33] Commissioners' Records, Book 1, p. 5.

[34] *The Wyoming Stockgrower and Farmer*," May 12, 1909, p. 1.

[35] "Election Returns," Commissioners' Records, Book 1, p. 7.

[36] *Park County Enterprise*, April 16, 1910, p. 4.

[37] "Clark Squibs," Park County Enterprise, April 16, 1910, p. 8.

[38] "Clark Squibs," *Park County Enterprise*, June 18, 1910, p. 8.

[39] *Park County Enterprise*, July 16, 1910, p. 7.

[40] "Clark Squibs, *Park County Enterprise*, July 30, 1910, p. 4.

[41] *Park County Enterprise*, November 2, 1910, p. 6.

[42] *Park County Enterprise*, November 12, 1910, p. 8.

[43] *Park County Enterprise*, November 19, 1910, p. 5 and 8.

[44] Commissioners Records, Book 1, p. 41.

[45] *Park County Enterprise*, October 28, 1911, p. 4; Note: In this time before paved roads the word, "adamantine," as used by Charlie Snow meant that the roadway would be very hard like steel or a diamond; a substance of extreme hardness. (Thorndike Century Junior Dictionary, [Chicago, Atlanta, Dallas, and New York, Scott, Forsman and Co., 1935]), p. 10; The plat for this town of Hyde-Clark was filed in 1911 at the Park County courthouse and their records indicated that it is held there. Despite an extensive search by the author and several of the county clerks, it was not located. Archivists at the State Archives in Cheyenne also reported that it is also not amongst the Park County records held there.

11
Gold, Coal, and Oil

"The Clark's Fork excitement still continues with unabated fury and
old placer miners say they never saw anything like it. The reports
of prospectors arriving from that field for grub are more flattering
every day and confirm the fact that the gold dust is there in quantities
to satisfy the most skeptic miners. As the gold is found on quite a large
scope of country efforts are being made by several old miners to ascertain
where it comes from and the foot hills are being carefully prospected.[1]

Gold Seekers

Not everyone coming into the Clarks Fork Valley was solely concerned with home-steading and agricultural pursuits. As early as the 1890's, there were gold seekers using sluice boxes and flumes in their pursuit of riches on the Clarks Fork River. One account in 1893 mentions that two men, working about four miles above the mouth of Bennett Creek, were averaging $1.50 a day for $8\frac{1}{2}$ hours of work each. [2]

Because the gold was too fine to work successfully with a gold pan, flumes and sluice boxes were used to handle the large amount of river bottom and bank dirt. Flumes were built to channel river water, which flowed over long sloping troughs, called the sluice boxes. These boxes had grooves in the bottom over which separated the gold from the gravel and sand. Potential miners were warned "poor prospectors without a grub stake and considerable money to start with should keep away, as they will not meet with success." [3]

These area miners were taking advantage of the United States Mining Law of 1872, which was enacted twenty years earlier when the government was encouraging settlement of the West. In summary the law, which is still in effect today, granted free access to individuals and associations to prospect for minerals on public domain lands, and allowed them, after a mineral discovery was made, to locate or "stake" a claim on that deposit. The claim gave the holder the right to develop the minerals after paying a fee of $2.50 to $5 per acre depending upon the type of claim and to satisfy an annual work requirement until a patent was issued.[4] There are two types of claims - lode and placer - depending upon the character of the deposit.[5]

The Red Lodge newspaper reported the placer mining claims that had been filed in the office of the county clerk. In November 1893 each of the claims filed were by associations of eight individuals filing for the 160 acre maximum allowed. All of these claims were located on the Clarks Fork River. Some of the familiar area names included: John Chapman, Andy Chapman, Hank Chapman and 5 others for their Mascot placer claim; Warren Sirrine, Earl Sirrine, Orton Sirrine, and 4 others for their Nugget Queen placer claim; and Warren Sirrine, Earl Sirrine, Orton Sirrine, Mary Sirrine, Mrs. R. O. Sirrine, and 3 others for their Lookout placer claim. [6]

To encourage mining efforts throughout the United States, a bill was passed by Congress and signed by the President in November suspending the required $100 worth of labor or improvements made for the 1893 year. [7]

The rush of gold seekers all along the Clarks Fork resulted in a petition being circulated in northern Wyoming and in Red Lodge to increase the tri-weekly mail service between that town and Meeteetse to a daily one, because of the increase in "placer diggers and the large number of settlers that are taking up land along the route." Their present mail service was considered inadequate. [8]

Individuals, who would later file for acreage under the Homestead and Desert Land Acts, were first working placer claims along the Clarks Fork. In 1894 John Bush and Eli Vickery were working and after five days of work had gold returns of $59.[9] Dave Simpson and Clarence Sirrine were building sluice boxes to work the river bordering Sirrine's property, while Hudson Darrah, who had just arrived in the area was working with Granville Berry and were going to commence sluicing operations as soon as the river's level dropped. Mining activity was going at quick pace and "the ring of the shovel and scraper and tap of the workman's hammer is heard on every hand." [10]

In April of 1895 Eli Vickery cleaned up $48 from his sluice boxes after a day and a half's work with two men and a team. Other placer miners working on the Clarks Fork near the mouth of Bennett Creek were making "making cleanups that exceed their largest expectations." Each outfit of two men and a team were making from $20 to $40 a day. Gold from along the Clarks Fork was arriving in Red Lodge each day for shipment to the Helena assay office. [11]

While placer mining activity was developing along the Clarks Fork, by the summer of 1897 lode mining activity was taking place in the Sunlight Basin. John R. Painter was making considerable headway with his Evening Star Mine and was freighting about 100 tons of high-grade silver ore to Red Lodge for further shipment to be smelted. His ore was running over 500 ounces to the ton. With the development in the Sunlight mining camp, there were plans to survey and construct a wagon road down the Clarks Fork Canyon or over Dead Indian Hill. [12]

That same summer Carbon County Attorney, Ludlow Reno who lived in nearby Chance, came to Red Lodge and reported the high number of placer miners along the Clarks Fork was far in access of anything he ever expected to see. "It appears that the placer miners of this section are beginning to realize that there is pay in the gravel along the Clark's Fork and their efforts have at last been turned towards securing some of it." Some of the irrigation ditches back from the river were also being using to wash gold out of the bench areas. [13]

Coal Mines

In 1905 two miners were prospecting for gold and nickel in the Clarks Fork Canyon, and brothers, Enoch and Joseph C. Brown also had a placer claim there. [14]

While gold was the primary driving mining activity in the area, there was also interest in coal. In 1909 Solomon Weathermon and Roy Wagoner opened up a coal mine on Lake Creek and expected to start furnishing "first-class quality of coal" to area ranchers.[15] Beginning in 1910 there were reports of the Tiger Gulch coal mine also being used to supply fuel to local residents. [16]

Gold Dredging Operations

In the late summer of 1914 gold mining procedures along the Clarks Fork changed with the arrival of a mining outfit from California who started a crew of sixteen men washing gold just above the mouth of Bennett Creek. Their California Mining Company would soon begin dredging operations there. [17] Companies that could afford to mechanize gold mining by the uses of dredging equipment quickly replaced individual efforts with their shovels and sluice boxes whose work output was a fraction of this improved method.

Dredges could scoop out several cubic yards of material at once. Through the use of an excavating crane, a large bucket could be dropped into the water, onto river gravel beds or banks and then dragged toward the crane base by a cable. In this way quantities of dirt, mud, and gravel possibly containing gold could be gathered. Some of these crane dredges were installed on long flat boats.

Other types of dredges used a different mechanism to gather material. Some used a continuous line of buckets attached to a belt which scraped the bottom then brought then brought the material up into the dredge where it was dumped into sluice boxes. Here water was pumped in to separate the gold from the bottom material, which was dumped out the back into the river as the dredge moved along. Other dredge techniques employed the use of large suction hoses, which gathered material from under the water's surface. [18]

By October Ed Fuson and Emerson Bunn were busy cutting timber for the company, and needed roadwork on the east side of the Clarks Fork had been completed. Their main piece of equipment was a dragline and it was being transported from the rail station in Belfry. Also in Belfry awaiting transportation south were 180 tons of freight including a 60 horsepower boiler, which was to be used in the electric light plant. Their plans were to work three shifts daily including during the night when the lights would be needed. [19] They were also planning a second dredge at the location. [20] This much larger mechanized mining operation caused some concern among many of "old prospectors and gold miners of this part of the country." [21]

In December it was announced that the California syndicate was planning to purchase the Ben Eckloe ranch of 160 acres for $20,000. By then there equipment consisted of 9 carloads of dredging equipment, which had the capability of working the banks and bars of the river including the moving of boulders. [22] In January when the Eckloe ranch was sold to Gagnon and Company for $24,000, assays from the river area claim had gone as high as $89 a ton for gold. [23]

The Powell Tribune in reporting about the dredging operation later that spring conceded that the operation for the most part was a well-kept secret. "Few people in this immediate vicinity know anything about this plant and there are many well-informed people in Cody who go so far as to insist that the whole thing is a myth, and who doubt the sincerity of those who have seen the plant and testify as to its reality." [24]

The Tribune article further reported that $10,000 worth of machinery was already in place and a large number of buildings were being erected. At that time the dredge was near the Vickery ranch (neighbor to the Eckloe place) and was planning to work upstream with the machinery being carried on immense flat boats which would allow work to be accomplished during when the river was high. "Where the dredge is now working an assay shows that $35 worth of gold is being taken from every yard of material handled. The promoters say there is enough ore in sight to keep the plant working for twenty years." [25]

In September 1916 sensational news reached Red Lodge of the "discovery of the source of all the placer gold in the Clarks Fork river." Two individuals had recently visited the claims of George Teeples located just below the mouth of Pat O'Hara Creek where they had washed out about two yards of dirt and gotten more than "$15 worth of gold and one ounce of platinum." It was reported " no gold had been discovered as far south as Pat O'Hara Creek before and "it was always the belief that the gold in the river had its origin several miles north of that point." Supposedly prospectors had searched the hills for years without any success to locate the source of the gold in the river. [26]

Possibly as a result of this publicity, Teeples got financial backing in early 1918 from Independence Mining Company of Greybull to develop his promising gold placer claims along the Clarks Fork. The corporation, which was organized under Montana laws, had a capital of $20,000, and its stockholders chose Teeples as president and manager in the "hopes of interesting local people in this enterprise." [27]

Two years later Teeples had interested some Denver capitalists in his project and made plans to install a $76,000 hydraulic pump and thirty houses for miners further south on the Clarks Fork at a site near the Hopkins Bridge and mouth of Pat O'Hara Creek. The plan was to use the pump to pull the river bottom and its gold to the surface for processing. In preparation for this activity, the former Charles Taylor house located on the north side of the river was purchase and remodeled into a garage for company use. Walter Braten was awaited a contract to deliver coal from his mine, and he with a force of men was busy hauling coal to the site. [28] In May a train car of mining machinery was received at Ralston for the Clarks Fork gold mine, which had been named the "Gold Placer Mine." [29]

Despite grandiose plans and "the most extensive" preparations to date, this venture was to be short lived and soon died like others before it. By then the old dredge down by Bennett Creek had also been abandoned because "while the enterprise was nominally successful, it scarcely paid a living wage to the day laborers employed." [30]

In the following years there was continued interest in recovering placer gold from the Clarks Fork or discovering its source. Roy Cecil (Shorty) Lowmiller of Clark spent much of his life in the effort "trying to scratch the natural resource in his neighborhood with the ideal of supplementing his farming activities until farm products started paying their own." [31] His prospecting search ended twenty-four years later when he was found dead in the hills four miles southwest of Clark. He had been dead for nearly a week. [32]

In 1933 prospectors from Butte, Montana were "again working the Clarks Fork vicinity for gold," [33] and the next year a gold dredge had been working the river above the Gloeckner place [34] (where Alan and Laurie Denney live today).

In 1935 the Robert Cole Gold Dredge Company was "working the river bed with a big steam shovel," [35] and the following year, an old-time prospector named Dave Williams, who had been living in the Clarks Fork Canyon, dislocated his hip and was taken to Cody for treatment. [36] At the end of 1938 signs of gold were also discovered in the Canyon near the George Ogden property line. [37]

Sometimes the persistent search for gold paid off in an unexpected way. In 1925 Andy Marler, a rancher on Skull Creek, reported his finding of a specimen of ore containing gold, silver, and copper on his property. He was sure that better ore would "be discovered upon following the lead." [38]

His interest in gold changed to oil after a government survey of his homestead ranch in 1943 indicated a high probability of gas and oil being found there. In 1950 he leased his mineral rights to the Heart Mountain Oil Company, and the next year drilling began on his ranch. A good grade of gas was found at 2456 feet. The Marler ranch also had an open coal mine not too far from their log house, and others undeveloped at that time. "Dry farming and white-faced cattle can be forgotten. Marler's ranch is paying off." [39]

Badger Basin Oil Field

While early gold-seeking activities were underway on the Clarks Fork River, oil placer mining claims were being staked and filed in the Sections 18, 20 and 30 to the east of the river in Badger Basin. Most of these were 160-acre claims filed by associations of 8 individuals – many of whom were involved with a number of claims. Granville (George) Berry was involved with the Jaybird, Cyclone, Skyscraper, Eagle Rock, Wild Cat, Rattlesnake and Whirlwind claims all filed on in April and May 1916. In the next two years his name also shows up as a part owner of the Last Placer, Lone Star, Glory, Dollar Mark, Chinook, and with claims named only by letters – D, G, H, L, P, S and R. [40]

Other placer claims in the same area were held by area residents Emerson Bunn, Fred Bunn, Jesse Bunn, J. D. Clark, Mr. and Mrs. Ben Eckloe, J. O. Higham, Mr. and Mrs. James Hunter, Ed Lindquist, Emil Olson, Oscar Olson, Mr. and Mrs. David Parker, Alfred Russett, Mr. and Mrs. Ira Toothaker, Mr. and Ms. J. H. Van Horn, and Mr. and Mrs. E. A. Vickery. [41] In March 1916 Oscar Lindquist, Ben Eckloe and Dave Parker went to Belfry to attend a meeting of the directors of the Badger Basin Oil and Gas Company. [42]

It was announced in June of 1917 that the Badger Basin Oil Company was expecting the arrival of a larger outfit, as they had only been running a small rig for their drilling activities. It was also announced that another company there was suspending operations there indefinitely due to the lack of funds. [43]

By the late 1920's oil drilling activities in Badger Basin were back on track. In the spring of 1928 brothers, Herbert and Gus Forsman consolidated a number of leases in the area after geologists, Charles T. Lupton and George S. Kearney had concluded favorable tests on the area. Gus Forsman had previously recognized the dome structure under the Elk Basin north of Powell and had drilled the first well there going down to 1,140 feet on October 8, 1915. [44]

The Forsman brothers leased the entire field to the Resolute Oil Company retaining a large royalty in return. The company began a test well, and by June of 1928 their crew had drilled to a depth of two hundred and fifteen feet. [45] Almost one year later they had had reached a depth of 2400 feet. [46]

Lena and Gus Forsman, about 1920
Photo courtesy of Juanita Smith Moore

The company had a setback in August when a fire, which started in the 'dog house' at the rig, got out of control and burned their wooden drilling rig to the ground. New tools were ordered to replace those damaged or destroyed in the fire, and work on building a new rig was started immediately. [47]

Less than a month later Jack Vickery was brought in from the well site with severe head injuries caused by some falling tackle from the oilrig. George Witherup, who was also injured in the same accident, lost some teeth, but was able to drive himself and Jack to the Cody hospital for medical care. [48]

By October the well in Section 17 having gone down in excess of 3,875 feet and was expected to yield light oil production at 4500 feet. It was reported that almost $100,000 had already been spent on this test, but geologists were confident that the Badger Basin dome had "all the features necessary to make it a commercially productive oil and gas field.[49]   Drilling operations had to be suspended during part of the winter due to the freezing of the surface water line from the Clarks Fork River. [50]

By August of 1930 the drillers had reached a depth of 6500 feet,[51] and in November considerable excitement was generated when the drilling hit gas at a depth of 8250 feet. New casing was ordered so that the drilling could continue. [52]

By March of 1931 the Resolute Oil Company's well had the distinction of being the deepest well ever drilled in the Rocky Mountain states as well as the deepest well ever put down with cable tools when it passed 8343 feet in depth in the Frontier sand layer. By then the well had shown some production but not in commercial quantities. The company

80

had lost some drilling time when the bailer dropped 7,000 feet taking 1200 feet of cable with it. It took more than a week to retrieve it. [53]

Drilling continued through April when they reached a formation, which required the changing of bits more often. By the end of the month they were below 8375 feet into the diamond sand of the second Frontier level and had struck considerable oil. By then it was flowing fifty to sixty barrels every ten hours. [54]

In the first week of May they had reached a depth of 8515 feet, [55] and by the end of June they had reached 8670 feet. [56]

In August the well was flowing about 40 barrels a day, and Harry Simpson's trucks were hauling it to Belfry where it was reloaded for further shipment to the Laurel refinery. [57] He did take some of it to his Pioneer area ranch where he had a small refinery. Because the crude oil was so light it, could be used in tractors and other vehicles. [58]

With the success of their first well, the Resolute Oil Company began building a small refinery of their own at the first Badger Basin well site the following May of 1932. [59] That July work on a second well began, as well as the building of a rotary oilrig, a number of cabins, and a cookhouse for the 25 men employed on the construction work force. [60]

Drilling on the new well began on Saturday, July 29th, [61] and within two weeks the well had been cemented, cased to 200 feet, and had been drilled to 1000 feet. [62] By early October the drillers had reached 2600 feet, while a crew was burying the water line so that drilling could continue through the winter. [63]

Later that month the oil well was down to 3300 feet, the level where oil was struck in the first well. [64] In late November the well was shut down for six weeks and most of the work crew went to Cut Bank, Montana to work for the Resolute Company wells there. [65]

Continued progress on the second well was put on hold for over two years due to insufficient funds. In June of 1936 after part of the drill hole that had caved in was cemented, drilling resumed. Work crews also laid additional waterlines and installed extra boilers. [66]

By mid-August the drillers had reached 6,000 feet, and two months later they were down below to 8,000 feet. Before they could continue additional casing and cement was required. [67]

After reaching a depth of 8400 feet in mid-November, high-grade oil began flowing from the well with the potential production for 2,000 barrels a day. Gus Forsman reported that the well was "one of the major strikes in recent years" and had "a potential production of 2,000 barrels daily." Julius Peters was then owner of the Forsman leases. [68]

The success of Well Number 2 was a shot in the arm for the Resolute Oil Company, and the following year in 1937 there was a flurry of development in Badger Basin. In February a water well was being drilled to alleviate the water shortage for the refinery, and by April the oil rig was being moved to a third well location. Construction was also underway for a house for the head driller, as well as 20 two-room houses, a cookhouse, a store, new roads and ditches. [69] In May drilling was started on a new well on John Large's permit, and a second well was to be started after a seismograph brought in from California had located the center of the oil pool beneath the surface. [70]

Badger Basin Refinery, 1940's
Photo courtesy of Elmer Bunn

In July a fourth well was started in Badger Basin on Northern Pacific Railroad land, while the third well was by then down to almost 6,000 feet. [71] The third well was completed in mid-October striking oil at 8600 feet. [72]

On December 1st, 1937 the first fatality in the oil field occurred when a falling timber from the "crow's nest" killed William O'Mara, a derrick man for the company, half way up the derrick on Well Number 2. [73]

There was a lot of activity in the Badger Basin in 1938, 1939, and 1940, as new wells were being drilled and others were improved and deepened down into the Frontier sands levels. [74] In August 1939 the company put in a cracking plant so that the oil residue could be processed further. [75] Before this the residue left after the gas and diesel oil was extracted from the crude oil was collected in an outdoor pit, then sold later. Elmer Bunn remembered that at one time the company sent some to Canada for sale where it was burned in boilers for heat. [76]

In late December of 1940 a post office was granted to Badger Basin and set up in the Althoff store where there was also a bar and service station. [77]

Oil operations at Badger Basin continued through the 40's with old wells being cleaned out and new ones drilled. New families were moving into area to work, [78] and additional housing was brought in from Bearcreek to accommodate them. The little houses were well kept, and many had small yards with flowers.

This was the beginning of the most active time for Badger Basin. While employees came and went, there were about 25 employees there at one time. Some of these lived in the 12 residences, or in their own trailers there, while others commuted from the nearby area. Also at the site were an office, the refinery, the ethyl-mixing plant, the combination store – bar – and post office, and the dance hall, where regular dances were held every two weeks. [79] Dances were also given in honor of Clark men going into the service during World

War II. [80]

In August 1943 the Olin Oil Company dug a test hole for water on the Clarence Pearson ranch in the Pioneer area. In early 1944 a work camp was established there to construct a pump house and reservoir to supply a water pipeline to the oil areas in Elk Basin. [81]

The second fatality in Badger Basin occurred on November 22, 1944 when 29-year old Joe Harkin was fatally injured when one of the boilers in the boiler house blew up destroying the building by fire. The force of the explosion sent the boiler "airborne over the telephone lines out to the road, before it went into the ground like a dozer." [82] Harkin was rushed to the hospital in Powell where he died of his injuries the following day. [83]

Two months later the stove in the water-pumping house on the Clarks Fork River exploded destroying the pump and the building. Work stopped at the wells and the refinery for a few days, while a tractor was put into emergency service to pump water to the Basin. [84]

In January 1947 the Leo Althoff family were left homeless when a leak in a gas pipe under their house caused an explosion blowing out three sides of their house. Luckily no one is the family was hurt during the early morning blast. That same week Lester Stidham and Donald Briner, who were working in the refinery, received second-degree burns and were taken to the Powell hospital where they spent two days. [85]

In September Mrs. Pete Nose started to drive from her Badger Basin house to go to town when her car burst into flames and was destroyed. She and her young son received surface burns before the fire was extinguished by workers with the company fire extinguisher. [86]

In September Mrs. Pete Nose started to drive from her Badger Basin house to go to town when her car burst into flames and was destroyed. She and her young son received surface burnsbefore the fire was extinguished by workers with the company fire extinguisher. [86]

Outside Althoff's store and bar in Badger Basin, 1942. (L to R): Kenneth Gairrett, Harold Clark, Ike Gairrett, Paul Gairrett, Leo Althoff, Weldon Althoff (in back), Wilkie Braten. Photo courtesy of Iva and Roberta Bunn Gairrett.

In February 1948 heavy snow resulted in blocked roads. As a result, Clark and Pioneer schools were closed and area children, including those living in Badger Basin, did not have school for three weeks. [87]

Community life continued in Badger Basin into the early 1950's when the oil reserve in Badger Basin began to become depleted. The flow from the wells decreased dramatically. As a result Resolute Oil Company closed their refinery on July 1, 1953. Some of the refinery employees went to work for Husky in Cody, while the field employees went to North Dakota and elsewhere to seek work. [88]

In August Williston Oil and Gas and Petroleum Operators took over the leases from Resolute Oil Company and hired Stub Manley as superintendent and Elmer Bunn as pumper. Ed Klaeger from Oklahoma was the manager for the two companies. [89]

In 1956 Williston Oil and Gas took over as the sole operator, and Elmer Bunn was in charge of the field as the company's only employee in Badger Basin. Husky Oil began buying oil from the field that year using it for blending purposes with their own oil because it was so light. The remaining oil was trucked to Laurel and to Mosby, Montana for refining. That summer Walter and Virginia Teichert, who had continued to rent their house from the company, moved from the Basin. Their residence was the last one occupied at the site. It was purchased by them and moved to the Pioneer area ranch. [90]

Today only concrete foundations, discarded equipment, and vacant streets remain to give a hint of the company town that had occupied the site for almost twenty-five years. When the wind is calm, the sound of the few wells still pumping can be heard. Their oil is collected and trucked to the pipeline near Frannie and Deaver for further transit elsewhere.

Badger Basin, 1948
Photo courtesy of Elmer Bunn

Elmer Bunn provided the following list of the employees whom he remembered worked at Badger Basin: [91]

Refinery Employees (pre-1953)

Stub Manley – Superintendent
Tommy Moore – Foreman/welder
Everett Kelsey – Gas mixing plant
Walter Teichert – Operator
Walter Lowe – Operator
Kenneth Gairrett – Loader
Ike Gairrett – Loader
Pat Lineback – Welder
Jack Felton – Operator
Neal Bean – Pumper
Jack Kanvick
Jake Cameron – Operator
Harold Brown
Fred Bunn
Walter Cochrane

Pete Manley
Baldie Maze – Operator
William Teichert - Operator
Elmer Bunn - Operator
Lester Stidham - Loader
Don Briner - Loader
George Moore - Loader
Bill Appleton - Loader
John Cameron - Loader
Louis Carter - Loader
Pete Nose - Operator
Joe Hardee
Ray Bunn
Eddie Schock
Randall Braten

Other Employees at Badger Basin

Wilbur Bunn – Roustabout (winter)
Jody Brown - Roustabout (winter)
Lee Wayman
Johnny Large
Jim Vickery
Paul Parker
Leo Vanderendonk
Eddie Schock – Foreman
Frank Deville, Sr.
Del Coorough
Verne Vaught

Ray Black - Roustabout
Clarence Black - Roustabout
Merton Walters - Loader
Bud Bean
Albert Peters - Field Super. last 5 yrs.
Jack Hardin – Field Foreman
William Vazanko - Pumper
Hugh Rough - Pumper
Fred Harkin - Pumper
Jiggs Sinnock - Pumper
Glen Brown

Field Employees (post July 1953)

Byrne (Stub) Manley
Jack Harkin (30 days)
William Vazanko (30 days)
Elmer Bunn (total 6 yrs. refinery/ 30 yrs field)
Fred Hartnik (Badger Oil owner)
Jack Van Norman (Badger Oil owner

Hugh Rough (30 days)
Ray Martin
Robert Marney

Kenney Van Norman (Badger Oil owner)
Bud Lanning - Geologist

85

Chapter 11 notes:

[1] *Red Lodge Picket,* November 11, 1893, p. 3.

[2] *Red Lodge Picket*, October 14, 1893.

[3] *Red Lodge Picket*, November 11, 1893, p. 3.

[4] "Regulations Pertaining to Mining Claims Under the General Mining Laws of 1872, Multiple Use, and Special Disposal Provisions," brochure, Bureau of Land Management, United States Department of the Interior, no date; "The General Mining Law of 1872," www.greatbasinminewatch.org/mining law.html; and "The 1872 Mining Law," IB89130, Congressional Research Service, January 22, 2001.

[5] Lode claims are staked on veins or lodes in a defined boundary of rock, while placer claims are all other claims not confined in a lode. They are usually found in loose sand or gravel from an ancient or active stream or river, which have probably been washed down from a vein or lode. A placer claim could be no larger than 20 acres for an individual, but an association of eight persons could locate multiple claims of 20 acres each totally no more than 160 acres. ("Overview of the Mining Law of 1872," www.mosen.net/mining_law.html).

[6] *Red Lodge Picket,* November 25, 1893, p. 3.

[7] The bill stipulated that "no mining claim which has been regularly located and recorded as required by local laws and mining regulations shall be subject to forfeiture for non-performance of the annual assessment for the year 1893... provided that the claimant or claimants shall file and record a notice in the office where the location notice is filed before Dec. 21, 1893 that they intend to hold and work said claim." ("New Assessment Law," *Ibid.*).

[8] *Red Lodge Picket,* March 31, 1894, p. 3.

[9] *Red Lodge Picket*, April 14, 1894, p. 3.

[10] *Red Lodge Picket*, September 1, 1894, p. 3.

[11] *Red Lodge Picket*, April 13, 1895, p. 3 and April 20, 1895, p. 3.

[12] *Red Lodge Picket*, June 19, 1897, p. 3.

[13] *Red Lodge Picket*, August 14, 1897, p. 3.

[14] "Paint Creek Items," *Wyoming Stockgrower and Farmer,"* August 30, 1905, p. 1.

[15] "Clark Squibs," *Wyoming Stockgrower and Farmer*, October 22, 1909, p. 2.

[16] "Clark Squibs," *Wyoming Stockgrower and Farmer,* January 28, 1910, p. 8; "Clark," *Wyoming Stockgrower and Farmer,* November 27, 1912, p. 4; December 17, 1913, p. 5; August 1, 1914, p. 8, August 26, 1914, p. 2; and October 24, 1914, p. 2.

[17] "Clarks Fork," *Park County Enterprise,* August 1, 1914, p. 8; "Clark," *Park County Enterprise,* August 26, 1914, p. 2; and September 16, 1914, p. 7.

[18] Murray Lundberg, "Gold Dredges in the North," www.explorenorth.com/libraryweekly; Elliott – World's Leading Dredge Producer – Gold Dredging, www.dredge.com/casestudies/ alludepo.htm; Willie, Zach and Skip Via, "How Gold Dredges Work," www.northstar.k12.ak.us/schools/upk/gold/facts/dredge/dredge.html; Dave McCracken "Suction Dredging for Fun and Gold," www.goldgold.com/suctiondredging.htm.

[19] "Clark," *The Park County Enterprise,* October 3, 1914, p. 8.

[20] *Bridger Times,* October 9, 1914, p. 3.

[21] "Clark, *Park County Enterprise,* October 24, 1914, p.8.

[22] *Bridger Times,* December 11, 1914, p. 1.

[23] *Bridger Times*, January 15, 1915, p. 8.

[24] "Park County Rich in Gold-Bearing Sand," *The Powell Tribune,* April 2, 1915, p. 3.

[25] Ibid.

[26] "Finds Clark Fork Placer Gold Feeder, *Carbon County Journal,* September 27, 1916, p. 1.

[27] *Bridger Times,* March 22, 1918, p. 1 and *Carbon County Journal,* April 12, 1918, p.1; April 17, 1918, p. 4: and *Park County Enterprise,* April 24, 1918, p. 1.

[28] *Northern Wyoming Herald* article republished in *The Picket-Journal,* March 21, 1920, p. 1.

[29] Park County Enterprise, May 19, 1920, p. 5.

[30] *The Picket-Journal,* March 21, 1920, p. 1)

[31] "Park County Agent Notes by F. A. Chisholm," *The Cody Enterprise,* March 2, 1932, p. 5.

[32] "Find Prospector Dead Near Clark," *Carbon County News,* November 22, 1956, p. 1.

[33] "Clarks Fork, *The Cody Enterprise,* May 24, 1933, p. 6.

[34] "Lower Clark Fork," *The Cody Enterprise,* August 8, 1934, p. 6.

[35] "Lower Clark Fork," *The Cody Enterprise,* April 17, 1935, p. 6.

[36] "Clarks Fork," *The Cody Enterprise,* December 9, 1936, p. 8.

[37] "Clarks Fork, *The Cody Enterprise,* December 14, 1938, p. 6. (Note: the Singer property today).

[38] "Andy Marler Finds Specimen of Rich Ore," *The Park County Herald,* July 22, 1925, p. 8.

[39] "Drilling Starts on Marler Land," *The Cody Enterprise,* March 22, 1951, p. 6; "Gas Reached on Marler Ranch," *The Cody Enterprise,* April 5, 1951, p. 1; "Skull Creek Ranch Pays Off With Gas," *The Cody Enterprise,* April 12, 1951, p. 1.

[40] Park County Book 24, pgs. 203, 204, 207, 208, 254, 256, 498, 562, 566, 570, 572; and Park County Book 32, pgs. 507, 509, 511, 512, 513, 515, and 516.

[41] Park County Book 24, pgs. 203, 204, 206, 207, 208, and 209.

[42] "Clark," *Park County Enterprise,* March 22, 1916, p. 8.

[43] *Carbon County Journal,* June 13, 1917, p. 4.

[44] "The Forgotten Man, *The Powell Tribune,* March 4, 1982, p. 9.

[45] "Clarks Fork," *The Cody Enterprise,* June 20, 1928, p. 4.

[46] "Clarks Fork," *The Cody Enterprise,* May 29, 1929, p. 3.

[47] "Clarks Fork," *The Cody Enterprise,* August 21, 1929, p. 4; and "Badger Basin Oil Rig Burned to Ground," *The Cody Enterprise,* August 28, 1929, p. 1.

[48] "Oil Men Injured Badger Basin Well," *The Cody Enterprise,* September 25, 1929, p. 1.

[49] "Badger Basin Test Awakens Interest," *The Cody Enterprise,* October 9, 1929, p. 5.

[50] Elmer Bunn, interview with the author on driving tour of Badger Basin, August 12, 2000.

[51] "Clarks Fork," *The Cody Enterprise,* August 20, 1930, p. 6.

[52] "Clarks Fork," *The Cody Enterprise,* November 26, 1930, p. 4.

[53] "Deepest Well Goes Deeper and Deeper," *The Cody Enterprise,* March 4, 1931, p. 2; and "Lower Clarks Fork," *The Cody Enterprise,* March 11, 1931, p. 7.

[54] "Lower Clarks Fork," *The Cody Enterprise,* March 25, 1931, p. 4 and 6; April 15, 1931, p. 6; and April 29 1931, p. 6.

[55] "Lower Clarks Fork, *The Cody Enterprise,* May 13, 1931, p. 6.

[56] "Drilling Continues Resolute Well in Badger Basin," *The Cody Enterprise,* July 1, 1931, p. 3; and "Clarks Fork," *The Cody Enterprise,* July 1, 1931, p. 8.

[57] "Lower Clarks Fork," *The Cody Enterprise,* August 5, 1931, p. 11.

[58] Elmer Bunn interview, August 12, 2000.

[59] "Lower Clark Fork," *The Cody Enterprise,* May 18, 1932, p. 6,

[60] "Clarks Fork," *The Cody Enterprise,* July 12, 1933, p. 3 and July 26, 1933, p. 6.

[61] "Clarks Fork," *The Cody Enterprise,* August 2, 1933, p. 6,

[62] "Lower Clarks Fork," *The Cody Enterprise,* August 9, 1933, p. 6 and August 16, 1933, p. 6.

[63] "Lower Clarks Fork, *The Cody Enterprise,* October 4, 1933, p. 7.

[64] "Lower Clarks Fork," *The Cody Enterprise,* October 25, 1933, p. 5.

[65] "Lower Clarks Fork," *The Cody Enterprise,* December 6, 1933, p. 5.

[66] "Lower Clarks Fork," *The Cody Enterprise,* July 1, 1936, p. 6.

[67] "Lower Clarks Fork, *The Cody Enterprise,* August 19, 1936, p. 6 and October 21, 1936, p. 5.

[68] "Forsman Claims Fine Well Badger Basin," *The Cody Enterprise,* November 18, 1936, p. 1.

[69] "Lower Clarks Fork, *The Cody Enterprise,* February 3, 1937, p. 6; April 14, 1937, p. 6; and "Clarks Fork," *The Cody Enterprise,* April 14, 1937, p. 6.

[70] "Lower Clarks Fork, *The Cody Enterprise,* May 5, 1937, p. 6.

[71] "Lower Clarks Fork, *The Cody Enterprise,* July 14, 1937, p. 3.

[72] "Lower Clarks Fork," *The Cody Enterprise,* October 20, 1937, p. 3.

[73] "Clarks Fork," *The Cody Enterprise,* December 8, 1937, p. 8; and Elmer Bunn, interview, August 12, 2000.

[74] "Lower Clarks Fork, *The Cody Enterprise,* May 4, 1938, p. 7; July 6, 1938, p. 6; August 31, 1938, p. 5; September 1938, p. 2; November 2, 1938, p. 7; November 16 1938, p. 2; January 18, 1939, p. 6; February 8, 1939, p. 3; April 5, 1939, p. 8; September 27, 1939, p. 7; and February 28, 1940, p. 6; **Note**: On October 10, 1939 the four stockholders of the Badger Basin Corporation, H. H. Forsman, his wife, Louise Forsman, Gus Forsman and his wife, Lena Forsman met in Billings and decided to sell or dispose of all of the property of the corporation in the Badger Basin area that had been assigned to the corporation on January 12, 1931. As a result of this meeting the corporation's holdings were divided up as follows: One half to Herbert Forsman, one-fourth to Gus Forsman, and the other one-fourth to Lena Forsman. All of the stockholders voted in favor of the resolution voting 500 shares. (Articles of Incorporation, Park County Book 52, pgs. 301-302)

[75] "Lower Clarks Fork," *The Cody Enterprise,* August 2, 1939, p. 2.

[76] Elmer Bunn interview, August 12, 2000.

[77] "Lower Clarks Fork," *The Cody Enterprise,* December 25, 1940, p. 3.

[78] "Lower Clarks Fork," *The Cody Enterprise,* June 11, 1941, p. 2; and August 11, 1943, p. 6,

[79] Elmer Bunn interview, August 12, 2000.

[80] "Clarks Fork," *The Cody Enterprise,* March 25, 1942, p. 3.

[81] "Lower Clarks Fork," *The Cody Enterprise,* August 18, 1943, p. 6; and February 2, 1944, p. 3.

[82] Elmer Bunn interview, August 12, 2000.

[83] "Clarks Fork and Lower Clarks Fork," *The Cody Enterprise,* November 29, 1944, p. 2; and *Carbon County News,* November 30, 1944, p. 1.

[84] "Clarks Fork," and Lower Clarks Fork," *The Cody Enterprise,* January 31, 1945, p. 6.

[85] "Badger Basin," *The Cody Enterprise,* January 29, 1947, p. 11.

[86] "Badger Basin, *The Cody Enterprise,* September 10, 1947, p. 11.

[86] "Badger Basin, *The Cody Enterprise,* September 10, 1947, p. 11.

[87] "Badger Basin," *The Cody Enterprise,* February 11, 1948, p. 3; and February 18, 1948, p. 11.

[88] Elmer Bunn, conversation with the author, Clark, March 22, 2004.

[89] Ibid.

[90] Ibid; and Rayola Teichert Fink, telephone conversation with the author, March 27, 2004.

[91] Elmer Bunn, "History of Badger Basin Oil Field, notes given to the author, December 9, 2002.

Harry Temple house in Clark
Photo courtesy of Marian Fricke Bainter

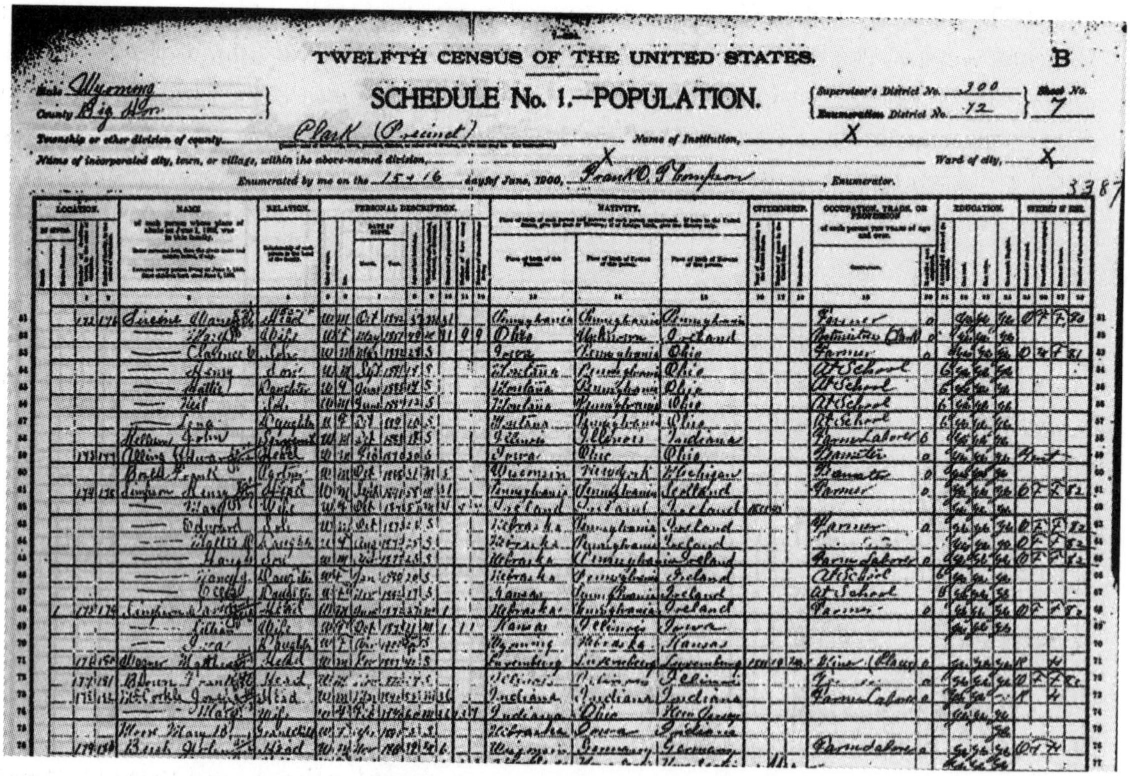
TWELFTH CENSUS OF THE UNITED STATES.

B

State Wyoming
County Big Horn

SCHEDULE No. 1.—POPULATION.

Supervisor's District No. 300
Enumeration District No. 72
Sheet No. 7

Township or other division of county Clark (Precinct)
Name of Institution, X
Name of incorporated city, town, or village, within the above-named division, X
Ward of city, X

Enumerated by me on the 15 & 16 day of June, 1900, Frank O. Thompson, Enumerator.

Clark's first census record, 1900

12
Who Was Here in 1900?

Not every Clark area individual or family completed the homesteading requirements to acquire ownership of their land, and thus those residents would not be found in the title transfer records.

A better reflection of who was living in Clark can be found in the United States Census records. This survey, which takes place every ten years, reflects all of the members of a family and others who were living in a household.

Almost the entire 1890 government census was destroyed in a records building fire, so the 1900 census is the first one from which we can learn who some of the early Clark families were. At that time the Clark precinct included the Sunlight and Crandall areas, and all were part of a larger Big Horn County. Below are listed the 129 Clark residents from that census taken on June 15th and 16th, 1900.[1] Husbands and wives are listed with their children and others living in the same households. Those who were single or living by themselves are listed separately.

1 - Warren and Mary Sirrine
    Clarence E. Sirrine – son
    Henry Sirrine – son
    Hattie Sirrine – daughter
    Neal Sirrine – son
    Lena Sirrine – daughter
    John Kelliam – servant
2 - Edward Alling
    Frank Bostic – partner
3 - Henry M. and Mary Simpson
    Edgar Simpson - son
    Mattie Simpson - daughter
    Harry Simpson – son
    Nancy J. Simpson - daughter
    Ellen Simpson - daughter
4 - David and Lillian Simpson
    Iva Simpson - daughter
5 - Matthew Wagner
6 - Frank Brown
7 - Joseph and Mary McCorkle
    Mary Moore – granddaughter

8 - John and Jennie R. Bush
    Louisa M. Bush - daughter
    Louis S. Bush - son
9 - James and Anna Worley
    Pearl Worley daughter
    George Worley - son
    Guy Worley - son
10 - William and Margaret J. Fouse
    Ralph L. Fouse - son
    William J. Fouse – son
    Samuel P. Fouse - son
11 - Emery and Victoria Cunningham
    Russell Cunningham - son
    Lloyd Cunningham - son
    Hiram Thompson - boarder
    Charles E. Galford - boarder
12 - George Leatherman
13 - John McGonegal
14 - John C. McCleary
15 - S. Judson Hubbard

16 - James Smith

17 - Solomon and Marinda Weathermon
  Josie Weathermon - daughter
  Anna Weathermon - daughter
  Christopher Weathermon - son
  Mark Weathermon - son

18 - Mark and Dorothy B. Frizzelle
  Elva Frizzelle - adopted daughter
  Violet Moore - servant

19 - James and Anna Hogan
  Willard Hogan - son

20 - John W. Moore - servant

21 - William L. and Alice Barber
  Walter Barber - son
  Pearl Barber - daughter
  Floris Barber - daughter
  Blanche Barber - daughter
  Merrill Barber - son
  Fay Barber - daughter

22 - Emerson Bunn
  Electia Watson - mother-in-law
  Fred Bunn - son
  Jesse Bunn - son
  Wilbur Bunn - son

23 - John and Sarah W. Fry
  Ephraim Fry - son
  John Fry, Jr. - son
  Lillie Fry - daughter
  Sarah Fry - daughter
  Willis Fry - son
  Eva Fry - daughter

24 - Eli and Carrie Vickery
  Edgar Vickery - son
  Mary A. Vickery - daughter
  Emma Vickery - daughter
  Dorothy Vickery - daughter
  Carol Vickery - daughter
  Elizabeth Vickery - daughter

25 - George L. Berry

26 - Charles F. Curtice

27 - Andrew Minch

28 - Joseph Wood

29 - Orton Sirrine
  Harold Silvas - servant

30 - Charles Hohntetter

31 - John and Alphia Chapman
  William Miller - servant
  Albert Ureley - servant
  Osborne Williams - servant

32 - David and Ora McCarty
  William McCorkle - boarder

33 - James Shorey
  Percy Shorey - son

34 - M. and Carrie Boughton
  Jessie Boughton - daughter

35 - Henry Davis
  Lola Davis - daughter

36 - Russell Kimball
  Farley Kimball - brother
  Riley L. Lay - servant
  Fred Denton - servant
  Michael Hewett - servant
  Joseph Wallace - servant

36 - Marcus and Maggie Davenport
  James Coltsera - boarder

37 - Archie and Grace Beaton
  Glenn Beaten - son
  Mary J. Palmer - mother-in-law
  Bertha Palmer - niece

Chapter 12 notes:

[1] *Twelfth Census of the United States, Schedule No. 1 - Population*, Big Horn County, Wyoming, Clark (Precinct), Enumeration Dist. 72, p. 189B - 191A (*Family History Library Microfilm* #1241826)

13
Who Was Here in 1910?

Ten years later the number of families living here had increased dramatically when the next U.S. Census was taken here in 1910. The Clark, Pioneer, Pat O'Hara and Paint Creek areas were now located in the newly created Park County. It took the census takers from April 22nd to May 12th to locate and record all of the families living in this enumeration district. The following are the 390 area residents listed in that census.[1]

1 – Walter E. Bates
    Gordon Kneisley – partner
2 – George and Laura M. Schnitker
    Laura A. Schnitker – daughter
    George H. Schnitker – son
3 – Joseph E. and Cora Skipper
    Gladys Skipper - daughter
    Janet Skipper – daughter
    Ross Skipper – son
4 – Bert L. and Esther Card
    Alice Card – daughter
5 – Edward M. and Gerta Card
    Edna R. Card – daughter
    Florence L. Card – daughter
6 – Frank G. Hopkins
    Louise Hopkins – daughter
    George T. Hopkins - son
7 – Simon C. Kimball
    William B. Kimball – brother
    Ellsworth Hauth – hired man
    Ralph W. Barr – hired man
    Frank T. Ives – hired man
    Ike Terekawa – hired man
8- Edwin T. and Bessie Fuson
    Evelyn Fuson – daughter
    Clytie Fuson – daughter
9 - Miles and Sadie Decker
    Lawrence Kane – boarder
10 - James and Annie H. Hogan
    Willard E. Hogan – son
    Harold G. Hogan – son

11 – Solomon F. Weathermon
    Vernon Weathermon – son
    Josie Weathermon – daughter
    Christopher Weathermon – son
    Mark Weathermon – son
12 – Bruno Becker
    Herbert L. Sweet – partner
    Benjamin Pendergast – hired man
    Joe Mellenos – hired man
13 – Albert A. Owens
14 – Emma H. Wilson
    Charles A. C. Snow - son
    Sylva Denson – grandson
15- Matt Wagner
16 – William H. and Edith M. Schmidt
    Ethel M. Schmidt - daughter
    Alvin R. Schmidt – son
    Eliza J. Johnston - mother-in-law
17 – Frederick J. and Margaret Richards
    Alfred J. Richards – son
    Henry Hughes – father-in-law
18 – David Parker
19 – Oskar and Emma Lindquist
    Edward Lindquist – son
    Howard O. Reese – hired man
    Lulu Reese - servant
20 – William H. Woods
    Emile Blanchard - hired man

21 – Lemuel and Rosa V. Standley
    Amanda J. Standley – daughter
    William B. Standley – son
    Minnie Standley – daughter
    Frances B. Standley – daughter
    Charles W. Standley – son
22 – Benjamin and Helga Eckloe
    Marion Eckloe – daughter
23 – Julius Kling
24 – William F. and Alice Davis
    Myrtle Davis – daughter
    Floyd Davis – so
25 – Harry O. and Mayme Temple
    Helen E. Temple – daughter
26 – John E. and Everetta E. Ricketts
    John L. Ricketts – son
    Dwight E. Ricketts – son
    Ruth E. Ricketts – daughter
    Edward G. Ricketts – son
27 – Lulu E. Johnston
    William E. Ricketts – nephew
28 – Frank and Mamie Miller
    Frederick Laurentz – boarder
29 – Eli J. and Carrie Vickery
    Edgar A, Vickery – son
    Mary A. Vickery – daughter
    Emma C. Vickery – daughter
    Dorothy Vickery – daughter
    Carol L. Vickery – daughter
    Elizabeth Vickery – daughter
    Theodore Vickery – son
    Elsie Vickery – daughter
    Frederick Vickery – son
    James V. Vickery –son
    Jack M. Vickery – son
30 – Emerson Bunn
    Fred A. Bunn – son
    Jessie E. Bunn – son
    Wilbur Bunn – son
    Rosella Snyder – sister-in-law
31 – Charles B. and Rachel Hubbard

32 – William G. and Augusta Brough
    Glenn Brough – son
    Frank Brough – son
    Helen Brough – daughter
    Jay Brough – son
    Vera Brough – daughter
    Marcus T. Davenport – hired man
    Henry Elder – hired man
    Hugh C. Henry hired man
    Denis Brennan – hired man
    Amile Bosley – hired man
    August Vedel – hired man
    Albert Simeral – hired man
33 – Charles B. and Fannie Taylor
    Vinita Taylor – daughter
    Denver Taylor – son
    Sanford Taylor – son
    Howard Taylor – son
34 – Fred Hodges
35 – Joseph C. and Josephine Brown
    Bertha Brown – daughter
    Clarence Brown – son
    Verna A. Brown – daughter
    Ethel Brown – daughter
    Joseph Brown – son
    Roy Brown – son
36 – Willard D. Ruscher
37 – Edwin and Emma Manning
38 – Owen C. Bevelhymer
39 – Jacob C. Bevelhymer
40 – Thomas J. and Julia Davenport
    Joseph O. Davenport – son
41 – George Heald
    Walter Heald – brother
    Edward P. Heald – brother
    Mary C. Heald – sister
    John H. Jones – hired man
    Harden Spicer – hired man
42 – Russell and Ina Kimball

43 - Farley and Mina Kimball
    Mary Kimball - daughter
    Florence Kimball - daughter
    John Spicer - hired man
44 - Perceval Fullerton
45 - Harrison and Hettie Wogoman
    Mabel Wogoman - daughter
    Bryan Wogoman - son
    Emma Wogoman - daughter
    Monroe Wogoman - son
    Molly Wogoman - son
    John Wogoman - son
    Charley Wogoman - son
46 - Melvin B. and Emma Lowe
    Clarence Lowe - son
47- Thomas E. and Anna B. Frasure
48- Minnie Rieman
    Otto A. Rieman, Jr. - son
    Oscar Olson - hired man
    Alfred Olson - hired man
    Charles S. Frasure - boarder
    Henry McDade - hired man
49 - Walter D. and Grace D. Brown
50- Jay D. Clark
51 - George W. and Mary C. Ballard
    Nancy T. Ballard - daughter
    Willis Ballard - son
    Martin Ballard - son
    Joseph L. Ballard - son
    Carrie J. Ballard - daughter
    Grace G. Ballard - daughter
    Lily F. Ballard - daughter
    Hazel M. Ballard - daughter
    Della F. Ballard - daughter
52 - John and Jennie Bush
    Louisa M. Bush - daughter
    Louis S. Bush - son
53 - Ebenezer and Mary E. Huntington
    Myra Huntington - daughter
    Morris E. Huntington - son
    Stella Huntington - daughter
    Lucretia Huntington - daughter
    Lloyd Huntington - son

    Arthur Huntington - son
    Frederick Huntington - son
    Charlotte Huntington - daughter
54 - Daniel D. and Emma F. Wildman
    Jessie Wildman - daughter
55 - Jenna and Daniel D. Wildman, Jr.
    Dwight R. Wildman
56 - Orton and Amelia Sirrine
    Katherine R. Sirrine - daughter
    Robert M. Mandeville - father-in-law
    Rebecca Mandeville - mother-in-law
    John H. Pugh - brother-in-law
    George Pugh - brother-in-law
57- Melissa J. Green
58 - James Green
    John J. Green - son
59 - Mary Simpson
    David M. Simpson - son
    Lilly Simpson - daughter-in-law
    Iva Simpson - granddaughter
    Robert Simpson - grandson
    Edgar Simpson - son
    Harry G. Simpson - son
    Edith Simpson - daughter-in-law
    Nancy Simpson - daughter
    Ella Simpson - daughter
    Philip Livingston - hired man
    Julius Hanson
60 - Mary G. Sirrine
    Neil Sirrine - son
    William Sullivan - hired man
61 - Jacob Gloeckner
    Martin Gloeckner - brother
    Ferris Palmer - nephew
62 - Peter and Effie Greenwald
    Lydia Greenwald - daughter
    Clara B. Greenwald - daughter
63 - Clarence and Martha A. Sirrine
    Hazel Newman - niece
    George Baumgartner - hired man
    David R. Petitt - hired man
    Frank L. Clark - hired man
    Joseph H. Berry - hired man

Frederick Hildebrand – hired man
Lucy Hildebrand – boarder
Hazel Hildebrand – boarder

64 – William H. and Margaret Fouse
Ralph Fouse – son
John Fouse – son
Samuel Fouse – son

65 – John Olson
Fridolf Olson – son
Emil Olson – son
Jennie Olson – daughter
Walter Olson – son
Myrtle Olson – daughter

66 – Daniel and Mary Mason
Roy Mason – son
Clyde Mason – son
Ethel Mason – daughter
Melvin Mason – son
Alice Mason – daughter

67 – George W. and Martha D. Johnson
Iona Johnson – daughter
Clifford L. Johnson – son
Mary K. Johnson – daughter
Martha L. Johnson – son

68 – Frank A. and Grace Huggins
Arden Huggins – son
Earl Huggins – son
Altie Huggins – daughter

69 – James D. and Maggie Owen
Edwin E. Owen – son
Cecil O. Owen – son
Fernan E. Owen
Irene Owen - daughter

70 – Ulyses and Nellie Tucker
Percy L. Tucker – son
William E. Tucker – son
Elsie Tucker - daughter
Sylvia Tucker - daughter

71 – Sidney B. and Emma Henry
72 – Ira and Edith Edna Toothaker
73 – Joseph B. and Joannash Hundley
Virginline Hundley - daughter
74 - Elizabeth Denney

Russel Denney – son
Edith Denney – daughter
Cornelius Denney – son
Linda Denney – daughter
Eva Denney – daughter
Ethel Denney – daughter

75 – Elisha M. Clark
Nellie Goodno – servant

76 – Peter O. and Estella Simpson
John Simpson – son
Earl Simpson – son
Frank Simpson – son
Vern Simpson – son
Stella Simpson – daughter
Robert Simpson – son
Kate Newton – granddaughter

77 – Albert W. and Lina S. Connell
Etlor Connell – son
Charles Taylor – father-in-law
Pheby Taylor – mother-in-la

78 – Peter and Emily Johnson
Mathilda Rittel – mother-in-law
Carl M. Johnson – brother
William Rittle – brother-in-law

79 – Benjamin and Ida Steen
Thomas W. Goff – boarder

80 – Andrew J. McCleary

81 – James M. Hunter
John Vallet – hired man
William L. Henry – nephew
Roy L. Ballard – hired man
Blanch Ballard – servant
Lillian Ballard – Roy's daughter

82 – George L. Berry

83- Ira Sparhawk

84- James and Caroline Pugh
James R. Pugh – son

85 – John H. Frasure
William Green - (no designation)

86 – John E. and Gertrude Brown
Edith M. Brown – daughter

87 – Milton E. and Olive Gorsuch
Lois Gorsuch – daughter

Milton E. Gorsuch, Jr. – son
88 – Allen Campbell
89 – John P. and Lizzie A. Allison
Hatta A. Bervis – daughter
90 – Martin A. and Nellie Jobe
John T. Jobe – brother
Charles Hadley – hired man
Augustus La Fond – hired man
H. J. Ives – hired man
John Staib – hired man
Jack Johnson – hired man
Florence Johnson – servant
Tony Burkett – hired man
George Hall – hired man
Daniel McClanenan – hired man
Bert Oliver – hired man
Charles Beard – hired man
Alfred Blackstone – hired man
Joseph C. Spicer – hired man
Emil Embert – hired man
Oscar Thompson – hired ma
91 – Edgar P. Jandell
92 – David C. Collins
93 – Henry A. and Maude G. Luce
George Prell – hired man

Chapter 13 notes:

[1] *Thirteen Census of the United States: 1910 Population, Park County, Wyoming*, Election District #26, Painter Precinct and Election District #1, Clark Precincts #1 and #2, and Paint Creek Precinct; Enumeration District #28, pgs. 134A – 137B. (*Family History Library Microfilm* #1375760) **Note:** Names are spelled exactly as they were recorded by the enumerator.

Dorothy Pearson and her brother, Edward, 1921
at the Pioneer area ranch. Photo courtesy of Carol
Briggs Joy and Dorothy Pearson Williams.

Esther Weathermon with her children: Mark, Lee, Marge, and Ada.
Photo taken at the Mattie Simpson ranch in Pioneer area about 1927,
courtesy of Ada Weathermon Eckerman.

14
Who Was Here in 1920?

The number of area households declined slightly during the ten years from 1910 until the next census was taken in 1920. When the census was collected between January 8th and February 6th, 1920, the area's population was listed as 302. [1]

1 - Edmond B. Groom

2 - Emma H. Wilson
    Charles A. C. Snow – son
    Sylva L. Wilson – adopted son

3 - Charles H. and Allia B. Trumbo

4 - Albert A. Owens

5 - Solomon F. Weathermon
    Josie Cooper - daughter
    William H. Cooper – son-in-law

6 - Mary M. Cravens
    Genoa G. Miller – sister
    Henry D. Miller – brother-in-law

7 - Oscar F. and Emma Lindquist
    Emma V. Hasselstrom – niece
    Philip J. Herman – hired man

8 - David and Emma G. Parker –
    Paul A. Parker – son
    Dale Parker – son

9 - Otis W. and Ethel S. Gould
    Eleanor V. McHugh – lodger

10 - Edwin T and Bessie E. Fuson
    Evalyn L Fuson – daughter
    Clytie V. Fuson – daughter
    Della A. Fuson – daughter
    Thornton E. Fuson – son

11 - Emerson and Lucy Bunn
    E. Ray Bunn – son
    Ella B. Bunn – daughter

12 - Andy and Evlena Marler
    Erma Marlier – daughter
    Saber Marler – daughter
    Johnnie A. Marler – daughter

13- Preservid O. and Jeannie A. Fish
    Sadie C. Fish – daughter
    George H. Fish – son

14 - Dwight G. and Alexia S. King
    Virginia F. King – daughter
    Charles G. King – son

15 - Andrew B. Chapman
    Jasper N. Parker

16 - Granville L. Berry

17 - Henry McDade
    Nevada V. Wolfe – lodger

18 - Peter and Leone M. Delamonica
    George Delmonica – son
    Leopold G. Delmonica – son
    Marguerite Van Wouter – niece

19 - Harrison and Hettie Wogoman
    Mollie Wogoman – daughter
    Monroe Wogoman – son
    John Wogoman – son
    Charlie Wogoman – son
    Ezra Wogoman – son
    Bessie Wogoman – daughter

20 - W. Frank and Lila D. Marlin
    Eli J. Marlin – son
    Ruth E. Daws – cousin
    John G. Bell – hired man
    Nannie R. Bell – cook

21 - David Robertson

22 - David D. and Mable Mecklenburg
    Mable O. Mecklenburg – daughter
    Bernard A. Mecklenburg – brother
    Walter Hylar – hired man
    Matt Wagner – lodger

23 – Edgar Simpson
    Nannie Simpson – sister
    Fred L. Myers – hired man
    Grace L. Lee – servant
    Max C. Yeoman – hired man
    Frank Lasater – hired man
    John Weir – lodger

24 – David M. and Lillie B. Simpson
    Iva G. Simpson – daughter
    Robert H. Simpson – son
    Florence L. Simpson – daughter
    Cal M. Underwood – hired man
    Aaron L. Baker – hired man
    Earl Dusell – hired man

25 – Carl H. and Emma E. Carlson

26 – Frank O. and Bessie E. Sparhawk
    Helen L. Sparhawk – daughter
    Howard E. Sparhawk – son
    Richard P. Sparhawk – son
    Andy Dudas – hired man

27 – Lindley M Clark
    Charles Watts – hired man
    Mrs. Caroline Watts – housekeeper
    Burt Watts – hired man
    Halvor Howeland – hired man
    Frank Chamberlain – hired man
    Oscar Olson – hired man
    Jack Whitney – hired man
    Nick Dura – hired man

28 – William H. and Margaret J. Fouse
    Ralph L. Fouse – son
    W. John Fouse – son
    Samuel P. Fouse – son
    Isabel Fouse – mother

29 – Andrew and Ellen Madison
    Ben Madison – son
    Alice L. Madison – daughter
    A. Emil Madison – son
    Frances R. Madison – daughter
    Ove Arthun – brother-in-law

30 – Ira Toothaker
    Ove Toothaker – daughter
    Helen G. Toothaker – daughter

31 – Martin G. and Belle Gloeckner
    Jacob Gloeckner – brother
    Matthew B. Brown – hired man

32 – Clarence A. and Hannah E. Pearson
    Edward P. Pearson – son
    Dorothy S. Pearson – daughter

33 – Charles E. and Elsie M. Townsend
    Eva C. Townsend – daughter
    Zylpha M. Townsend – daughter

34 – Walter G. Cochrane

35 – Russell and H. Grena Oliver
    John D. Underwood – lodger

36 – Wrightis W. and Nannie M. Hardee
    M. Leonard Hardee – son
    Wilburn W. Hardee – son
    Joseph H. Hardee – son
    Myrtle V. Hardee – daughter
    Dorothy M. Hardee – daughter
    Cleo B. Hardee – daughter
    Billy Hardee – son
    Purl J. Hardee – daughter
    Walter R. Hardee – son

37 – George W. and Mattie D. Johnson
    Iona Johnson – daughter
    Clifford Johnson – son
    Marion G. Johnson – daughter
    M. Eleanor Johnson – daughter
    Minnie E. Johnson – daughter
    E. Allan Johnson – son
    John H. Pugh – lodger

38 – Harry G. and Cora E. Simpson
    Mabella Godfrey – lodger
    John DeRoadt – hired man
    Harry Underwood – hired man

39 – Orton N. and Amelia A. Sirrine

40 – Robert M. and Rebecca Mandeville

41 – Daniel S. and Panayiota A. McCorkle
    Antonio E. McCorkle – son

42 – Charles Bratrsovsky
    Leo Bratsovsky – brother
    Rudolph Millfait – lodger

43 - Albert DeForest and Ruth L. Wilkinson
- Albert Wilkinson, Jr. - son
- Daisy R. Wilkinson - daughter
- Rose H. Wilkinson - daughter
- Dora E. Urfer - sister-in-law
- John L. Armstrong - partner

44 - Josiah E. and Olivia E. Earl
- Clarence M. Earl - son
- Myrtle V. Earl - daughter
- Albert Bush - hired man

45 - Carl M. Johnson

46 - Peter and Emily M. Johnson
- Eric S. Alanko - ward
- Maria S. Alanko - ward

47 - Andrew J. McCleary
- Charles S. DeGraw - lodger

48 - William H. and Edith M. Schmidt
- Ethel Schmidt - daughter
- Alvin Schmidt - son
- Frederick W. Schmidt - son
- Hazel Schmidt - daughter
- Florence Schmidt -daughter
- Harold H. Schmidt - son
- John Johnston - father-in-law

49 - Victor R. and Bertha Robbins
- Chester A. Robbins - son

50 - Fred W. Schmidt

51 - John N. Tolman
- Mary Tolman - daughter
- Bronson Tolman - son
- Mary G. Howard - housekeeper
- Frank Davis - hired man
- Peter E. Weber - hired man
- Arl Walters - hired man
- Joe Zugarmande - hired man

52 - Lars E. Skorr

53 - Robert G. Hopkins
- Farney H. DeRaymond - lodger
- Leonard A. Olson - hired man

54 - George Coleman

55 - Albert L. and Esther R. Card
- Floyd A. Card - son
- Marguerite J. Card - daughter
- Lee E. Card - son

56 - Edward M. and Gerta R. Card
- Edna R. Card - daughter
- Clyde E. Card - son
- Malvin A. Card - son
- Aileen A. Card - daughter

57 - David F. Good
- John E. Simpson - lodger

58 - Owen C. and Grace J. Bevelhymer
- Orin K. Beaton - stepson
- Lucinda M. Francisco - adopt. dau.

59 - George M. and Mary P. Heald
- George M. Heald, Jr. - son
- Louis W. Lowe - hired man
- Fred G. Hodges - hired man
- Fred A. Bunn - hired man
- William Dwyer - hired man
- Joseph Spinhirny - hired man

60 - Jacob J. Bevelhymer

61 - Edwin and Emma E. Manning

62 - Glenn and Jessie M. Bosley
- Glenn E. Bosley - son
- Gwendolyn C. Bosley - daughter
- Verda Bosley - daughter

63 - Calvin G. and Gertrude Bosley
- Mildred G. Bosley - daughter

64 - Alvin and Emma G. Bosley
- Phyllis M. Bosley - daughter
- Bessie Bosley - daughter
- May Bosley - daughter
- James R. Blowers - lodger

65 - Frederick W. and Josephine Schultz
- Leona S. Schultz - daughter
- Lorene M. Schultz - daughter
- Henry H. Schultz - brother

66 - John T. and Rena Jobe
- Gordon A. Kneisley - partner

67 – E. Harold O'Donnell
    Leon V. O'Donnell – brother
    Harley E. Brant – hired man
    Carrie K. Brant – cook
    William Green – hired man
68 – J. Edward and Gertrude Brown
    Edith M. Brown – daughter
    L. Pearl Brown – daughter
    Irene Brown – daughter
69 – Joseph C. and Josephine Brown
    Joseph D. Brown – son
    Roy G. Brown – son
    Wilbur E. Bunn – son-in-law
    N. Ethel Bunn – daughter
    Virgie A. Bunn – granddaughter
    Viola E. Bunn – granddaughter
70 – Frank L. and Olive M. Brough
    William Brough – son
    Clyde W. Brough – son
71 – William G. and Augusta Brough
    E. Chloe Reynolds – grand daughter
    Allan W. Reynolds – grandson
72 – Walter and Orpha E. Braten
    Hiram M. Abshire – lodger
73 – Peter C. Everett

Chapter 14 notes:

---

[1] *Fourteenth Census of the United States: 1920 – Population, Park County, Wyoming*, Election Districts No. One and Ten, Enumeration District No. 101, pgs. 65A – 67A. (*Family History Library Microfilm* #1822028) **Note:** Names are spelled exactly as they were recorded by the enumerator.

15
Who Was Here in 1930?

The economic decline throughout Wyoming, Montana, and the rest of the country during the 1920's was felt in Clark too. Many families, unable to repay bank loans, lost their property, and were forced to move elsewhere. Other long-time residents died, and their children, after marrying, were living elsewhere. Even though there were new residents moving into the area, there was still a decline in the Clark population by 1930 when the next government census was taken between April 18th and April 22nd, 1930. At that time there were 254 residents living here. [1]

1 – Ralph and Beulah Fouse
    Margaret - daughter
    William Fouse - father
    Arthur L. Robinson – father-in-law
    Wilbur Holtz – hired man
2 – William E. and Iva Clark
    Margaret Delaney – housekeeper
    Arthur D. Carpenter – hired man
    Lindley M. Clark – hired man
    William A. Clark – hired man
    Arthur C. Taylor – hired man
    William C. Taylor – hired man
    Dan H. Noville – hired man
    George F. Nye – hired man
    Virgil Masterson – hired man
    James S. Virgil – hired man
    Ralph F. Gilbertson – hired man
    Martin Kasath – hired man
    Otto Lovset – hired man
3 – Thomas K. and Ruth D. Mathews
    David D. Mathews – son
    Thomas K. Mathews, Jr. – son
    Jim Lee Mathews – son
    David M. Mathews – brother
4 – David and Amanda Gloeckner
    Jacob Gloeckner – brother
    Claude S. Daby – hired man
    Joseph Zalorski – hired man

5 – Clarence A. and Hannah Pearson
    George Keiss – hired man
6 – George F and Annie R. Hays
    Honier A. Hays – son
    Charlie Hays – son
    Lizzie Hays – daughter-in-law
    Betty Hays – granddaughter
    Arnold Hays – nephew
    K. Hays – nephew
    Billy A. Hays – nephew
7 – Andrew and Ellen Madison
    Ben Madison – son
    Alice L. Madison – daughter
    Emil E. Madison – son
    Frances L. Madison – daughter
8 – Carl H. and Emma E. Carlson
    William K. Weller – lodger
9 – Frank O. and Alice Peterson
10 – Arthur T. and Mabel A. Huntington
    Helen M. Huntington – daughter
11 – Morris E. Huntington
12 – Orton N. Sirrine
13 – William M. and Minnie Standley
    Robert Standley – son
    William Standley – son
    Rosa Standley – daughter
    Charles Standley – son

14 – Dave M. and Lillie C. Simpson
   Robert H. Simpson – son
   Florence Simpson – daughter
   Dorothy M. Hardee – lodger
   William A. Reynolds – hired man
15 – Edgar Simpson
   Ella Simpson – sister
   Jay Herriman – hired man
   Ann Herriman – servant
   Joseph Gregory – hired man
   Albert Weimer – hired man
   William O. McConvill – hired man
   Larry King – hired man
16 – George W. and Mattie S. Johnston
   Clifford Johnston – son
   Ella Johnston – daughter
   Ernest A. Johnston – son
   Minnie E. Johnston – daughter
17 – Harry G. and Edith M. Simpson
   Ruth Newman – niece
   Charles Newman – nephew
   Lee Wayman – lodger
   Charles O. Farrell – hired man
18 – Dave L. and Eva K. Gard
   Dean F. Gard – son
   Helen Meyer – servant
19 – Lambert W. and Faye Holthues
   Violet D. Holthues – daughter
   Neil Holthues – son
   Carl Holthues – son
   Jack Holthues – son
   Jean Holthues – daughter
20 – William and Antje Holthues
   William Holtheus, Jr. – son
21 – Fred and Lydia Walter
   Theodore F. Walter – son
   Marian Walter – daughter
   Marjorie E. Walter – daughter
   Jake A. Anderson – hired man
22 – Guy and Dora Fowler
   Theodore Fowler – son
   Donald Fowler – son
   Theodore Fowler – brother
   E. R. Baskies – lodger

23 – Frank & Lila Marlin
   Eli Marlin – son
   Cecil Lowmiller – hired man
24 – Wilbur E. and Ethel Bunn
   Virgie Bunn – daughter
   Viola Bunn – daughter
   Iva Bunn – daughter
   Roberta Bunn – daughter
   Elmer Bunn – son
25 – Andrew and Edwina Holthues
   John Holtues – son
   Andrew Holthues – son
26 – Marion P. and Mollie Stine
27 – Edward and Thelma Vine
28 – Lena Forsman
   John K. Large – son
   Evalyn Large – daughter-in-law
   Betty Large – granddaughter
   Jack Large – grandson
   Clytie Fuson – lodger
29 – Emerson and Lucy Bunn
   Ray Bunn – son
   Ella Bunn – daughter
30 – Benjamin and Helga Eckloe
   Ben M. Eckloe – son
   John J. Eckloe – son
   Marguerite Eckloe – daughter
   Virginia D. Eckloe – daughter
   Oscar Olson – lodger
31 – Jasper N. Parker
32 – Granville Berry
33 – Newton H. and Mary Castle
   Royce Castle – son
   Chester Castle – son
   Leon Keuevais – hired man
   Mary Keuevais – hired girl
34 – Jody D. and Vera Brown
   Verla B. Brown
   Lois F. Brown
35 – George B. Ryder
   Alexander Gillespie – lodger
   Fred W. Schmidt – lodger
   Rex V. Posten – lodger
   William D. McCune – lodger

36 - Edward C. and Esther Weathermon
    Margaret Weathermon – daughter
    Lee Weathermon – son
    Ada Weathermon – daughter
    Mark Weathermon – son
    Jean Weathermon – daughter
37 - Jesse H. and Bessie Smith
    Vernon Smith – son
    James Smith – son
    Terry Smith – son
    Darrell Smith – son
    Bruce Smith – son
38 - Bert and Ethel Stidham
    Lester L. Stidham – son
    Margie Stidham – daughter
    Florence Stidham – daughter
39 - Oscar F. and Emma Lindquist
40 - Edward and Florence Lindquist
    Geraldine Lindquist – daughter
41 - William H. and Irene J. Cooper
    Eva E. Cooper – daughter
42 - Vernon H. Weathermon
43 - Peter and Emily Johnson
    Maria Alanko – adopted daughter
    Eric Alanko – adopted son
    Dave Elder – hired man
44 - George Coleman
45 - Albert and Ruth Wilkinson
    Rose H. Wilkinson – daughter
46 - Joseph C. and Viola Anderson
    Thomas Miller – stepson
    Wesley Miller – stepson
    Emma Miller – stepdaughter
    Theodore Miller – stepson
47 - Logan E. and Myrtle Bostic
    Loyd Bostic – son
    Orval Bostic – son
    Charlotte Bostic – daughter
    Lyman Bostic - son

48 - Bronson Tolman
    Richard Sisco – hired man
    Grace Sisco - servant
    Arrel Walters – hired man
    Joe Wilson – hired man
    A.E. Kepford – hired man
    Joseph M. McKenzie – hired man
    Joe E. Earl – hired man
    Oscar Gredean – hired man
    Lou E. Stein – hired man
    Carrie Stein – hired man's wife
49 - William C. and Gladys Mardis
    James W. Mardis – son
50 - George L. and Bessie Briner
    Phyllis Briner – daughter
    George Briner – son
    Donald Briner – son
    Helen Briner – daughter
    Mary Ann Briner –daughter
51 - William and Marie Turk
    Gladys M. Turk – daughter
    William Turk, Jr. – son
52 - William and May Cochrane
    Addie Cochrane – stepdaughter
    Hazel Cochrane – stepdaughter
    Clayton Cochrane – stepson
    Wilma Cochrane – daughter
    Jack Cochrane – son
53 - James R. Owens
54 - John Poulson

Chapter 15 notes:

[1] *Fifteen Census of the United States: 1930 Population Schedule*, Park County, Wyoming, Election District # 1, E. D. 15-1, p. 1A – 3B. (*Heritage Quest Microfilm* T626-2625) **Note:** Names are spelled exactly as they were recorded by the enumerator.

Clarks Fork River looking north toward State Ditch head gate
on opposite shore

Head gate at Clarks Fork River entrance to State Ditch

16

Water Rights and Ditches

"All of the settlers along the Clark's Fork have water world without end. If there are any quarrels in that neighborhood they must be worked up over some other question than the over-appropriation of by any selfish user. Well improved land on Clark's Fork with perpetual water right can be purchased for about $25 an acre and will be worth double that sum in a few years." [1]

Water Rights

Wyoming water law is based on the doctrine of prior appropriation and dates back to Territorial Days. Under this doctrine the first to put the water to beneficial use had the first right to use it, and water rights are based on priority. Those with the earliest rights are entitled to use the water during periods of limited supply, while those whose rights date later are denied. [2]

One of the advantages of Wyoming statehood in 1890 was the state's control of its water, land and mineral resources. Local control with better law enforcement and with services provided by the state was more inviting to new settlers than were the conditions under territorial rules made from beyond its borders.

Article # 8 of the Wyoming constitution is concerned with irrigation and water rights. In summary it states that all water of natural streams, springs, and lakes within the boundaries of the Wyoming are property of the State, which regulates its use through a State Board of Control headed by the State Engineer. Water can be appropriated for beneficial uses, and none shall be denied except when it is demanded by public interests. [3]

The regulated use of Wyoming's water helped to transform this region, and gave its early settlers the chance to remain on the land, which they had filed on under the Land Purchase and Homestead Acts. With hard work, dedication, and water, they transformed sagebrush and rock into ranches and farms with planted hay, food crops, orchard and shade trees. Irrigation water from the Clarks Fork River and the area creeks became their life's blood of survival.

The First Ditches

Ditches were constructed to get water to areas away from major watercourses using gravity as the transporting agent. As early as June 1889 C. F. Curtis had a territorial permit to draw from Line Creek and irrigate 110 acres. [4] Three years later Warren and Mary Sirrine and two of their adult children, Clarence and Orton, as well as neighbor, William H. Fouse, had constructed the Sirrine Canal received permits to draw water from the Clarks Fork River and to irrigate a total 1390 acres. [5]

By March 11, 1893 John N. Tolman held permits to irrigate 300 acres with 2 ditches named Nutting No. 1 and Nutting 2 from Bennett Creek, while James Kimball was drawing water in 1897 on a single permit for 384.35 acres from Paint Creek. [6]

By April 1898 the Sirrine Canal Extension had been built which provided additional water to Clarence Sirrine's property, then was extended by May of the following year to the ranches of Harry, Henry, Edgar, and David Simpson and their sister, Mattie Simpson Johnson for a total of 1065 acres. Seven more ditches were built in the Pioneer area from February 1900 until December 1913. [7]

There were 14 permits issued for ditches drawing water from Line Creek by April 1912, 22 permits from Bennett Creek by 1910, 14 permits for Little Rocky Creek by 1906, 11 permits for water coming from Pat O'Hara Creek by 1906, and 32 ditch permits for Paint Creek by 1910. [7a]

These later permits were issued after the amount of water in the river and creeks was determined. It was noted that in June 1903 "the waters of the Clark's Fork River and its tributaries are being measured, and the work on Bennett Creek will be completed the following week. There will be this satisfaction in having the waters adjudicated at his time so we will know the amount of water available and act accordingly." [8]

In 1909 Lou Blakesley, a water superintendent, was in the area making a thorough inspection of the ditches and the irrigation needs of this locality. He "was also trying to get an insight into the mysteries that seem to surround some of the water appropriations. The time is not far off when every ditch and the tillable land it is to water will be personally examined by the state engineer or his representative and the excessive amounts taken from the appropriator.[9]

The Paint Creek Ditch and Reservoir Company

This company was organized by N. M Huntington, Archy Beaton, Josephine Brown, E. M. Brown, and George Schnitker who took out state permits on October 16, 1902. [10]

By April 1905 the Paint Creek ditch and reservoir had 135 feet of pipeline finished with standpipe and water gate, and all laterals ditches were finished. The ditch was flowing with 7 feet of water upon which to draw.[11] Others area ranchers desiring to hook up to this source of water joined the Paint Creek Ditch and Reservoir Company whose shares were "becoming gilt-edged property." [12]

A week later Red McCawley and James Hogan were "building laterals for about 5000 acres to be irrigated from the Paint Creek reservoir."[13] Rancher Milton Gorsuch joined up in June, and in December another permit was taken out by the company to use 567 acre-feet for irrigation of lands under their ditch. [14] Joseph C. Brown, president and E. M. Brown, secretary, called an annual meeting of the company at the Paint Creek schoolhouse on December 16th to elect officers and transact business. [15] By March of 1909 the company had completed a 300-foot flume across Sheep Creek. [16]

The Luce Reservoir

In May of 1905 Henry A. Luce and Milton Benedict purchased 60 head of cattle and were looking for land to file on in anticipation of having an "extensive stock farm" as "the Paint creek country is progressing rapidly." [17] They had visions of having "a ranch equal to the famous Bent & Allison ranch or Pat O'Hara," with a general store and post office on the property. In anticipation of their impending ranch they signed a contract to have

10,000 fence posts made ready. [18]

By the end of June they had moved onto the Roy Huntington place on Paint Creek and were "laying the foundation for a fine ranch, and next year hope to get 200 acres into crops." [19] Stock arrived from Iowa for their Spear Head Ranch, which included "a 4-year old Clyde-Cleveland Bay stallion, two registered Hereford bulls, and two Chester White hogs." [20] All they needed was a good supply of water to meet their Spear Head Ranch's needs

In early February 1906 activity started on the construction of the Luce Reservoir when Milt Benedict came into Cody to get a load of large water pipe. [21] Two weeks later Ed Hutsonpiler of Cody arrived in Paint Creek with four teams to begin the actual construction. [22] His crew dug down ten feet and found no boulders or rocks so they were able to proceed quickly. It continued through the spring and summer and was finally complete in mid-September. [23]

The Hubbard Ditch – The Ditch that Went Nowhere

In April of 1905 ambitious plans were in place to construct a ditch from the entrance of the Clarks Fork Canyon to cover several hundred thousand acres of land on the Chapman Bench and Big Sand Coulee areas. It was to be called the Hubbard Ditch after Judson Hubbard, its principal promoter. At that time a civil engineer from Sheridan with a corps of surveyors was in the area laying out the route of the planned water way. [24]

In October Hubbard and his partner, A. R. Williams transferred their rights of the Hubbard Ditch Company with its 490,000 acres to E. M. Mack and Co. of Iowa, who took charge and proceeded with the project. [25]

Work on the project stalled for over three years as no further reports of process reappear in print until June of 1909. At that time some work was progressing. [26]

In July a couple of the surveyors fell off a log into the swollen waters of Pat O'Hara Creek, and "it was nip and tuck for the rest of the boys to get them out." It was also reported that a telephone line was to be built from the Hubbard Canal surveyor's camp on the Clarks Fork below Pat O'Hara Creek to the Allison ranch where the line would be connected to the line from Cody. [27] Later that month Russell Kimball, a civil engineer, was put in charge of the Hubbard Canal surveying party. [28]

In February of 1910 on a trip to Cody, Kimball reported that the preliminary surveys had been made, and after suitable weather transpired, that work would begin which he thought would be of "incalculable value to Cody." He estimated that when the project was completed, nearly 50,000 acres would be available for cultivation. He stressed the need for telephone service with Cody, a bridge across the Clarks Fork near Pat O'Hara Creek, and improved roads wherever necessary. He said it was up to Cody "to see that this telephone line is built and that roads and bridges are provided where necessary." [29]

On October 14, 1910 F. H. Blodgett of F. H. Blodgett Construction Company, of Wheeling, West Virginia entered into an agreement forming the Clarks Fork Irrigation Company. By the agreement "work was to be begun on or before January 1st, 1911 and to be completed on or before March 23, 1914.[30]

Work plodded along for another year until the following February of 1911 when the contract to begin work on the Chapman canal was "only awaiting favorable weather to begin work." [31]

The following month it was reported that the project was expected to cost between $500,000 and $600,000, and that a diversion dam would be constructed at the mouth of the canyon from where the 30-mile ditch would begin. The main canal, which would be thirty feet wide at the bottom, and its laterals ditches, would provide water cover for 50,000 acres on Chapman Bench. Contracts had been let and quarters for the workers were being built at the mouth of Pat O'Hara Creek. It was further reported that machinery and supplies were being shipped to Belfry, which was the nearest and most accessible railway station to the work site. [32]

Later in March it was announced that F. H. Blodgett had arrived to oversee the movement of machinery necessary to begin work, as well as to build a commissary building for the workmen. In order to transact business more easily within Wyoming, a new company was incorporated in Cody known as the Hayden-Lorentz Corporation to handle all financial matters, and Blodgett assigned the company all of his rights. [33]

J. L. D. Queen, Secy. and Treasurer of the Blodgett Company said that they would begin the canal at Pat O'Hara Creek and work towards the Clarks Fork Canyon having that section done in the early part of 1912. Preliminary steps were being taken to establish a post office at the ditch camp at the Hopkins ranch [34]

Four days later local rancher, James Hogan, was in Cody on business and reported that three steam shovels had been brought in, two work camps have been established, and the company was advertising in Montana for three hundred men to work on the ditch. At that time "the force at the head of the canyon is mainly engaged in blasting rocks." [35]

A month later Mr. Queen reported that forty Blodgett Company men were arriving, and that a Vulcan Steam Traction Shovel was on its way from Toledo, Ohio and was expected any day in Ralston where it would be brought to the work site under its own power. He added that the commissary building was being rushed to completion and that the company was "now in the market for any produce the ranchers had to sell." [36]

On May 6 it was reported that F. H. Blodgett, his family, and 15 staff employees and their families of the Hayden-Lawrentz Construction Company, which would build the canal had arrived from recently-completed construction work in Louisiana. Blodgett said in an interview that his first efforts would be to get the steam shovel from Ralston to the work site, and that the main canal would now be 50 miles in length, requiring the movement of 1,500,000 yards of material. He "expected the work would occupy two years and that 200 laborers would be required after the task was fairly started." [37]

He also said that the canal would be 26 feet wide at the bottom and would carry six feet of water with a capacity of 500 feet per second. Twenty miles of laterals would radiate from the main canal carrying water to an area of 50,000 acres, which would be sold under the provisions of the Carey Act. [38]

On June 24, 1911 operations on the irrigation ditch suspended operations while F. H. Blodgett went East to oversee progress on other projects. As a result over one hundred workers were laid off. He returned to the work camp in December with the news that a

French syndicate was interested in supporting the project, and would send a representative to meet with him. While he waited, he and his wife, J. L. D. Queen and his wife, and Blodgett's brother-in-law were the sole occupants of the camp. [39]

On March 23, 1912 a lawsuit was filed in the Park County's District Court on behalf of the Hayden-Lorentz Construction Company against the Clarks Fork Irrigation Company and F. H. Blodgett to recover nearly $80,000. Filed against the two defendants were eleven causes of action amounting to $23,587.67 and $55,972.77 on the twelfth cause. "This includes damages in the amount of $25,000 on account of the defendant's alleged failure and refusal to perform the terms and conditions of their obligation." [40]

Because the Court was on vacation at the time the petition was filed, the Court Commissioners appointed Henry A. Luce the sole receiver to take control and conserve all the property, goods and effects belonging to the Clark's Fork Irrigation Company the same day. This was confirmed by an order of the Court on April 13th. [41]

On July 24th Gibson Clark, an attorney and statutory agent of the Clarks Fork Irrigation Co., whose corporation offices were in Cheyenne, made a motion to discharge the court appointed receiver claiming that he had never been notified of the previous action. He further claims that the company has endeavored "to raise the means to carry out and construction of the irrigation works" and its failure was due solely slowness and indifference of their Eastern investors to advance the needed money for the irrigation securities. [42]

The following day a new order was issued by District Judge Craig who vacated all the previous orders, as well as ordered that the Honorable C. H. Parmelee be the new judge to preside over at the trial. [43]

On August 19, 1912 the defendants answered the plaintiff's petition refuting the financial claims made against them, and cited the original contract signed between them on March 11, 1911 that any disagreement between them would be settled by three arbitrators and the decision of the majority "to be accepted as full and final." They also presented a motion to strike out the majority of the plaintiff's petition because it "is immaterial and irrelevant to any issue in this cause," and that "none of the matters alleged in said petition furnish or constitute any foundation or basis for any complaint...." [44]

That summer of 1912 while the court case was still ongoing, interest was shown by a French syndicate in taking over the ditch construction. But after some consideration they decided that the estimated one million dollar cost was too small of a project for their undertaking. [45]

The following June the attorneys for both parties in the lawsuit signed a stipulation that the case might be continued into the fall term of the court. [46] No further action was taken in this matter. The lawsuit died, and so did the Hubbard Ditch.

Ditches Today

Ditches and reservoirs are the life's blood of any farming or ranching endeavor, and today many of the original ditches of the past are still being utilized in Clark.

Wyoming law regarding ditch rights and easements is separate from that of water rights. The Wyoming Supreme Court spelled this out in 1912 in the Collett vs. Morgan decision. In that landmark decision the Court said that the Board of Control had no power or authority to determine the ownership or right to the use of a ditch. Rather its duties are confined to the distribution of waters, the granting of permits for the use of that water for beneficial purposes, the granting of certificates and the supervision of the waters. Ditch ownership questions are not under the authority of the Board and must be settled between the parties or by the court. [47]

Today's farmers and ranchers in Clark, as elsewhere in Wyoming, continue to abide by the appropriation amounts and dates of priority for their ditches, which were established long ago. They also continually measure the amount of the water being applied to their fields so as not to infringe on the rights of others using the same ditch water.

The flow of water in an irrigation ditch is measured in cubic feet per second. That amount is the volume of water, equal to 1 foot wide by 1 foot long by 1 foot high passing by a given point in a second.

Water flow in a pipeline is measured in gallons per minute. One cubic foot per second of water equals about 450 gallons per minute, about 1 acre -inch per hour, and about 2 acres-feet per 24-hour day.

Measuring the amount and depth of water passing through irrigation ditches can be accomplished through the use of different-shaped weirs and flumes in conjunction with a staff gauge and flow tables. Now irrigators are also using pipelines to direct irrigation water to their fields either by pumps or gravity flow. Measuring water flow through a pipeline is most commonly accomplished with a propeller-type meter within the pipe itself.

Today and is the past, the efficient use and application of irrigation water is paramount for the continuation of this limited resource and the resulting crops that benefit from it. [48]

Opening ditch from Clarks Fork into Badura reservoir, Oct. 1961
Photo courtesy of Ina Badura.

Chapter 16 notes:

[1] J. K. Calkins, Editor and Proprietor, "Clark's Fork Valley," *The Wyoming Stockgrower and Farmer,* June 9, 1903.

[2] Jacobs, Fassett, and Brosz, *Wyoming Water Law: A Summary,* (Cooperative Extension Service, College of Agriculture and Wyoming Water Research Center, University of Wyoming), June 1995, p. 2.

[3] The legislature further divided the State into four water divisions and provided for the appointment of a superintendent in each which along with the State Engineer, who is appointed by the governor and serves as the president of the board of control. "Constitution of the State of Wyoming," *Wyoming Blue Book, 50th Legislature Centennial Edition,* (Wyoming State Archives and Historical Department, Cheyenne, *1990), Vol. 2, p. 34).*

[4] Julia Bartlett Freeborn, Secretary of the State Board of Control, *Tabulation of Adjudicated Rights in Water Division Number Three,* (State Board of Control, Cheyenne), July 1, 1919, p. 4.

[5] The permit's date of priority was October 10, 1892. (Ibid, p. 3).

[6] Ibid, pgs. 4 and 6.

[7] Ibid, p. 3.

[7a] Ibid, p. 3-7.

[8] Bennett Creek Briefs," *The Wyoming Stockgrower and Farmer,* June 9, 1903, p. 1.

[9] "Clark Squib," *The Wyoming Stockgrower and Farmer,* October 1, 1909, p. 8.

[10] Tabulation of Adjudicated Rights in Water Division Number Three, p. 6.

[11] "Paint Creek Points," *The Wyoming Stockgrower and Farmer,* April 26, 1905, p. 3.

[12] *The Wyoming Stockgrower and Farmer,* May 3, 1905, p. 1.

[13] "Paint Creek Points, *The Wyoming Stockgrower and Farmer,* May 10, 1905, p. 3.

[14] *Tabulation of Adjudicated Rights in Water Division Three,* p. 6.

[15] *The Wyoming Stockgrower and Farmer,* December 6, 1905, p. 2.

[16] "Local News Items, *The Wyoming Stockgrower and Farmer,* March 18, 1909, p. 8.

[17] *The Wyoming Stockgrower and Farmer,* May 10, 1905, p. 1.

[18] "Paint Creek Items," *The Wyoming Stockgrower and Farmer,* June 7, 1905, p. 4.

[19] "What They Said," *The Wyoming Stockgrower and Farmer,* June 28, 1905, p. 1.

[20] "What They Said," *The Wyoming Stockgrower and Farmer,* July 5, 1905, p. 1.

[21] *The Wyoming and Stockgrower,* February 14, 1906, p. 4.

[22] *The Wyoming Stockgrower and Farmer,* February 28, 1906, p. 4.

[23] "Paint Creek News," *The Wyoming Stockgrower and Farmer,* September 13, 1906, p. 4, and September 20, 1906, p. 4.

[24] "Paint Creek Points, *The Wyoming Stockgrower and Farmer,* April 26, 1905, p. 3.

[25] "Paint Creek Items," *The Wyoming Stockgrower and Farmer,* October 18, 1905, p. 1.

[26] "Clark Fork Squibs," *The Wyoming Stockgrower and Farmer,* June 4, 1909, p. 7.

[27] Ibid, July 2, 1909, p. 2.

[28] Ibid. July 22, 1909, p. 4; Russell Kimball, and his brother, Farley were both mining engineers and graduates of Lehigh University in Pennsylvania. Their father was a Ph.D. mining geologist, and with his two sons, purchased in 1902, the former Andy Chapman ranch on Pat O'Hara creek. Russell Kimball did contract surveying jobs for the city of Cody until they hired him as the city engineer in 1910. He held this position until he and his wife moved to Casper in 1923. The following year he was hired by Mrs. Gertrude Whitney to build the base for the Buffalo Bill statue in Cody.

[29] *Park County Enterprise,* February 26, 1910, p. 1.

[30] Agreement signed in Pickering, LA on February 1, 1911 by W. D. Becker, president, Clark's Fork

Irrigation Co., and F. H. Blodgett, contractor, copy in Park County Civil Case #73 documents; *Park County Enterprise,* March 27, 1912, p. 1.

[31] *Park County Enterprise,* February 11, 1911, p. 2.

[32] Park County Enterprise, March 4, 1911, p. 2.

[33] *Park County Enterprise,* March 11, 1911, p. 1.

[34] Ibid.

[35] *Park County Enterprise,* March 15, 1911, p. 5.

[36] *Park County Enterprise,* April 19, 1911, p. 3.

[37] *Park County Enterprise,* May 6, 1911, p. 2.

[38] Ibid. Note: The provisions of the Cary Land Act were explained in depth in an earlier article in *The Wyoming Stockgrower and Farmer* - "The Carey act provides for the segregation of land from the public domain, the patenting of said land by the U. S. government to the state, its irrigation by an individual or irrigation company, its settlement and reclamation by an entry man and the issuance of patent from the state to the settler after compliance with the provisions of the state law which is passed in order to carry out the provisions of the Carey act.

"After the irrigation company has complied with the law and is ready to furnish water for the reclamation of its segregation, it may contract with settlers to furnish water rights for such land as the settler may desire to file upon.

"Within 30 days of the date of such contract the settler must file his application with the state land board, designating the land he desires to enter, and enclosing with his application a copy of the contract entered into with the water company. The fee for this filing is $1.00 for recording and a payment of 25 cents an acre must also be made to the state, and a small fee to the officer who fills out and transmits the papers to the board.

"Within six months of the date of filing entry man must make settlement upon the land, and within three years from said date must offer his final proof showing compliance within the law and pay an additional 25 cents an acre, $1.00 for recording and $1.00 for issuing patent, together with a small fee to the officer taking and transmitting the final proof.

"The qualifications of an entry man under the Carey act are similar to those under the Homestead Act. The limit to any one entry man is 160 acres. Where a claimant has taken less than 160 acres he may make a second entry, after receiving patent for his first, for an amount of land, which together with his former entry will not exceed in the aggregate more than 160 acres.

"A former Homestead entry will not debar a settler from entering land under the Carey act, but the two claims can not be held simultaneously.

"Final proof may be offered before all the payments for the water right have been made, and patent will issue, but the irrigation company is granted by law a first lien on the land until such payments are made in full.

"Title to the land itself is never vested in the irrigation company. The entry man buys the land from the state and the water right from the company. The chain of title to the land is from the United States to the state, and from the state to the entry man.

"But after the water right is secured and final certificate issued, the owner must continue to use it for the beneficial purposes for which the right was granted. A failure to do so for three consecutive years subjects the water right to cancellation and the title to the water will revert to the state.

"Entry men should be sure and familiarize themselves with the law and rulings. A strict compliance therewith will save them expense trouble and possibly loss of their rights." ("THE CAREY LAND ACT – How to Secure and Assign Title to Land and Water Rights Under This Law.

Facts Entry men Should Know," By J. K. Calkins, U. S. Commissioner, Cody, Wyoming," *The Wyoming Stockgrower and Farmer,* December 18, 1906, p.1).

[39] *Park County Enterprise,* December 23, 1911, p. 1.

[40] Petition of Hayden-Lorentz Construction, a corporation, Plaintiff vs. Clark's Fork Irrigation Company, a corporation and F. H. Blodgett, Defendants, District Court of the State of Wyoming, Park County, Civil Case #73, filed March 23, 1912; *Park County Enterprise,* March 27, 1912, p. 1.

[41] Order of Court Commissioners Appointing Receiver and Oath of Office signed by Henry A. Luce, March 23, 1912; and Order of the Court signed April 13, 1912, Park County Civil Case #73.

[42] Motion to Amend Motion to Discharge Receiver, July 24, 1912, Park County Civil Case #73.

[43] Order, July 25, 1912, Park County Civil Case #73.

[44] Answer from Defendants and Motion to Strike Out Parts of Plaintiff's Petition, both filed August 19, 1912, Park County Civil Case #73.

[45] *Park County Enterprise,* July 31, 1912, p. 1.

[46] Stipulation signed by the attorneys for Hayden-Lorentz Construction Co, and the Clark's Fork Irrigation Co., dated June 18, 1913.

[47] Twenty-two of the most commonly asked questions about ditch rights and responsibilities are addressed in a small pamphlet entitled, "Legal Aspects Relating to Irrigation Ditch Rights and Easements," available from the Wyoming State Board of Control. (*Legal Aspects Relating to Irrigation Ditch Rights and Easements,* (State of Wyoming, State Board of Control, rev. 1994).

[48] For a detailed explanation of this subject as well as measuring devices and flow tables, please see: *Irrigation Water Measurement: Irrigation Ditches and Pipelines,* (Cooperative Extension Service, College of Agriculture, Bulletin 583R, University of Wyoming, no date)

The State Ditch – looking south

Horses crossing repaired Sirrine Bridge early 1920's. Photo courtesy of Carol Briggs Joy and Dorothy Pearson Williams.

Wooden bridge across Bennett Creek near Henry V. Weathermon's cabin in the late 1920's. Photo courtesy of Marian Fricke Bainter.

17

Roads and Bridges

"A party consisting of Postmaster Thompson, Linc Rife and Banker Peters and brother came up from Bridger Wednesday, in Mr. Rife's touring car for a fish in Rocky creek. This was the first automobile to travel over the adamant roads of Rocky creek."

"A carload of automobilists had the 'nerve' to tackle the trail into the Clark's Fork canyon Wednesday."

"Automobiles going into the Clarks Fork canyon are getting as numerous as jack rabbits on the flat." [1]

Roads

With a population increase in the early 1900's many residents saw the need for better roads and bridges to cross the Clarks Fork River and area creeks. As early as April 1905 Paint Creek residents J. S. Huntington, Joseph C. Brown and E. Walters were working on a new road between Paint Creek and Pat O'Hara. [2]

On a visit to Cody in July 1907 Sirrine (Pioneer) resident, John Bush, made the comment that "new settlers are coming in on Clark's Fork, more land is being cultivated, and the community needs are constantly changing." He also said that the lack of county roads worked against Cody as a trade center, since residents from this part of the county find it more convenient to travel and trade in Red Lodge. He mentioned that the only bridge out here at that time was the one across the Clarks Fork River at the old Sirrine place, and that badly needed a new floor. "If it is neglected much longer it will be unsafe." [3] With the explosive population increase and development on Clark's Fork, this area of the county "certainly deserves attention." [4]

Bush's comments were echoed by others, who thought, "the people of Paint Creek need a post office and a county road badly." In February 1909 Joseph Brown reported the roads between Paint Creek and Cody were pretty bad. [5]

Even the Belfry newspaper was making disparaging remarks about Clark roads to which local resident Charlie Snow added his return comment:

"The Belfry News speaks of the roads around Clark as having no beginning and no ending and that they go nowhere, and says among other abusive - among other abusive - that the man who laid them out was drunk. We would advise our neighbors across the line that if they would leave their jugs and bottles back in Montana, the ditches encountered around Clark would be more crossable and the roads more passable and have a beginning and an ending. [6]

For more than ten years Emerson Bunn took care of the area roads as the local roads supervisor with limited equipment and a small work crew when available. His duties took him from Sirrine to Paint Creek to repair the area's dirt roads. In November 1909 he was working in Sirrine (Pioneer) "putting the roads in a passable condition." A year later it was noted that he and Park County Commissioner Woods "are doing a fine job on the north and south road by their places, and at their own expense, too." The following month he had completed roadwork on Paint Creek winding up his work for that year. [7]

When the weather was bad either from rain or snow, area roads were often impassable. Another problem was faced when melting winter snows in the mountains or heavy rains storms caused the Clarks Fork and area creeks to flood. The only way to cross the Clarks Fork before 1910 was to ford it, as only the Sirrine area had a bridge crossing. During flood conditions crossing the Clarks Fork to travel between Paint Creek and Clark could be dangerous and impossible:

> "The Clarks Fork river has been very high for sometime and most of
> the people of this country will be glad to see it go down as they have
> not been able to get their mail from the Clark Post Office. [8]

> "The Clark Fork River is rising fast and communication with the opposite
> side is about at an end for a few months." [9]

Before area residents faced another summer's high water problems, county, federal and Cody city funds were promised in 1910 to construct two bridges across the Clarks Fork River – one at the Dredge ford and the other near the entrance to Pat O'Hara Creek. The story of the building of those bridges follows later in this chapter.

In the spring of 1911 the Park County Enterprise in several articles stressed the importance of improving the road between Cody and Clark, which had long been ignored by the former Big Horn County Commissioners. Now that Park County had been established, it was time to correct the situation. The time was critical, as Belfry residents had recently subscribed $1200 to help build a proposed bridge at the Heald ford. If Carbon County Commissioners agreed, a new road down to the state line would follow. All this was being considered to make it more attractive for Clark area residents to do their business in Belfry. [10]

Later in the month the Enterprise editor interviewed "a prominent resident of the Clark's Fork neighborhood" who stated that the needed road improvements consisted of changing the road from the west side to the east side of Skull Creek, and the granting of a road through the Allison ranch to the Chapman Bench. He said that the present Skull Creek road on the east side was a catching place for snowdrifts and remained wet and slippery until late in the winter season. It was also cited that the present ascent to the Chapman Bench was a veritable boulder bed and another grade was needed. Clarks Fork residents have paid a reasonable share of taxes, and with the exception of one bridge, "they have never had one cent of improvement money from Fremont, Big Horn or Park county, and they think their turn is about due." [11]

An editorial followed this article requesting that the Park County Commissioners at their next meeting meet the demands of the Clarks Fork residents for better road facilities, which would honor the promises that were made before the last election. [12]

At the May session of the County Commissioners a petition was received asking "for a public road commencing at the bridge across the Shoshone river at Cody, thence west and north-west via Cottonwood creek, west of Hart Mountain and on the most practicable and feasible route to the Clarks Fork river and terminating near that river at the most feasible point selected by the viewers." They appointed four viewers who would accompany the county surveyor to look at the proposed route. [13]

When the Commissioners met in June, the petition for the new road was granted and "O. C. Bevelhymer, supervisor of the district was instructed to proceed with the necessary work." Two months later in August the Forestry Department set aside $2,000, the County Commissioners $1,000 and area residents another $1,000 so that work could start immediately. [14]

By December the road between the Woods and Chapman ranches had been graded and was in "fine shape," and a bridge on Bennett Creek had been raised several feet and two smaller ones put in place. This piece of road has been almost impassible in the winter on account of ice and money spent on it is a great benefit to the community." [15]

The following spring it was noted "Emerson Bunn, Clark's Fork efficient and worthy road supervisor, has been very busy during the past week fixing roads and bridges." In June after a cloudburst washed out the road leading to the Hopkins Bridge at the ditch camp, Mr. Bunn and his work team "succeeded in putting it in fine shape again." [16]

Later that month the Forestry Service began improving the trail in the Clarks Fork Canyon. Frank Sparhawk was in charge of a crew of five or six men who worked on the trail, which was "the main thorofare to Crandall creek, especially during the winter months." [17]

The following March Supervisor Bunn was securing the bridge timbers to begin work on the Sand Coulee road. [18]

In August of 1921 it was reported that, "the road to Cody is in fine shape, just like a boulevard, with the exception of two places. The one from the Two Dot ranch to the bench is bad, but the one going down to the Hopkins bridge is actually dangerous." The road supervisor was under strict orders to "do nothing except repair work and that only on the orders from the county commissioners." [19]

In May of 1923 Walter Braten was "the new efficient road supervisor in the Clarks Fork country," and he reported that he was "getting his section of road in first class condition." [20]

By the fall with the arrival of winter roads between Cody and the Clark area became "all but impassable." Six horses were required to pull a wagon over Dead Indian Hill to Sunlight, and Mr. and Mrs. Bob Hopkins on a return trip to Clark "bogged down in Sand Coulee where they spent the night." Clark area residents suggested that the County Commissioners consider building roads "that can be traversed in winter." [21]

The roads continued to be bad all that winter making travel difficult. In March Mrs. Walter Hoffman was required to make a trip into Cody by horseback and reported that "there are no roads left," and there was "two or three feet of snow on the Skull Creek Divide." The total on Bald Ridge increased by 26" between the 16th and 21st of March. When O. C. Bevelhymer came to Cody from Paint Creek he said it was the first time in the last six months that" he had been able to come to town on account of the heavy snowfall in the Paint Creek district." [22]

As weather improved, Road Supervisor Walter Braten and his crew once again resumed their work from the State line to Skull Creek blasting out rock, widening, and making needed repairs to area roads. At the last legislative session that year, a new county road supervisor's position was created making the entire Park County into one district under one head. At the August election Walter Braten, George Schnitker and Fred Schmidt ran against two nominees from Powell. J. B. Wright of Powell defeated all three Clark candidates. [23]

Local area roadwork continued as before in the summer months, with bad weather causing problems for residents in winter. Cody newspapers were full of complements, as well as complaints about the condition of the roads.

In December of 1930 there was renewed interest in the construction of a highway up the Clarks Fork Canyon, through Sunlight and on to Cooke City and Yellowstone National Park. Members of the Cody Club met with a group of men from the Clarks Fork to discuss the feasibility of soliciting the support of the State Highway Commission to construct the highway. By mid-January a resolution had been adopted by the club and forwarded to the Wyoming delegation in Washington, DC. In mid-April it was reported that the Forest Service had passed favorably on the proposed highway and that construction would commence as soon as the Secretary of the Interior allocated the necessary funds. [24]

In October of 1933 possibilities looked good for the early building of the first unit of the Cody-Clark road under the secondary road plan of the State Highway Department, who was leaning towards building the middle unit first so that "the greatest good would be received from the money expended." Bids were to be let soon so that work could start in the spring. The following April the Taggart Construction Company was the low bidder at $40,619.00 to built a very high standard road up Skull Creek Hill. It was the most expensive part of the route from Cody to the Montana State line. [25]

After years of inactivity, the possibility for a road through the Clarks Fork Canyon came to light again in March of 1945. Fifteen years earlier efforts had been made to secure federal funding, but the costs were considered excessive at the time and "a long-range program of improving the road over Bald Ridge and down Dead Indian Hill was initiated." While that route was in good condition, it could never be maintained during winter months. It was thought that an alternate route through the Clarks Fork Canyon could more easily be kept open during the entire year. [26]

In December 1949 it was announced that the contract to construct the ten miles of highway between Cody and the top of Skull Creek Hill had been awarded to Taggart Construction Company whose bid of $110,249 was $20,000 lower than the next bid of fourteen others. [27]

In March 1958 bids were let for an additional 9.4 miles of all weather road to complete the road from Clark to the Montana State Line. The State Highway Commission had earlier awarded the segment from the base of Skull Creek Hill to Clark to Forgey Brothers Construction Co. of Casper. This additional 9.4 miles would complete the approximately 24 miles of remaining highway remaining to be completed. There would also be a four-mile surfaced spur road into Clark. Towards the end of May work started on the road across Chapman Bench. [28]

On January 1, 1959 it was announced that Studer Construction of Billings had been the successful bidder for grading, special embankment and surfacing of 9.5 miles of highway as well as four culverts and one concrete cattle guard. The following month Charles Smith Construction of Thermopolis who was building the two highway bridges that crossed the Clarks Fork River. [29]

By mid-July as work on the highway was progressing, cars were already crossing the two completed bridges. A month later the highway was completed as far as the two bridges, while the remaining road had a good gravel surface. The Wyoming Highway engineer urged careful driving. On August 4, 1959 the County Commissioners made a formal resolution to establish the Clark Spur Road. [30]

The following June of 1960 a crowd of over 60 people gathered on the highway to dedicate the bridges. The group included representatives from Billings, Red Lodge, Bridger, the State Highway Department, and a large group from Cody. In ceremonies that day the bridges were named in honor of Stanley Quick "for the effort he had put forth while county commissioner for Park county in gaining final completion of the project which had been pushed by interested Cody people for over 20 years." [31]

Three weeks later on June 21 bids were opened for the 4.09 miles of road into Clark from Highway 120 between the Quick Bridges. Lamb Construction Company was the successful with a bid of $153,576 for grading, surfacing and other work, while Mclean and McQueen of Worland had the successful bid of $20,130 for construction of two bridges on the spur road. Work was also progressing on a new highway in Montana from Belfry to the Wyoming State Line. [32]

A year later on June 28, 1961 the Montana Highway Commission let a contract to pave with blacktop hot mix the 10.5 miles of highway south from Belfry to the State Line. [33]

On October 12th Congressman James Battin spoke at the dedication of the new Belfry-Cody highway which was completed just three hours before the well-attended ceremony, saying, "Let us use our new highway to the advantage and good of the people."

Henry Hecht, Cody Club president, served as master of ceremonies and introduced the special guests present, which included a number of representatives from both the Montana Highway Department and the Wyoming Highway Commission. The Rev. George Wollenburg of Bridger gave the invocation, then Bronson Tolman of Belfry and Clark welcomed visitors. The Belfry high school band played 'The Star Spangled Banner' and Montana,' and the Belfry American Legion color guard presented the United States and Montana state flags. Mr. Roy Sorrells of Billings, president of the Montana Highway Commission and Mr. T. D. Cowgil of Cody, a member of the Wyoming Highway Commission cut the barbed wire to officially open the road. The ceremony concluded with the benediction given by Reverend R. N. Buswell of Cody. [34] The long-awaited highway from Cody to the Montana State Line was finally realized.

The Sirrine Bridge

Sometime in the early 1900's a wooden bridge was built about fifty yards downstream from where Warren Sirrine had his ferry crossing. This bridge over the Clarks Fork became known as the Sirrine Bridge.[35]

The first mention of the bridge in local newspapers was in July of 1907 when Joe Bush made a visit to Cody. In discussing the needs of the forming community, he said that the only bridge out here "needs a new floor very badly, and that if it is neglected much longer, it will be unsafe." [36]

In late June of 1917 this bridge collapsed while Rev. Daniel McCorkle and his wagon team were crossing over it. Only the circuit minister's quick action, as well as his horses' strength pulled the wagon to safety as the bridge went into the river. [37]

On October 16, 1917 the Park County Board of County Commissioners took up the matter of rebuilding the Sirrine Bridge. Plans for the construction were presented with an estimate of $3,793, and J. F. Allen and George C. Zimmerman were awarded the contract to rebuild the bridge to the plans and specifications presented. [38]

In late December after new pilings were driven, Clarence Pearson, Pioneer area rancher, came to Cody to pick up some lumber for the project. The Sirrine Bridge was a crossing between Pearson's ranch on its east side and Ira Toothaker's on the west side of the Clarks Fork River. The new bridge was completed in early February 1918. [39]

Today a pre-stressed concrete single lane bridge without side-rails is located at this long-used Clarks Fork River crossing in the SW $\frac{1}{4}$ of Section 20, T. 58N, R. 101W. It was built in late in 1972 after the Board of County Commissioners entered into a written agreement with the State Highway Commission of Wyoming.[40]

Pearson family members and guests watch the rising flood waters of the Clarks Fork River from the Sirrine Bridge on July 4, 1915. Photo courtesy of Carol Briggs Joy and Dorothy Pearson Williams.

The Bridge Near Pat O'Hara Creek (The Hopkins-Simpson Bridge)

In March 1910 construction work began on a bridge at the fording site to the east of where Pat O'Hara Creek flows into the Clarks Fork River. Local residents Dave Parker and Chris Weathermon (Lee's dad) were among the workers who cut and hauled logs to the bridge site. [41]

Toward the end of April the pile driver had finished its work at the Dredge ford bridge site downstream and had been moved to this site to start putting in log pilings here. It was reported that "work on both is being rushed and enough material is already assembled to complete both with the exception of the decking for each," which "will be forthcoming thanks to the efforts of certain Cody citizens, and both bridges completed in due course of time." [42]

Local rancher, James Hogan, whose untiring efforts with the construction of the Pat O'Hara Bridge, said that it would be ready for public travel on May 18th and expressed his gratitude to local sheep men and Cody business interests for providing money without which the bridge could not have been completed. "For the first time in 16 years there is now open travel afforded by this bridge which makes it possible for ranchers to be in direct and sure connection with the now County seat of Park County." [43]

The third week of May 1910 the Clarks Fork River was fordable again due to a second drop in water level since the spring's high water began. That same week the bridge near Pat O'Hara Creek as completed, which totally eliminated further worries about fording the river there for travel north or south. [44]

By March of 1911 the bridge was being called the Hopkins Bridge for the Frank G. Hopkins family whose property it touched on the south side of the river.[45] During that month the bridge was being refloored so that heavy loads of coal, lumber, machinery, and other materials needed for work on the Hubbard Canal could cross safely.[46]

In early August 1945 despite signs indicating a six-ton load limit, two heavily-laden oil trucks proved too much for the bridge. This resulted in the middle span giving away and causing one of the trucks to land in the river. No one was hurt in the accident, and two days later the truck was removed. [47]

Rebuilding the bridge hadn't started by the middle of October and area residents were "still hoping to get the Hopkins bridge in again before bad weather makes the Sand Coulee road unfit for travel." It wasn't until the first week of January that some of the bridge material had been salvaged from the river and new materials hauled in to start repairs, which were finished by the end of the month. [48]

In September the bridge needed additional repairs, and then again in April 1953 when "some much needed work was being done" on the bridge. [49]

As the new highway across the Chapman Bench moved steadily northward to the Montana State Line during the late 1950's, north-south traffic switched to the new route and the crossing near Pat O'Hara Creek was mainly used by locals. Finally the condition of bridge deteriorated and it was not being used because of its unsafe condition. On January 4, 1961 in the interest of public safety, the Board of County Commissioners decided to abandon and vacate the old bridge rather than have it repaired. [50] It was torn down and removed.

For fifty-one years the Hopkins-Simpson Bridge continued to serve the needs of the community, as well as travelers going north and south between Cody and the Montana border. Today travelers on County Highway 7RP can still see the former approach to the bridge and the continuation of the old road on the opposite side of the river. Only a few wooden pilings remaining on either shore bear testimony to the former bridge, which made year-round crossings possible across the Clarks Fork.

Clark teacher, Ronald Reese and his family standing on the Hopkins-Simpson Bridge, 1959.
Less than 2 years later the bridge was declared unsafe and abandoned. Photo courtesy
of the Florence Wogoman Collection, Cody Branch of the Park County Library.

The Bridge at the Dredge Ford Site

This shallow ford across the Clarks Fork, located near today's Clark Fork Fish Hatchery, was named for gold extraction activities that took place along this section of the Clarks Fork River beginning back in the early 1890's. [51] Dredging outfits, as well as placer mining, were still taking place in the river near here in 1914 and 1918. [52]

The original wooden bridge at this location was started in March 1910 with the hauling of logs to the building site. This was being built at the same time as the bridge near Pat O'Hara Creek. [53]

By mid April the work was progressing, and by the third week all of the pilings were in for the Dredge Ford Bridge, and the pile driver had been moved south to the Pat O'Hara site. With the exception of the floor decking lumber, all other material was at the site to complete this bridge quickly. [54]

Further work on the Dredge ford bridge stopped in late April when $500 in building funds promised by the Forest Reserve service was diverted to roadwork on the North Fork. Questions were raised as why the promised money had been given to another locality after the work was well under way, the solution of which was "going to take a whole lot of smooth explanation and genuinely brotherly love on the part of certain persons over Cody's way to put the matter straight." [55] The controversy continued without a solution for almost a month with lengthy reporting in the Cody newspaper. [56]

At the end of June the bridge at the Dredge ford location was completed and open for use. It was described as "one of the best bridges on the upper end of the Clarks Fork river and is a fine testimony of the energy and pluck of the citizens of this basin." [57]

The story of how the Dredge Ford Bridge was finished came to light in September when E. M. Clark, W. H. Woods, and J. N. Hunter presented their unpaid claim against the County for money they advanced to complete its construction. It was learned that these three men and others on both sides of the river had donated money for the project, after they were given a promise that additional funds would be contributed from both the Forest Reserve and the County

Construction was stopped when it was learned that there was no money available to install ironwork to reinforce the bridge against high water. Rather than to lose what had already been done, Clark, Woods and Hunter along with Mr. Boulware, a blacksmith, advanced the needed $555. Part of the money was needed for the cost of iron, while Mr. Boulware donated his labor for the project. It was stressed by the newspaper editor that it was up to the County Board of Commissioners to see that the bill was paid. "If the county is to own this bridge it should help pay for it, or the ownership should rest with the men who built it." [58]

The following March Road Supervisor Bunn had a force of men at work on the west approach to the bridge so that "the summer's high water" could be "held off and not endanger the approach." Later that month the bridge was being refloored to further insure it against heavy loads crossing over it. [59]

Marlin (Line Creek) Bridge in a late 1920's winter with snow on shore.
Photo courtesy of Carol Briggs Joy and Dorothy Pearson Williams.

At the beginning of March, 1928 construction work began to replace the Dredge Ford Bridge with a new one when lumber milled at the Freeman sawmill was hauled from Cody to the river site. The bridge remained closed while work progressed until early June when it reopened to traffic.[60]

The new bridge, now called the Marlin Bridge, because of its location near the Marlin ranch, was only temporarily opened. In early August when a threshing machine attempted to cross the new bridge, the timbers gave way sending the center span of the structure along with the steam engine and tractor into the streambed below. The threshing outfit, owned by a Billings firm, was returning there when the accident happened. Road Supervisor J. B. Wright said "he could give no explanation of the bridge giving away other than that possibly the timbers had been green when placed in use, and the natural shrinkage had caused the bridge to weaken." Soon a crew of men was "replacing the Marlin bridge over the Clarks Fork river that fell in two weeks ago." [61]

In early February 1944 one span of the Marlin Bridge gave way when Eldon Denney, who was home on leave from the Navy, struck the end of the bridge causing it to slide out of place. The car went over the side of the bridge and landed upside down with its wheels up on the riverbank below. Eldon and Elmer Bunn, the other occupant of the vehicle, were both "somewhat bruised" by the experience but "were not hurt and were able to climb out and walk to the Frank Badura home." [62]

Within days of the accident, work was begun on clearing away the timbers in order to rebuild the bridge. It was reported that the temporary closing of the bridge was "a great inconvenience to people on Line creek and Bennett creek as they have to go several miles out of their way over very bad roads. Mr. Gallentine meets the mail stage at the bridge and gets the mail for Clark." [63]

Collapsed span of the Marlin Bridge after Eldon Denney and Elmer Bunn's automobile accident in February 1944. Photo courtesy of Elmer Bunn.

Carl Carlson hauled timbers from Cody for his crew to rebuild the fallen span, which took more than two weeks. After being closed for almost a month the Marlin Bridge opened again to traffic. [64]

In January 10, 1967 a section of the old 300-foot wooden bridge, which was then known as both the Badura Bridge and the Line Creek Bridge, collapsed under the weight of a herd of about 40 head of cattle crossing over it. The middle span of the bridge gave way when the Badura ranch cattle bunched up in one area of the three-span bridge plunging that section and some of the cattle 15 feet below into the river. Area school buses and the mail car from Belfry had to be rerouted. [65]

In late January after the old bridge was burned, a temporary one was put into place at the site, which could be used until high water. [66]

Abutments for a concrete bridge were poured in April at a cost of more than $30,000, but the county did not have enough money in their budget to purchase the decking until the next fiscal year. [67]

Ten months later in February 1968 the County Commissioners opened sealed bids for the decking and awarded the contract to Otto Madsen of Cody whose bid of $33,168.00 was the lowest. The new bridge was to be completed by May 1st. The decking was composed of six pre-stressed concrete spans each weighing 33,000 pounds, which were set in place with the help of a 40-ton crane and a 25-ton crane hired from Billings. The river had to be diverted during part of the installation process which was completed by the May contract date.[68]

Sometime after the summer of 2004, a new Line Creek Bridge and approach is planned to be constructed. This will be ninety-six years after the first bridge was built on the old dredge fording site. [69]

Line Creek Bridge, 2003

Chapter 17 notes

[1] 'Clark Squibs,' *Park County Enterprise*, June 18, 1910, p. 8; July 16, 1910, p. 8; and July 23, 1910, p. 1.

[2] "Paint Creek Points, *The Wyoming Stockgrower and Farmer*, April 26, 1905, p. 3.

[3] This was the former wooden bridge west of today's Sunlight feed lot in Pioneer. Today a concrete bridge crosses at that site.

[4] *The Wyoming Stockgrower and Farmer*, July 18, 1907, p. 1.

[5] "From Paint Creek," *The Wyoming Stockgrower and Farmer*, August 8, 1907, p.2; and "Locals News," *The Wyoming Stockgrower and Farmer*, February 25, 1909, p. 5.

[6] "Clark's Fork Squibs, " *The Wyoming Stockgrower and Farmer*, July 16, 1909, p. 2.

[7] "Clark Squibs," *The Wyoming Stockgrower and Farmer*, November 26, 1909, p. 8; "Clark Squibs," *Park County Enterprise*, November 2, 1910, p. 8 and December 10, 1910, p. 6.

[8] "Pulse of Paint Creek," *The Wyoming Stockgrower and Farmer*, August 22, 1907, p. 1.

[9] "Clark Fork Squibs," *The Wyoming Stockgrower and Farmer*, June 4, 1909, p. 7.

[10] *Park County Enterprise*, April 8, 1911, p. 4.

[11] *Park County Enterprise*, April 29, 1911, p. 1 and 4.

[12] "Editorial – The Clark Road," *Park County Enterprise*, April 29, 1911, p. 4.

[13] *Park County Enterprise*, June 8, 1912, p. 4.

[14] *Park County Enterprise*, June 8, 1912, p. 4; and "Four Thousand Dollars for Clark's Fork Road Work," *Park County Enterprise*, August 2, 1913, p. 1.

[15] "Clark," *Park County Enterprise*, December 17, 1913, p. 5.

[16] "Clark," *Park County Enterprise*, May 23, 1914, p. 6 and June 13, 1914, p. 5.

[17] "Will Improve Trail in Clarks Fork Canyon," *Park County Enterprise*, June 30, 1915, p. 1.

[18] "Clark," Park County Enterprise, March 22, 1916, p. 8.

[19] *Park County Enterprise*, August 10, 1921.

[20] "Mainly About People," *The Cody Enterprise*, May 2, 1923, p. 8.

[21] *The Cody Enterprise*, October 10, 1923, p. 5; November 21, 1923, p. 2 and p. 4 and "Paint Creek," *The Cody Enterprise*, January 30, 1924, p. 2.

[22] "Mainly About People," *The Cody Enterprise*, March 5, 1924, p. 8; March 26, 1924, p. 8; and "Off Bald Ridge," *The Cody Enterprise*, April 2, 1924, p. 5; and "Mainly About People," *The Cody Enterprise*, April 2, 1924, p. 8.

[23] *The Park County Herald*, August 6, 1924, p. 6 and August 20, 1924, p. 1.

[24] "Editorial," *The Cody Enterprise*, December 10, 1930, p. 2; January 7, 1931, p. 1; January 14, 1931, p. 1; and April 8, 1931, p. 8.

[25] "Will Survey Skull Creek Road Project," *The Cody Enterprise*, October 18, 1933, p. 1; and *The Cody Enterprise*, April 17, 1935, p. 10.

[26] "Road Through Clarks Fork Canyon May be Post-War Job," *The Cody Enterprise*, March 21, 1945, p. 1.

[27] "State Highway Commission Awards Contract for Clarks Fork Work," *The Cody Enterprise*, December 20, 1949, p. 1.

[28] "New Surfaced Road Will Serve Clark," *The Cody Enterprise*, March 13, 1958, p. 1 and "Clarks Fork by Emma V. Simpson," *The Cody Enterprise*, May 29, 1958, Sec. 2, p. 11.

[29] *The Cody Enterprise*, January 1, 1959, p. 1; and "Bridge Jobs Progress on Area Roads," *The Cody Enterprise*, February 12, 1959, p. 6.

[30] "Clarks Fork by Emma V. Simpson," *The Cody Enterprise*, July 23, 1959, Sec. 2, p. 2; and Park County Commissioners Records Book 6, page 350.

[31] "Quick Bridges Dedicated on Clarks Fork River," *The Cody Enterprise*, June 2, 1960, p. 1.

[32] *The Cody Enterprise*, June 23, 1960, p. 1.

[33] *The Carbon County News*, June 8, 1961, p. 1.

[34] "New Belfry Road is Dedicated," *The Carbon County News*, October 19, 1961, p. 1; "Montana, Wyoming to Dedicate Road Today," *The Cody Enterprise*, October 12, 1961, p. 1; and "No Ceremonial Ribbon for This Occasion," *The Cody Enterprise*, October 19, 1961, Sec. 2, p. 8.

[35] The ferry was still in use in 1899 from a dated photo at Park County Archives.

[36] "Clarks Fork Needs," *The Wyoming Stockgrower and Farmer*, July 18, 1907, p. 1.

[37] "Belfry Items," *Carbon County Journal*, July 4, 1917, p. 3; Note: This former wooden bridge crossed over the Clarks Forks River to the west of today's Sunlight Feed Lot in Pioneer. Nearby to the southeast is the former Gloeckner ranch now occupied by Allen and Laura Denney. Ira Toothacher's ranch was on the northwest side of that bridge, which today is part of the Earl Holding ranch properties.

[38] Board of County Commissioners, Book 2, p. 98.

[39] "Belfry Items," *Carbon County Journal*, January 2, 1918, p. 2; and "Chance," *Carbon County Journal*, February 6, 1918, p. 3.

[40] Special Meeting of the Board of County Commissioners held on August 16, 1972. (Commissioners Records, Book 8, p. 342)

[41] "Clark Squibs," Park County Enterprise, March 26, 1910, p. 8 and April 9, 1910, p. 8.

[42] *Park County Enterprise*, April 23, 1910, p. 1.

[43] "Clark Squibs," *Park County Enterprise*, May 7, 1910, p. 2; and *Park County Enterprise*, May 21, 1910, p. 4.

[44] "Clark Squibs," *Park County Enterprise*, May 21, 1910, p. 8.

[45] Sometime in the 1930's locals started calling the bridge the Hopkins-Simpson Bridge adding the Simpson name for John and Emma Simpson who began living and working on the Hopkins ranch in November 1927. They remained there as caretakers living in a small house near the main house, after Bob Hopkins's death in January 1934, and his widow, Josephine, married Dr. Jesse D. Lewellan. The Lewellans lived in Cody most of the time, and also spent time in California. The Simpsons continued to live on the property even after it was sold to become part of the Two-Dot Ranch. After John's death in February 1961, Emma moved to Belfry and died in January 1964. The former bridge is still known by old-timers as the Hopkins-Simpson Bridge because of both families' long association near the former crossing site.

[46] *Park County Enterprise*, March 25, 1911, p. 3.

[47] *The Cody Enterprise*, August 8, 1945, p. 4 and 7.

[48] "Clarks Fork," *The Cody Enterprise*, October 17, 1945, p. 6; "Clarks Fork," *The Cody Enterprise*, January 02, 1946, p. 2; January 9, 1946, p. 7; and January 30, 1946, p. 9.

[49] "Clarks Fork," *The Cody Enterprise*, September 25, 1946, p. 11; and April 2, 1953, p. 9.

[50] County Commissioners Records, Book 6, p. 487.

[51] *Red Lodge Picket*, October 14, 1893; April 14, 1894, p. 3; April 13, 1895, p. 3; and April 20, 1895.

[52] "A Mr. Scanlan of California is starting a crew of sixteen men washing gold on the Clark Fork river just above the mouth of Bennett creek. They are building a large dredge for the purpose." ["Clarks Fork," *Park County Enterprise*, August 1, 1914, p. 8]; "Baxter Zachary, Belfry reports activity in the placer camps up the river, one outfit operating at the mouth of Bennett creek having ordered two dredges which they propose getting in operation soon." [*Bridger Times*, October 9, 1914, p. 3; also December 11, 1914, p. 1]; and "Expensive dredges were located at several points on the river above Chance..." ["*Bridger Times*," *Carbon County Journal*, April 17, 1918, p. 4].

[53] "Clark Squibs," *Park County Enterprise*, March 26, 1910, p. 8)

[54] *Park County Enterprise*, April 23, 1910, p. 1.

[55] "Clark Squibs," *Park County Enterprise*, April 23, 1910, p. 8.

[56] "Clark Squibs," *Park County Enterprise*, May 7, 1910, p. 2.

[57] "Clark Squibs," *Park County Enterprise*, June 18, 1910, p. 8; June 25, 1910, p. 5; and July 16, 1910, p. 8.

[58] *Park County Enterprise*, September 16, 1911, p. 1; Note: A reading of the County Board of Commissioner's minutes of meetings between August 1911 and January 1916 revealed no payment was authorized to pay the four individuals their requested $555. No mention of the bridge or of the owed money was found in the minutes. If either were discussed, nothing was recorded.

[59] *Park County Enterprise*, March 25, 1911, p. 3.

[60] "Clarks Fork," *The Cody Enterprise*, March 7, 1928, p. 8); March 28, 1928, p. 8; April 11, 1928, p. 5; and June 13, 1928, p. 7.

[61] "Marlin Bridge on Clarks Fork Breaks," *The Cody Enterprise*, August 7, 1929, p. 4; "Clarks Fork," *The Cody Enterprise*, August 21, 1929, p.4.

[62] "Clarks Fork," *The Cody Enterprise*, February 23, 1944, p. 3; Note: Looking at photos of the wrecked vehicle and the distance it fell to the bank, it is surprising that the Eldon and Elmer were not more seriously hurt.

[63] "Clarks Fork," *The Cody Enterprise*, February 23, 1944, p. 3; and March 1, 1944, p. 6.

[64] Ibid. and March 8, 1944, p. 3; March 15, 1944, p. 6; and March 22, 1944, p. 7.

[65] "Line Creek Bridge Falls," *The Powell Tribune*, January 13, 1967, p. 1; "Clark's Fork News, by Virgie Teichert," *The Powell Tribune*, January 20, 1967, p. 3.

[66] "Clarks Fork News by Mrs. Walter Teichert," *The Powell Tribune*, February 3, 1967, p. 8.

[67] "Fund Shortage Holds up Bridge," *The Powell Tribune*, April 7, 1967, p. 1.

[68] Commissions Records, Book 7, pgs. 559-60; "Badura Bridge Contract Let," *The Cody Enterprise*, February 15, 1968, p. 1; "Madsen to Build Badura Bridge," *The Powell Tribune*, February 16, 1968, p. 1; "New Clark's Fork Bridge Going Up," *The Powell Tribune*, April 9, 1968, p. 1.

[69] David Hoffert, Park County Roads Commissioner, conversation with the author, Cody, Wyoming, March 25, 2004.

Line Creek Bridge, 2004

18
Schools

"At the annual school meeting the voters of that district (Paint Creek)
decided to improve the schoolhouse before the opening of the next term,
and to have a six months' session." (*Wyoming Stockgrower and Farmer*,
May 10, 1905, p. 1)

In the 1890's with the arrival of more homesteaders with families in the Clarks Fork Valley, it was clear that formal schools were needed to replace home teaching. County school districts were formed to fund and to oversee the operation of these early one-roomed log schoolhouses, which were scattered through this area's communities of Sirrine (later Pioneer), Bennett Creek, Paint Creek, Line Creek and Pat O'Hara.

These rough log buildings offered few amenities to their students other than desks, a blackboard, and a wood or coal stove to try to keep the room warm during the harsh winters. Then in the late teens and early 1920's the log buildings were replaced by more modern school facilities which had a standardized design, frame siding, a much larger floor plan, high ceilings, better lighting through banks of windows, and an anteroom or cloak room where students could store their lunches and coats during class. Some of these newer schools even had basements and much improved jacketed stoves, which were better suited to heat these larger buildings.

What follows is a brief history of each of the schools and a list of the teachers, who provided an education to the children of the area's communities. In some years other staff members, when known, are added.

The Sirrine School (School District #24)

In the 1890's with the arrival of more homesteaders with families, it was clear that a formal school was needed to replace home teaching. In 1895 a school was established on the Sirrine ranch in a log building with material and labor donated by Henry M. Simpson, his sons, Harry, David and Edgar Simpson, and by William Fouse and Warren Sirrine. While the coalhouse and the two closet buildings were built at the expense of the district, the expense of a needed water well was too much "to be ordered done now." The Sirrine School became known as Big Horn County School District #24. [1]

The following year in 1896 Mattie Simpson taught for 3 ½ months for which the District paid her $172. During their annual school meeting held in May the following trustees were elected: Warren O. Sirrine, Director, William H. Fouse, Clerk, and David M. Simpson, Treasurer. [2]

In 1897 Matte Simpson's father, Henry M. Simpson, served as teacher for a three-month term in February, March and April, and was paid $150. There were 13 students - 8 boys and 5 girls, and the county paid the operating expenses for the school at $3.85 per student per month. Some of the schools expenses included 4 tons of coal, 1 load of wood, schoolhouse repairs, and the building of two outhouses. Warren O. Sirrine, Frank Thompson and William H. Fouse were elected trustees of the district. From 1898 through 1904 the annual meeting's minutes reflected positive changes and improvements for the school with the purchase of a classroom globe and new stove, teacher's chair, the plastering of the schoolhouse, the building of a new coal house, and in 1902 the increase of the teaching term to 6 months.[3]

On May 21, 1904 a special meeting was held at the Sirrine school house to discuss the possibility of bonding the district for a new school house, a shed, two outhouses, one cistern, one coal house and to purchase and fence a new school site. Bonds were set at $1500 and a new larger school house 40 feet long by 24 feet wide was erected on the Ed Simpson ranch a mile or so to the south. It was built during the summer and opened in September. The name of the school district was changed to Pioneer School District #24. After Park County was created in 1910, and the school districts were reorganized, it became Park County School District # 4. [4]

By 1913 the small building on the Simpson ranch had outgrown its usefulness. At the end of the 1913 school year there were 22 students (12 males and 10 females) attending the school being taught by Mable T. Jones. She received a salary of $60 a month for a 9-month school year. Operating costs included: $30.40 for repairs to the building, $14.00 for books, $11.00 for paper and $32.83 fuel to heat the building. [5]

Minutes of School Board Meeting, Sirrine District #24, May 1896

132

2nd Sirrine School was at the Ed Simpson Ranch.
Photo courtesy of Ina Badura.

By then it was realized that small building on the Simpson ranch had outgrown its usefulness, and a larger school building was needed. Board members W. W. Ballard, Clarence Pearson and Edith Simpson held an election to determine whether the voters in the district would support a bond issue to fund a new school. The voters approved the resolution and 20 bonds were to be sold for $125 a piece to secure the needed $2500 to erect a new, larger building. [6]

The Pioneer School (District #4)

On June 12th, 1914 Josephine Green Lukes gave the School District 2 acres of her land for the erection of a new school, [7] and three weeks later on July 1st a request for building proposals for "the construction of a frame school house near Chance Montana" was advertised in local newspapers. [8]

The new Pioneer School was designed by architect Curtis Oehme and built by H. P. Anderson. It was accomplished during that fall. The original building had one large classroom on the ground floor with a double door entry and storage closest. On January 27, 1915 a dedication dance was held in the new building. [9]

On the 18th of February 1937 the wind was so strong that part of the roof was torn off of the Pioneer School and the rest so badly damaged that it had to be removed. While the new roof was being installed, the students temporarily attended classes in the basement of the nearby Carl Carlson house for over two weeks. Before the students returned to their school, a new well was drilled on the property. [10]

In 1953 a two-room teacherage was added on the east end of the building. This consisted of a combination kitchen, living room and one bedroom. Three years later the building was upgraded again and a music room was added on the north side. [10a]

WARRANTY DEED

SCHOOL DISTRICT NO. 4, Park County, Wyoming

grantor___, of ____Park_____County, and State
of _Wyoming_____, for and in consideration of _Ten and no/100=======================
===($10.00) DOLLARS
in hand paid, receipt whereof is hereby acknowledged, CONVEY AND WARRANT TO_____
_____PIONEER SERVICE GROUP, a Wyoming Corporation_____

grantee___, of _____Park_____County and State of ____Wyoming_____
the following described real estate, situate in_____Park_____County and State
of Wyoming, hereby releasing and waiving all rights under and by virtue of the homestead exemption laws of the State,
to-wit:

A tract of land situate in the SW¼, SW¼ of Section 29,
Township 58, North, Range 101 W, of the 6th p.m., Park
County, Wyoming, more particularly described as follows:

Beginning at the SE¼ of the SW¼, SW¼ of
Section 29, thence W 295.17 feet along
the South boundary of said Section, thence
N 295.17 feet parallel to the East boundary
of said Section, thence E 295.17 feet parallel
to the South boundary of said Section, thence
S 295.17 feet parallel to the East boundary
of said Section to the point of beginning
containing two (2) acres more or less together
with all improvements thereon and all appurtenances
and hereditaments thereunto anywise appertaining

WITNESS____OUR____hand S____this__14th__day of__August_____, 19 70.

SCHOOL DISTRICT NO. 4

Mrs David Denney TRUSTEE

Thurman A Biggs TRUSTEE

Don M Fraker TRUSTEE

State of ____Wyoming_____
County of ____Park_____ }ss.

The foregoing instrument was acknowledged before me this 14th day of __August__, 19 70.
Witness my hand and official seal.

James P Feather
Signature
NOTARY PUBLIC
Title of Officer

My Commission Expires: _November 1, 1973_

Recorded August 19, 1970 at 9:25 A M
In Book 348, Page 87 Park County, Wyo.
No. 134605 Eva E. Larson, County Clerk

Deed to the Pioneer Service Group, 1970

Pioneer School

The Pioneer School served the needs of area children through the end of the school year in the spring of 1969 when it closed and School District #4 consolidated with Powell District #1. On August 14, 1970 the District Trustees: Mrs. David Denney, Thurman A. Briggs, and Don M. Fraker deeded the building and its 2 acres of property to the Pioneer Service Group, to serve the area as a community center. [11]

Since 1970 the Pioneer Service Group, made up of interested community members and governed by a board of three elected directors, has painted and cleaned the building from time to time and made needed repairs as their budget permitted. In the 1990's the Park County Historical Society proposed the building to be added to the National Register of Historic Places. The school that contributed so much to the education of the Pioneer community received this status on October 5, 1993.[11a]

The Bennett Creek School (District #16 & later #8)

In the early months of 1901 the Clark School District was established as Big Horn County School District #16. A log bunkhouse was selected as a temporary school on the R. L. Davis ranch in the southwest corner of Section 23, T57N, R102W. [12] Because of the building's proximity to Bennett Creek, the school became known as the Bennett Creek School.

Miss Zoë Wheeler was the teacher during that first summer term, and twenty students - eight boys and twelve girls were enrolled. She was paid $40 a month for her 65 days of teaching. [13] The first District Trustees elected were Eli A. Vickery, W. H. Woods, Clerk, and Granville L. Berry, Treasurer. [14]

The following year in 1902 the District was given funds to build a larger log building in Section 23 about a half mile south of the first school near the present Chet Bell Ranch. The new school was built for a cost of $400 with more than half of that amount given in donated labor and materials, and the name of the former school traveled with it to its new location. [15] In 1903 there were fourteen families sending their children to the one-room school on this side of the valley. [16]

The one-room log building had a wood floor and its walls were chinked inside and out. There were doors on the north and south sides, neither of which had an entrance porch. There were also four windows, two on the east and two on the west sides. Inside a blackboard hung on the west wall behind the teacher's desk, and a big belly stove kept the room warm in winter. The roof was covered with dirt, and in the fall or whenever it was needed, members of the community would see that more was added to it. It never did leak. [17]

As more families were moving into the area, community needs were also increasing. Petitions had already been sent to Big Horn County officials requesting county roads in the northern part of the county, and by 1907 there were also voices desiring a change in the boundary lines between the Clark and Pioneer Districts. This was needed, because "as now laid out children are ten miles from the schoolhouse in their own district and at the same time are within a mile and a half of the schoolhouse in another district." If size of the Clark District could be increased on the west side of the Clarks Fork River, then a bond could be raised to build a new larger schoolhouse. [18] This problem would be lessened in 1911 with the creation of the Line Creek School District.

The student population of the Bennett Creek School remained constant through the first decade of century, and did not seem to be influenced by the amended law enacted in 1909 by the Wyoming State Legislature requiring compulsory school attendance for children ages seven to fourteen. [19] There was regular news of the school, its teachers, its student and other activities in Cody newspapers during this period, which was always positive. The building was also being used for church services, community meetings, and dances. [20]

Bennett Creek School, 1908
(Front) Johnnie McKeever, Mildred Carter, Wilbur Bunn, Fay Barber, Merrill Barber. (Back) Teacher, Mildred Anderson, Jesse Bunn, Blanche Barber, Fred Bunn. Photo courtesy of Elmer Bunn.

At the District's annual school meeting in May 1910 Emerson Bunn was re-elected as a Trustee, and a motion was passed authorizing the board to furnish free textbooks to its students. [21] In September a social was held to help raise money for a school bell, and by November enough money had been raised and it was purchased. The only problem for the Trustees was how to get the 450-pound bell onto the schoolhouse. [22]

After Park County was organized, the Clark School District became District # 8. [23] At the annual school meeting that year in 1911 William H. Schmidt, Ben Eckloe and Charles A. C. Snow were elected Trustees. At that meeting a resolution was adapted that the "Trustees were to use their best judgment in allowing dancing in the school house, but in case they did give permission for a dance, a bond was to be required of one or more responsible parties covering all damages to the school house or fixtures that might occur while the house was in their possession." [24]

Faced with a continually growing student population, the district trustees made plans to finance a new schoolhouse. In May of 1915 school trustees voted to plan for a new schoolhouse, and at the annual meeting in 1916 they voted to call an election to vote on bonds to finance the new building. [25]

On December 4th, 1918 all of the schools in Park County reopened after two months of enforced vacation due to the epidemic of Spanish influenza that was felt all across the country. [26]

On September 8, 1921 Oscar and Emma Lindquist gave to School District 8 a tract of land 200' by 220 feet in Section 21 for use as a new site for the Clark school. [27] By mid-October the contractor, Howerton & Scholes, had "the basement of the new school and community building completed" and were working on the main building which they expected to have enclosed by October 20th. [28]

In early 1922 the Bennett Creek students left their one-room log school behind and moved into their new $5,000 school building northwest of the Bennett Buttes. It took two years before the school's former name was finally abandoned and the name changed to the Clark School. [29] In formalized ceremonies in May 1924 the Clark School was added to the list of rural schools in Park County, which were standardized. [30]

The Paint Creek School (District #31 and #5)

In the fall of 1901 a petition was circulated and signed by Paint Creek residents requesting that a school be built in their area for the twelve school aged children there, as their nearest school was over ten miles away on Bennett Creek. [31]

The following August a meeting of Paint Creek area parents was held to petition the County Superintendent of Schools to establish a new school district in their area. A motion was also made and passed to build an 18' x 28' x 8' wall schoolhouse on K. L. Gilland's ranch. [32]

Meetings were held in September to form a new Paint Creek School District and in October to elect H. J. Huntington, George Schnitker, and Mrs. William G. Brough as it first trustees. A vote to raise a special tax of $300 for a teacher's fund passed unanimously. [33] On October 14, 1902 the Paint Creek School District # 31 in Big Horn County was created from School District 24. [34]

School began in a temporary log building with 20 students - 9 boys and 11 girls - at the Paint Creek school, [35] which was located on the south side of Section 26 of T56N, R102W about one mile from Paint Creek. The first teachers were David H. Teel and Sibyl Easton.[36]

In May 1903 new trustees were elected: James Hogan, Director; Joseph Brown, Clerk; and Mrs. Brough as treasurer.[37]

On May 1, 1905, the annual school meeting was held at the Paint Creek School and Mrs. J. Roy Huntington was elected director to serve three years. At that meeting it was decided to rebuild the schoolhouse and make other repairs. When the school term ended 10 days later, it was said that it had been a very successful school year.[38]

In February 1906 Paint Creek residents were surprised to learn that David Teel, their former teacher for the school's first two years, was sentenced in U. S. Court in Helena, Montana to six years in prison for "raising one dollar bills to ten." [39]

In 1907 Paint Creek residents felt that "the Paint Creek school is still a thing of the future," because that fall they could not secure a teacher until the next year when Ranna Brown taught.[40]

After Park County was established in 1910, the Paint Creek School District number changed from 31 to 5, [41] and by October 1913 plans were back on track when the District's trustees announced the sale of negotiable coupon bonds in the amount of $1500 to "erect a School House in said District and furnishing same." [42]

After Park County was established in 1910, the Paint Creek School District number changed from 31 to 5, [41] and by October 1913 plans were back on track when the District's

Paint Creek School, 1910
(Rear) Olive Decker, Ethel Brown, Dolly Brown, Mary Decker, Jody Brown.
(Front) Dana Decker, Lois Waters, Gladys Skipper, Janice Skipper. Photo courtesy of Elmer Bunn.

trustees announced the sale of negotiable coupon bonds in the amount of $1500 to "erect a School House in said District and furnishing same." [42]

By 1920 a new larger frame school building had replaced the former log one, and during the summer of 1923 it underwent some improvements due to a special tax of $500 that had been levied. The building was painted inside and out, and running water and a lavatory were installed. A swing and other equipment were added to the playground. [43]

In the winter and spring of 1924 the Paint Creek School was in the local newspapers twice. Word was received at the school that the mid-year examination grades that they had taken ranked them second in the county. [44]

The second occurred two months later when Mrs. Flossie Wood, the Paint Creek teacher, who was very popular with area parents, flew into a rage during class. She gave one of her students, Joe Darcy, a merciless beating with a thick willow switch because "he had missed some words in the spelling lesson."

As a result, she was arrested, and soon after resigned from her Paint Creek position. Mrs. Minnie Ide, the County Superintendent of Schools felt the newspaper stories were exaggerated. Nevertheless Clarks Fork residents were "much incensed over the affair and the unmerciful beating she gave the boy." [45]

Joe Darcy, from Bridger, Montana, was under the guardianship of Walt Braten, and returned to attend Paint Creek School until he graduated in 1928. [46]

The only problem that the next teacher, Margaret O'Donnell, encountered the following fall, was getting her car stuck on Paint Creeks' muddy roads.[47]

Georgia Frame was hired to teach at the Paint Creek School in the fall of 1942. She only had three students. She remembered, "that the place was pretty bare. There was just the schoolhouse, the outside toilets and a cistern which was filled out an of irrigation ditch. When you stop and think about it, that wasn't very sanitary." [48]

Four unidentified men paint interior of Paint Creek School, 1933,
as teacher, Nedra Shinn watches. Photo courtesy of Elmer Bunn.

She was the first teacher to live at the school, and her quarters consisted of a small, narrow 10' by 6' storage room, which had just enough room for a bed, a cook stove and the wardrobe trunk that her grandfather had fixed for her. There were also some small cubbyholes in the room that she used for storage. [49]

When she first arrived, she brought fresh meat, which needed to be kept cool. "There was a pool of water out there and I didn't realize it was an irrigation ditch. I put an apple box out there and kept my meat cool in it in that irrigation ditch. Well, that plugged up the irrigation ditch a bit. Mr. Lundvall who owned the land on which the school was located didn't say anything much about it, but the neighborhood dogs got my meat. So that didn't last very long." [50]

When you first came into the school building you passed through an anteroom where the kids put their coats and lunch buckets. One day when Georgia was teaching, one of her students forgot to close the outside door and three or four dogs came in and ate all of the lunches. She soon discovered the dogs belonged to Harold Close who lived nearby with his father. [51]

Later in December 1942 Georgia married Harold and gave up teaching the next spring. She only taught one school year at the Paint Creek School. She said, "I had been raised away from town and I was used to doing things for myself. Still I was 21 and a lot of young girls wouldn't go to a place like that. But that didn't bother me." [52]

When the Paint Creek School was closed in the spring of 1952, 8 students attended it during its last year. [53]

Line Creek School (District #7)

Concerns over increasing numbers of school aged children and the large size of the Clark and Pioneer School Districts, prompted local residents to request a new school district. In March 1907 Joseph B. Hundley, a lower Line Creek area farmer, wrote such a letter to the Big Horn County Superintendent of Schools and attached a petition signed by other local residents. [54]

In July John Bush on a trip to Cody, expressed his own opinion about the districts boundaries and if changes were made, then bonds could be raised for a new schoolhouse. [55]

In May of 1909 the Big Horn County Superintendent of Schools received another petition signed by more area residents. With the creation of Park County a new Line Creek School District # 7 was established from parts of the Clark and Pioneer Districts. [56]

At the May 10th 1911 annual school meeting of the Clark School District, "patrons of the new Line Creek district met and organized and elected Charles Trumbo, Ed Fuson and Peter Johnson as Trustees. Two locations for the schoolhouse were chosen which the Trustees will choose from later." [57]

In less than three weeks a special election of the new District 7 was called to decide on the school site from the two locations, and "the corner between E. M. Clark's and E. T. Fuson's places was chosen." [58]

The site was just west of the Clarks Fork River in the northwest corner of Section 12 on the hillside above the old Dredge Ford Bridge. Today's residents know the bridge at this location as the Line Creek Bridge, while the former school site is about a quarter mile north of the Clarks Fork Fish Hatchery.

The new schoolhouse was built during the summer, and in the fall eleven students (9 boys and 2 girls) started classes there. The following year in 1912 the number increased to sixteen students in the District. [59]

School records from teacher, Berthe E. Weyeneth, reflect that 22 students attended the school from 28 ½ days to 120 days during the 6th month 1913 – 1914 school year with an average daily attendance of 15 students. Six-year-old Evalyn Fuson and fifteen-year old Katie Newton had perfect attendance for the entire term. [60]

At the May 4th, 1914 school election, Elisha M. Clark was elected by an overwhelming majority as a Trustee to serve a three-year term. J. S. Gilles was elected for two years and Carl Busch was to finish the remaining year of his term. The voters felt that they had "a board which will exercise every power within their means to build up the school system in our community, of which, we have long been in need." [61]

In February 1932 the Line Creek School, with an enrollment of ten students, was one of only two rural schools in the County having perfect attendance for the month. [62]

When Pioneer and Line Creek schools had their "last day of school' picnic on the Clarks Fork across from the Pearson ranch (near the present Sunlight Ranch feed lot), the two schools had a sports contest and Line Creek carried off most of the honors. [63]

In the fall of 1940 the District Trustees bought a trailer house for the teacher, Elsie Mailander, to live in. The following month, Lee Halverstadt, an 8th grader at the school, caused an in- school emergency when he accidentally swallowed a thumbtack and had to be rushed to a doctor who "put him on a soft milk diet." [64]

A community meeting was held in early November 1946 at the Line Creek School to discuss the consolidation of the area's three schools. Alice Patterson, the County Superintendent, was there. [65] As a result of that and later meetings, it was decided to consolidate the Line Creek and Clark School Districts.

The Line Creek School closed when the spring term was over in May 1947. In June a new school board was elected due to the consolidation [66] In mid-July the Line Creek School building was moved to the Clark school grounds to provide additional use there as a classroom. [67]

The Pat O'Hara School (School District #29)

District #29 with its school at the Two-Dot Ranch was formed from Paint Creek School District #5. It was to serve the ranch and the residents of the Upper Pat O'Hara drainage area. Don Tolman in his Park County school history believed that the district was formed about 1917. [68] This is collaborated by the earliest roster for District #29 found at the Wyoming State Archives, which lists the names of fifteen students for 1918. Included in the listing were the children of the Two-Dot Ranch owners and employees, as well as the children of residents who lived nearby on Skull Creek and up on Bald Ridge. [69]

In August 1921 the Park County Enterprise announced, "Miss Dorothy Matthews of Powell will teach the school at the Two Dot this coming year." In the same issue it was announced that School District # 29 would be giving a picnic on Pat O'Hara Creek on Labor Day, and

Clark School with former Line Creek School building (after it was moved), and teacherage, 1958. Photo courtesy of Carol Brown Christiansen.

that everyone was invited. [70]

The following May it was reported that the school board had a very good meeting, that Mrs. Jesse M. Lowe had been elected treasurer, and that the new school building for the district was expected to be completed early in the fall. [71]

As predicted the new Pat O 'Hara schoolhouse was dedicated on November 3rd, 1922 at the Ganguet and Barth ranch. An admission charge of $1 a couple provided a supper and music. Unfortunately the dedication was not a big success as only fifteen people were able to get there due to the bad condition of the roads. [72]

The Two-Dot School gave a Christmas program that year, and on the following February 9th, 1923, the girls of the school planned a pie social with a dance and supper to raise funds to buy school equipment. [73]

In May of that year pupils, parents, and teachers of Monument Hill, Paint Creek and Pat O'Hara Schools met in Cody for the county spelling contest. Teacher, Ann Derschell and pupils, Emily Reigle, Erma and Sabra Marler, and Victoria and Marie Ganguet represented Pat O'Hara. Victoria and Marie went on to the final County contest but did not win. [74]

In July a letter written by ten-year-old Bonnie Reigle appeared in *The Cody Enterprise* protesting the decision of the District #29 board to reduce the nine-month school term to eight. The vote had been eight to six for the shorter term. [75] Possibly as a result of the letter, an election was called for August 25th of all legal voters of the District to decide the matter. [76]

The results of that election were not in the subsequent newspaper issues, but in mid-May of the following year it was reported "Mr. Mathews, our school teacher, expects to give a dance at the end of the school term." [77] So the nine-month term must have passed!

After Flossie Wood was arrested for the beating incident at Paint Creek School in late March of 1924, Park County Sheriff Loomis received a request from Miss Helen Young, the Pat O'Hara teacher, for permission "to carry her 'shootin' irons to and from the Pat O'Hara school where there appears to be some friction." [78]

Miss Young stated that two residents of that district had threatened to come to the schoolhouse and 'make trouble' for her, and "she did not want to be caught unawares." Even though she assured the sheriff that she would not "use her shooting' iron unless she was put to it," the Sheriff was reluctant to start such a precedent with his approval. [79]

Mrs. Minnie Ide, the County Superintendent of Schools, who was still trying to smooth over the publicity in area newspapers concerning Mrs. Wood's behavior at the Paint Creek School, diplomatically stated that Miss Young had been the victim of poor advice by one of the District #29 directors when she proposed carry a gun while engaged in school duties. The Superintendent added that Miss Young had since resigned and returned to her home in Powell, and that Mr. Merle Mathews would finish out the remaining weeks of the term. [80] The students at the school "were sorry to have her leave here as she was a very competent teacher." [81]

Mr. Mathews was rehired to teach at Pat O'Hara in the fall of 1924, and the school " was glad to welcome him back." [82] Beside his regular teaching duties, he hosted a social and dance at the school the following March. [83]

The next month he was badly bruised when his horse fell pinning his leg underneath,[84] but he recovered to give another well-attended dance at the school in late May. "He was very much liked and had a successful school year." [85] Thelma Black succeeded him in the fall. [86]

In January of 1927 new desks and black boards funded by a recent box social, were installed at the school. [87] And in early April, Miss Gladys Horner, the Pat O'Hara teacher was taken ill and had to dismiss her class to go home. [88] Her illnesses continued, and at the end of the month she had a nervous breakdown and was unable to continue. Miss Geraldine Kindler from Powell came to finish out her term, [89] and her students wanted her to come back in the fall.[90] On the last day of school she took her students to the Walters ranch for a picnic.[91]

Coverage of the activities at the Pat O'Hara School in Cody newspapers during the 1930's was sparse and limited to occasional mentions of the teachers serving there. Starting in 1930 the schools in the Painter and Sunlight area became part of School District #29, and for the first time the names of these children appear on the District's census.[92]

Except for 1930 and 1931 when students at the Pat O'Hara School numbered 6 and 9 respectively, the total number each year varied between 4 and 6 until 1940 when it increased to 12 for that one year. Eleven of those students were members of the Ed L. Brown and Henry G. Cate families. [93] Tolman's school history mentions that in 1940 the at O'Hara school was no longer taught at its Two-Dot location but at the Ed Brown ranch on Pat O'Hara Creek. In 1946 that portion of District #29 was consolidated back with Paint Creek District #5. [94]

Pat O'Hara School

The Clark School (Clark District #7)

Classes were held in the Clark School and former Line Creek School building until 1968 when they were replaced by a new brick facility. The old Clark School was torn down and the other building was sold and moved to a Line Creek area ranch. The Clark District #7 consolidated with Powell District #1 in 1970, and the Clark School continues to provide an elementary education to the children of today's residents.

Clark School

---

[1] H. M. Simpson, Clerk of Board, *Description of School District No. 24 Big Horn County*, 1897.

[2] *Minutes of Annual School Meeting held in School District No. 24 on May the 4th, 1896;* List of Sirrine #24 and Pioneer #4 teachers 1896 – 1939 provided by Elmer Bunn, August 12, 2000.

[3] *Minutes of Annual School Meeting held in School District #24 on May 3rd, 1897;* and *Report of School District Clerk, District # 24, For the Year Ending the First Monday in September, 1897;* In 1898, Warren O. Sirrine was re-elected as Trustee, H. M. Simpson as Clerk, and W. H. Fouse, as Treasurer; (*District Officers Elected in Big Horn County at Election Held May 2nd, 1898);* Warren Sirrine was re-elected in 1900 to succeed himself as Trustee. (*Minutes of Annual School Meeting held in School District # 24 on first Monday in May, 1900;* and *District Officers Elected in Big Horn County at the Election Held May 7, 1900, District 24).* In 1901 William Fouse acted as chairman and Mrs. Mary Sirrine was appointed and acted as the Clerk pro-temp. (*Minutes of Annual School Meeting, School District #24 held in May 1901 and District Officers Elected in Big Horn County at the Election Held May 6, 1901).*

[4] Robert Holmes, Clerk, *Minutes District School Meetings, May 2, 1904; May 7, 1904 and May 21, 1904.*

[5] *Report of School District Clerk, District # 4, Park County, Wyoming for the Year Ending April 30, 1913.*

[6] *Park County Enterprise*, 1 November 1913, p. 6; Janet Hanson, *Pioneer School 1904 to 1969*, compiled 1992 from materials in the Park County Archives.

[7] "Commencing at the south east corner of the southwest quarter of the southwest quarter of Section twenty-nine in Township fifty-eight north of range one hundred one west of the Sixth Principal Meridian, Wyoming, thence running west 295.17 feet thence north 295.17 feet, thence east 295.17 feet; and thence south 295.17 feet to point of beginning, consisting of two acres more or less as the case may be." (Warranty Deed made on 12th day of June 1914. Filed in Park County Book 21, p. 147).

[8] The sealed bids for the construction were to be received by the Board of Trustees by 5 p.m. on July 10, 1914 at the office of the Architect, Curtis C. Oehme in Billings, and were to be submitted in accordance with the plans and specifications on file there. Mrs. Harry Simpson was Clerk of the Board, and Mrs. Ella J. Sirrine was chairman. (*Park County Enterprise*, July 01, 1914, p. 8).

[9] "Pioneer School," document, Wyoming State Historical Preservation Office; and *Park County Enterprise*, January 27, 1915, p. 3.

[10] "Clarks Fork," *The Cody Enterprise*, February 24, 1937, p. 6 and p. 8; March 10, 1937, p. 2; April 14, 1937, p. 6.

[10a] "Pioneer School," document, Wyoming State Historical Preservation Office.

[11] Warranty Deed, School District # 4, Park County, Wyoming to Pioneer Service Group, a Wyoming Corporation, signed on August 14, 1970 and filed on November 1, 1973 in Park County Book 348, page 87.

[11a] Plaque #313, Pioneer School, Enrolled October 5, 1993 (*Wyoming Register of Sites Enrolled in the National Register of Historic Places).*

[12] Don Tolman, *Park County School History*, manuscript, 1999.

[13] *Report of the School District Clerk, District No. 16 to the Superintendent of Schools, Big Horn County, Wyoming, for the Year Ending the First Monday in September, 1901.*

[14] "District Officers Elected in Big Horn Count at the Election Held May 6th, 1901," *School District Officers Report 1898, 1900-1901, Big Horn County, Wyoming.*

[15] Undated one-page document on the history of several Park County schools found in Park County

Archives.

[16] Attending the school in 1903 were children from the households of W. L. Barber, Emerson Bunn, John J. Frey, Alvin Dix, Frank W. Decker, J. E. Hundley, H. B. Henry, C. E. Leckie, John McKeever, August Myling, S. E. Rickards, Peter O. Simpson, Eli A. Vickery, and Solomon F. Weathermon families. While there were 43 children listed 7 were 17 years or older and probably not attending school. (*Big Horn County School Records, District 16*, Wyoming State Archives File 07.02.01).

[17] Clytie Fuson Williams, interview with author, Cody, Wyoming, December 01, 2003. Clytie attended the Bennett Creek School from 1914 – 1921, after which the log school building was abandoned and the students moved to the new Clark School.

[18] Joe Bush, who was in Cody and talked to the newspaper editor about conditions in the area, also complained that the County School Superintendent hadn't paid a visit to this area in seven years. ("Clark Fork Needs," *The Wyoming Stockgrower and Farmer*, July 18, 1907, p. 1).

[19] "Law Demands Children Must Attend School - Every parent, guardian or other person in this state having control or charge of any child or children between the ages of seven and fourteen, inclusive, shall be required to send such child or children to a public, private, or parochial school each school year, during the entire time that public schools shall be in session in the district in which the pupils reside." (*The Wyoming Stockgrower and Farmer*, October 01, 1909, p. 3).

[20] Charles A. C. Snow (1868 – 1930) spent the last 25 years of his life in Clark where he had a homestead and lived alone. He took quite an active part in community affairs serving not only as the justice of the peace, but also as a member of the school board for many years. His "Clark Squibs" columns, which were first appeared in 1909 in *The Wyoming Stockgrower* and continued in successor Cody newspapers, reported day-to-day area events that often were never reported anywhere else. Sometimes he even injected humor in his squibs, such as, "There was no school last week as the teacher was in Cody fighting it out with Superintendent Jessie Hitchcock." (*Park County Enterprise*, February 01, 1911, p. 5).

[21] "Clark Squibs," *Park County Enterprise*, May 07, 1910, p. 2.

[22] "Clark Squibs," *Park County Enterprise*, September 03, 1910, p. 5; November 19, 1910, p. 5; and December 24, 1910, p. 8; Clytie Fuson Williams who attended the Bennett Creek School starting in 1915 when she was 6. She continued there until the school closed and occupied the new school building at Clark where she finished the eighth grade before going high school in Cody. She told the author that she never saw the large bell. The only bell that she remembered at the Bennett Creek School was the small teacher's bell that was used to call students in from recess or to start class. (Clytie Fuson Williams, telephone conversation with author, January 09, 2004).

[23] *Park County School Records, District 8*, Wyoming State Archives File 07.02.01.

[24] "Results in Clark School Elections," *Park County Enterprise*, May 17, 1919, p. 7).

[25] *Park County Enterprise*, December 04, 1915, p. 2 and May 17, 1916, p. 8.

[26] *Park County Enterprise*, December 04, 1918, p. 5.

[27] By terms of their land donation, if it was ever abandoned for school purposes, it was to *"revert to the owner of the tract of land from which it is taken."* (Contract for Warranty Deed, Park County Book 50, p. 159).

[28] *Park County Enterprise*, October 12, 1921, p. 4.

[29] *Cody Enterprise*, November 01, 1922, p. 8 and *The Park County Herald*, April 09, 1924, p. 5; April 23, 1924, p. 7; September 24, 1924, p. 4; December 31, 1924, p. 6.

[30] Wyoming Deputy State Superintendent of Education, Georgia Earlandson and Park County School Superintendent Minnie Ide were both present when the Clark School and the Paint Creek School were standardized in formal ceremonies. (*The Park County Herald*, June 04, 1924, p. 5 and p. 8).

[31] Letter to Mr. Lester, Big Horn County Superintendent of Schools from Nonie Moxley, dated October 02, 1901.

[32] Paint Creek meeting minutes, J. C. Brown chairman, and H. J. Huntington, secretary on August 02, 1902.

[33] Paint Creek meeting minutes on September 1, 1902 and October 13, 1902.

[34] Tolman, 1999.

[35] *School Census, District 31, Big Horn County, School Year Ending 1903,* dated 15 June 1903; Phyllis Bosley who grew up in Paint Creek remembered, "there was a little log school house across from where the school was built. It was used for one year or so, and then the they built the school house." (Phyllis Bosley Lovercheck, interview with author, Powell, Wyoming, 25 January 2000); Mrs. August Brough remembered that the school opened in an abandoned cabin which had no floor, windows or door, but by the time cold weather set in, a door and window covered the openings. The 10 school children sat on nail kegs, used soap boxes for desks, and used books furnished by Mrs. Brough, as well as a few from the Cody school system. The children wrote on slates, and there was no blackboard in the building. Hallie Huntington, a man, was the first teacher for a six-month term, and she thought that he was the best teacher they ever had. ("Mrs. Augusta Brough Tells Story of the Early Days of Paint Creek," *The Cody Enterprise,* November 28, 1950, p. 2).

[36] Tolman, 1999.

[37] Minutes of School Election, District 31, Big Horn Co., Wyoming held May 04, 1903.

[38] Paint Creek Points," *Wyoming Stockgrower and Farmer,* May 10, 1905, p. 3.

[39] *Wyoming Stockgrower and Farmer,* February 28, 1906, p. 4.

[40] "From Paint Creek," *Wyoming Stockgrower and Farmer,* August 08, 1907, p. 1; "Pulse of Paint Creek," *Wyoming Stockgrower and Farmer,* August 22, 1907, p. 1; *Big Horn and Park County School Records, District 31,* Wyoming State Archives File 07.02.01; and "More Local News," *Wyoming Stockgrower and Farmer,* December 17, 1909, p. 4 and p. 5.

[41] Tolman, 1999.

[42] "Legal Notice of Sale of School Bonds, School District Number Five in the County of Park, in the State of Wyoming," *Park County Enterprise,* October 25, 1913, p. 6.

[41] Tolman, 1999.

[42] "Legal Notice of Sale of School Bonds, School District Number Five in the County of Park, in the State of Wyoming," *Park County Enterprise,* October 25, 1913, p. 6.

[43] *The Cody Enterprise,* September 25, 1923, p. 5.

[44] "Paint Creek Notes," *The Cody Enterprise,* February 20, 1924, p. 5.

[45] "Teacher Is Arrested for Beating Boy," *The Cody Enterprise,* April 02, 1924, p. 1; "County Superintendent Defends School Teachers," *The Powell Tribune,* April 10, 1924, p. 3.

[46] "Park County School Records: Paint Creek School, District 5, 1924 -1928," *Wyoming State Archives Box 07.02.01.*

[47] "Paint Creek," *Park County Herald,* October 15, 1924, p. 3.

[48] Georgia Close, interview with author, Clark, Wyoming, September 13, 2000.

[49] Georgia Close, interview with author, Clark, Wyoming, December 17, 2000.

[50] Georgia Close, interview with author, September 13, 2000.

[51] Georgia Close, interview with author, Clark, Wyoming, December 01, 1999.

[52] Georgia Close interview with author, September 13, 2000.

[53] "Park County School Records: Paint Creek School, District 5, 1952," *Wyoming State Archives Box 07.02.01.*

[54] Tolman, 1999.

[55] "Clark's Fork Needs," *Wyoming Stockgrower and Farmer,* July 18, 1907, p. 1.

[56] Tolman, 1999.

[57] *Park County Enterprise,* May 17, 1911, p. 7.

[58] *Park County Enterprise,* June 07, 1911, p. 4.

[59] RG 1130 Archives - County Government, Park County Superintendent of Schools, (Line Creek District #7), File 07.02.01 – Census, Wyoming State Archives.

[60] "Classification Report to Superintendent and District Clerk, District No. 7, Term began October 13, 1913 and closed April 2, 1914; teacher Berthe E. Weyeneth."

[61] "Clark Fork News," *The Powell Tribune,* May 08, 1914, p. 1.

[62] "The perfect attendance of the rural school children ranked high last year, but this year, with weather below zero, the percentage of attendance has been even higher. This says a great deal for those children who have to walk a long distance during the winter months." (*The Cody Enterprise,* February 17, 1932, p. 2).

[63] "Lower Clark Fork," *The Cody Enterprise,* June 01, 1932, p. 3.

[64] "Clarks Fork," *The Cody Enterprise,* November 06, 1937, p. 3.

[65] "Lower Clarks Fork," *The Cody Enterprise,* October 30, 1946, p. 19.

[66] "Clarks Fork," *The Cody Enterprise,* July 02, 1947, p. 11.

[67] Ibid. and 23 July 23, 1947, p. 10.

[68] Tolman, 1999.

[69] "Park County School Records, District #29," Wyoming State Archives File 07.02.01.

[70] "On Pat O'Hara," *Park County Enterprise,* August 24, 1921, p. 8.

[71] "Pat O'Hara News," *Cody Enterprise,* May 10, 1922, p. 5.

[72] *Park County Enterprise,* November 1, 1922, p. 8 and *The Cody Enterprise,* November 15, 1922, p. 5.

[73] The *Cody Enterprise,* January 31, 1923, p. 4.

[74] *The Cody Enterprise,* May 16, 1923, p. 1.

[75] *The Cody Enterprise,* July 4, 1923, p. 4.

[76] *The Cody Enterprise,* August 15, 1923, p. 4.

[77] "Pat O'Hara," *The Park County Herald,* May 14, 1924, p. 2.

[78] *The Cody Enterprise,* April 2, 1924, p. 1.

[79] Ibid.

[80] *Powell Tribune,* April 10, 1927, p. 3.

[81] *The Park County Herald,* April 16, 1924, p. 2.

[82] "Pat O'Hara," *The Park County Herald,* July 16, 1924, p. 6.

[83] "Pat O'Hara," *The Park County Herald,* March 4, 1925, p. 4.

[84] "Pat O'Hara, *The Park County Herald,* April 8, 1925, p. 7.

[85] "Pat O'Hara," *The Park County Herald,* June 03, 1925, p. 6.

[86] "Pat O'Hara," *The Park County Herald,* August 26, 1925, p. 6.

[87] "Pat O'Hara," *The Cody Enterprise and Park County Herald,* January 19, 1927, p. 6.

[88] "Pat O'Hara," *The Cody Enterprise and Park County Herald,* April 6, 1927, p. 9.

[89] "Buffalo Bill Town Doings," *The Cody Enterprise and Park County Herald,* May 4, 1927, p. 4.

[90] "Pat O'Hara," *The Cody Enterprise and Park County Herald,* May 11, 1927, p. 8 and May 18, 1927, p. 7.

[91] "Off Bald Ridge," The Cody Enterprise and Park County Herald, May 25, 1927, p. 3.

[92] *Park County School Records, District #29,* Wyoming State Archives File 07.02.01.

[93] Ibid.

[94] Tolman, 1999.

19
Teachers & Staff

1896 – Sirrine = Mattie Simpson
1897 – Sirrine = Harry M. Simpson
1898 – Sirrine = Eleanor Sabin
1899 – Sirrine = Bertha Hinds
1900 – Sirrine = Zoë Wheeler

1901 – Bennett Creek = Zoë Wheeler (summer term)
      Sirrine = Zoë Wheeler (Sep-Nov)

1902 – Bennett Creek = Lillie P. Holmes
      Paint Creek – H. R. Huntington
      Sirrine = Sarah Frances Cochrane

1903 – Bennett Creek = Gertrude F. Natson
      Paint Creek = David H. Teel and Mrs. Sibyl Easton
      Sirrine = Sarah Frances Cochrane

1904 – Bennett Creek = Minnie Whittington
      Paint Creek = David H. Teel
      Sirrine = Sarah Frances Cochrane

1905 – 1906
      Bennett Creek = Mattie Simpson
      Paint Creek = Mrs. Henderson
      Sirrine = Sarah Frances Cochrane

1906 – 1907
      Bennett Creek = Mattie Simpson
      Paint Creek = Miss Pettis
      Sirrine = Edith Newman

1907 – 1908
      Bennett Creek = Mattie B. Betty
      Paint Creek = Gertrude Scott
      Sirrine = Ella J. Sirrine

1908 – 1909
      Bennett Creek = Millie Anderson and Evelyn Rose (winter)
      Paint Creek = No teacher available
      Sirrine = Nellie Hughinbough

1909 - 1910
  Bennett Creek = Lucy Barnhart
  Paint Creek = Ranna Brown
  Sirrine = Nellie Huginbough

1910 - 1911
  Bennett Creek = Anna Tipton
  Paint Creek = Laurie Wenchell
  Sirrine = Mannie Winchell

1911 - 1912
  Bennett Creek = Mrs. C. E. Lord, Addie L. Mead (6 months)
  Line Creek = Addie L. Mead (3 months)
  Paint Creek = Mary E. Volk (resigned in Oct to go to Kane)
      and replaced by Edgar H. Davis (6 months)
  Pioneer = Duell, McCabe

1912 - 1913
  Bennett Creek = Mary Cravens
  Line Creek = (No data)
  Paint Creek = Effie Abrahamson
  Pioneer = Mabel T. Jones

1913 - 1914
  Bennett Creek = Mary Cravens
  Line Creek = Bertha E. Weyeneth
  Paint Creek = Effie Abrahamson
  Pioneer = Frances Scott

1914 - 1915
  Bennett Creek = Eugena Swift
  Line Creek = Mary M. Cravens
  Paint Creek = M .J. Martin (closed in Jan for rest of year)
  Pioneer = Jennie Powers

1915 - 1916
  Bennett Creek = Mary M. Cravens
  Line Creek = Mrs. Flora Swinas
  Paint Creek = Irma Den and Alice Babbitt
  Pioneer = Mary Paxton

1916 - 1917
  Bennett Creek =Effie Abramson (married Ernest Shaw in Nov);
      Mary Cravens finished year
  Line Creek = Ethel Earl
  Paint Creek = Jessie Corlett
  Pioneer = Nellie Underwood

1917 - 1918

 Bennett Creek = Thura Campbell
 Line Creek = Florence Nohr
 Paint Creek = Fern Isham , Elizabeth Vickery, and Blanca Dean
 Pioneer = Alpha Vogel

1918 - 1919

 Bennett Creek = Myrtle Underwood
 Line Creek = Ethel Earl
 Paint Creek = Lorraine Martin
 Pioneer = Mabelle Godfrey

1919 - 1920

 Bennett Creek = Marguerite L. Hatton (married); Eleanor McHugh finished last 3 months
 Line Creek = Vergil Wolfe
 Paint Creek = Vera Snyder
 Pioneer = Mabelle Godfrey

1920 - 1921

 Bennett Creek = Elizabeth C. Ellingson
 Line Creek = Mamie Goff
 Paint Creek = James P. Rigg and Russell Dick
 Pioneer = Mabelle Godfrey

1921 - 1922

 Clark = Elizabeth C. Ellingson
 Line Creek = (No data)
 Paint Creek = Gladys E. Holm (left) and Alice Bailey (finished term in May)
 Pat O'Hara = Dorothy Matthews
 Pioneer = Mabelle Godfrey

1922 - 1923

 Clark = Mabelle (Fay) Anderson
 Line Creek = Flossie Wood
 Paint Creek = Thelma Edmonds
 Pat O'Hara = Anna Derschell (new school house dedicated on Nov. 3, 1922)
 Pioneer = Fay Till

1923 - 1924

 Clark = Thelma Edmonds
 Line Creek = Vernon Brothers
 Paint Creek = Flossie Wood (resigned in late March);
 Pat O'Hara = Helen Young (resigned April 14); Merle Mathews of Powell finishes term
 Pioneer = Helen E. Peterson

1924 - 1925

 Clark = Claire Seyler

Line Creek = Lorraine Martin
Paint Creek = Margaret O'Donnell
Pioneer = Helen Peterson
Pat O'Hara = Merle Mathews

1925 – 1926

Clark = Blanche Gilbert
Line Creek = Nora Luttrell
Paint Creek = Geraldine Kindler
Pat O'Hara = Thelma Black
Pioneer = Margaret O'Donnell

1926 – 1927

Clark = Marian Kobe
Line Creek = Nora Luttrell
Paint Creek = Fern Ashley
Pat O'Hara = Gladys Horner (suffered a nervous breakdown);
    Geraldine Kindler finished school term in May)
Pioneer = Helen Peterson

1927 – 1928

Clark = Marian Castle
Line Creek = Nora Luttrell
Paint Creek = Carrie Myers
Pat O'Hara = Lorena Schultz
Pioneer = Fern Ashley

1928 – 1929

Clark = Marian Castle
Line Creek = Mildred Kysar
Paint Creek = Carrie Myers
Pat O'Hara = Florence James
Pioneer = Emily Anderson

1929 – 1930

Clark = Clytie Fuson
Line Creek = Nora Luttell
Paint Creek = Geraldine Werner
Pat O'Hara = Lorene Schultz
Pioneer = Dorothy Hardee

1930 – 1931

Clark = Lorene Schultz
    Bus driver – Lonnie Edgmond had his own large car
Line Creek = Roberta Garmon and Alice Moore
Paint Creek = Charles Kooner
Pat O'Hara = Pearl S. Schock

Pioneer = Dorothy Hardee

1931 – 1932

    Clark = Alta Askdal
    Line Creek = Gertrude Billing
    Paint Creek = Arthur Marshall
    Pat O'Hara = Lorene Schultz
    Pioneer = Alice Moore

1932 – 1933

    Clark = Florence Wogoman
    Line Creek = Ella Bunn
    Paint Creek = Orlando Major
    Pat O'Hara = Gertrude Billings
    Pioneer = Alice Moore

1933 – 1934

    Clark = Constance Cubbage
    Line Creek = Ella Bunn
    Paint Creek = Nedra Shinn
    Pat O'Hara = no data
    Pioneer = Miss Besedaq resigns in late Sep; Mildred McFarland takes over.

1934 – 1935

    Clark = Constance Cubbage
    Line Creek = Elizabeth Webster Spear
    Paint Creek = Leona Dorn (married Herald in Jan); Alice Moore completes term
    Pat O'Hara = Ella Bunn
    Pioneer = Mildred McFarland

1935 – 1936

    Clark = Constance Cubbage (4-8); Ella Bunn (1-4)
        Bus driver – Ray Bunn had contract and used own bus
    Line Creek = Nora Luttrell Rigby
    Paint Creek = Mollie Stillings moved to Sunlight in late Sep;
        Alice Moore comes from Sunlight; they switch schools
    Pat O'Hara = Wayne Lovewell
    Pioneer = Mildred McFarland

1936 – 1937

    Clark = Lucille Beatty (1-4); Ann Collins (4-8)
        Bus driver - Frank Thull driving new Clark School bus.
    Line Creek = Helen Thornberry
    Paint Creek = Mrs. Constance Cubbage
    Pat O'Hara = Gertrude Billings (15 days); Mrs. Ross Young (154 days)
    Pioneer = Mildred McFarland

1937 – 1938

        Clark = Elsie Mailander
            Bus driver - Frank Thull
        Line Creek = Helen Thornberry (35 days); Mary Reffner (135 days)
        Paint Creek = Dorothea Florida
        Pat O'Hara = Ella Bunn
        Pioneer = Mildred McFarland

1938 – 1939

        Clark = Florence Wogoman
            Bus driver - Frank Thull
        Line Creek = Mrs. Nora Luttrell Rigby (resigned for health reasons in early Nov.);
            replaced by Elsie Mailander
        Paint Creek = Mary Lee Duncan
        Pat O'Hara = Donald Manmen
        Pioneer = Bessie Travess

1939 – 1940

        Clark = Florence Wogoman
            Bus driver - Frank Thull
        Line Creek = Elsie Mailander
        Paint Creek = Mary Lee Duncan
        Pat O'Hara = Mary Ritter
        Pioneer = Bessie Travess

1940 - 1941

        Clark = Florence Wogoman
            Bus driver - no data
        Line Creek = Elsie Mailander
        Paint Creek = Mary Lee Duncan and Ethel Edmonds
        Pat O'Hara = Mary Ritter
        Pioneer = Wilma Mailander

1941 – 1942

        Clark = John Larmer resigns 6 Feb to go into service;
            Ethel Snyder Clark comes from Paint Creek to finish term
            Bus driver - Woody Thompson (till Feb), then Guy Pointer
        Line Creek = Elsie Mailander
        Paint Creek = Ethel Clark moves to Clark in Feb; Mrs. Jack Higham finishes term
        Pat O'Hara = Evelyn Painter Day
        Pioneer = Mary Humphrey and Florence Wogoman

1942 – 1943

        Clark = Mary Jane Roney
            Bus drivers - John Simpson & no data
        Line Creek = Olga Otonichar
        Paint Creek = Georgia Frame

Pat O'Hara = Evelyn Painter Day
Pioneer = Florence Wogoman

1943 - 1944

Clark = Violet Moorehead
    Bus drivers – no data
Line Creek = Olga Otonichar (Made one school at Pioneer)
Paint Creek = Elmarie Badura
Pioneer = Cora Harkin quit in Oct to care for mother;
    Olga Otonichar brings Line Creek students to Pioneer to finish year

1944 - 1945

Clark = Violet Moorehead
    Bus drivers – Bert Stidham & no data
Line Creek = Dahl Christopherson
Paint Creek = Grace Byrd
Pioneer = Elmarie Badura

1945 - 1946

Clark = Violet Morehead Pointer
    Bus drivers – Ed Lindquist & Terry Smith (comes in Nov)
Line Creek = Geraldine Lindquist
Paint Creek = Vera Johnson or Johnston?
Pioneer = Elmarie Badura

1946 - 1947

Clark = Marcile Hutchins; replaced by Wilda McLaughlin in late October;
    Kenneth Helm started teaching 4 upper grades with Wilda on 17 Mar 47
    Bus drivers – Del Gaines & no data
Line Creek = Geraldine Lindquist **(Line Creek School closes at end of school year)**
Paint Creek = Mrs. Nora Bugher
Pioneer = Elmarie Badura

1947 - 1948

Clark = Wilda Hoefer and Mildred Lowe
    Bus drivers – Del Gaines & John Gairrett
Paint Creek = No school
Pioneer = Elmarie Badura

1948 - 1949

Clark = Mildred Lowe upper grades; (168 days); Hilda Bauer, lower grades (73 days);
    Wilda Hoefer (95 days) came on in Jan after the Bauers left Clark.
    Bus drivers – Lester Brown and Del Gaines
Paint Creek = No School this year
Pioneer = Dorothy Legg

1949 – 1950

  Clark = Mildred Lowe and Mrs. Irma Svoboda Patrick
      Bus drivers – Buck Cox & no data
  Paint Creek = Mrs. Wayne Lyman; Violet Pointer
  Pioneer = Frances Townsend

1950 – 1951

  Clark = Edith DiVall (lower grades) and Blanche Tuttle (upper grades)
      Bus drivers– Walt Teichert, Buck Cox (wrecks bus in May)
  Paint Creek = Violet Pointer
  Pioneer = Frances Townsend

1951 – 1952

  Clark = Edith DiVall (19 days), resigned to get married in late Sept; Phyllis Jesse (148 days)
      replaced her and taught lower grades; Blanche Tuttle (167days) (upper grades)
      Bus drivers – Walt Teichert & Pate Pointer
  Paint Creek = Marian Sprouse **(School terminated at end of school year)**
  Pioneer = Helen Parrish

1952 – 1953

  Clark = Betty Leona Alexander (lower grades) Lois Townsend (upper grades),
      Bus drivers – Walter Teichert, Pate Pointer, Earl Davidson
  Pioneer = Helen Parrish

1953 – 1954

  Clark = Betty Alexander (lower grades) and Ella Bunn Taylor (upper grades)
      Bus drivers – Walt Teichert & Pate Pointer
  Pioneer = Helen Parrish

1954 – 1955

  Clark = Betty Alexander Gairrett, (lower grades) (94 days) resigned in January; replaced
      by Mrs. Addleman from Powell and Ella Bunn Taylor (upper grades)
      Bus drivers – John Gairrett, Pate Pointer, and Mickey Obert
      Cafeteria - Mrs. Julia (John) Gairrett begins cooking at new school cafeteria
  Pioneer = Helen Parrish

1955 – 1956

  Clark = Thelma B. Hetland (1-4) and Mary E. Lockhart (5-8)
      Cafeteria – Julia Gairrett
      Bus drivers – John Gairrett, Mickey Obert, and Ray Marney
          In Dec Pate & Violet Pointer bring new school bus back from Illinois for
          transport of students to high school to Belfry
  Pioneer = Helen Parrish

1956 – 1957

  Clark =Thelma Hetland (1-4) and Mary Lockhart (5-8)
      Cafeteria – Julia Gairrett

Bus drivers – John Gairrett, Ray Marney, Mickey Obert; Dennis Warren (sub)
Pioneer = Sylvia Dickson

1957 – 1958
Clark = Thelma B. Hetland (1-4) and Carol L. Brown (5-8)
    Cafeteria – Julia Gairrett
    Bus drivers – John Gairrett, Dennis Warren & Ray Marney
Pioneer = Marjorie Cushman

1958 – 1959
Clark =Ethel Skibby (1-4) and Ronald G. Reese (5-8)
    Cafeteria – Julia Gairrett
    Bus drivers – Dennis Warren (dies in Oct); Leo Spence & Ray Marney
Pioneer = Marjorie B. Cushman

1959 – 1960
Clark = Ethel Skibby (1-4) and Ronald Reese (5-8)
    Cafeteria – Julia Gairrett resigns in Dec for health;
        Virginia Teichert takes over and finishes school year
    Bus drivers – Ray Marney & John Eckerman
Pioneer = Carol Brown Thull and Nannie Walker (aid 1-2)

1960 – 1961
Clark = Ethel Skibby (1-4) and Helen Butler (5-8)
    Bus drivers – John Eckerman & Ray Marney
    Cafeteria – Ada Eckerman takes over lunch preparation
Pioneer = Betty J. Heaser and Nannie Walker (aid 1-2)

1961 – 1962
Clark = John Harney (1-4) and Helen Butler (5-8)
    Cafeteria – Ada Eckerman
    Bus drivers – John Eckerman & Ray Marney
Pioneer = Betty J. Heaser & Nannie Walker (aid 1-2)

1962 – 1963
Clark = Carol Wagner (1-4) and Tom Wagner (4-8)
    Cafeteria – Ada Eckerman
    Bus drivers – John Eckerman, Ray Marney, and Harold Lawson
Pioneer = Dorothy La Follette

1963 – 1964
Clark = Glada Cooper (1-4) and Hjordis Sorensen (5-8)
    Cafeteria - Ada Eckerman
    Bus drivers – John Eckerman & Earl Black
Pioneer = Dorothy La Follette

1964 – 1965

      Clark = Glada Cooper (1-4) and Hjordis Sorensen (5-8)
         Cafeteria – Ada Eckerman
         Bus drivers – John Eckerman & Earl Black
      Pioneer = Dorothy La Follette

1965 – 1966

      Clark = Bessie Travess. Hill (1-4) and Hjordis Sorensen (5-8)
         Cafeteria – Ada Eckerman
         Bus drivers – John Eckerman & Earl Black
      Pioneer = Margaret Dempster

1966 – 1967

      Clark = Bessie Travess Hill (1-4) and Hjordis Sorensen (5-8)
         Cafeteria – Ada Eckerman
         Bus drivers – John Eckerman & Earl Black
      Pioneer = Margaret Dempster

1967 – 1968

      Clark = Bessie T. Hill (1-4) and Hjordis Sorensen (5-8)
         Cafeteria – Ada Eckerman
         Bus drivers – John Eckerman & Earl Black
      Pioneer = Helen Walker

1968 – 1969

      Clark = Bessie T. Hill (1-4) and Hjordis Sorensen (5-8)
         Cafeteria – Ada Eckerman
         Bus drivers – John Eckerman, Lee Weathermon & Earl Black
      Pioneer = Helen Walker **(school closes end of term)**

1969 - 1970

      Clark = Bessie T. Hill (1-4) and Hjordis Sorensen (5-8)
         Cafeteria - Ada Eckerman
         Bus drivers - John Eckerman, Lee Weathermon & Earl Black
      (Clark consolidates at end of school year with Powell School District # 1)

1970 – 1971

      Teachers = Bessie T. Hill (1-4) and Hjordis Sorensen (5-8)
      Cafeteria = Edna Mae Smith
      Custodians = Leo T. Spence and Ruth Spence
      Bus Drivers = Earl Black, John Eckerman, Leon E. Sprinkle, and Lee Weathermon

1971 – 1972

      Teachers = Bessie T. Hill (1-3) and Hjordis Sorensen (4-6)
      Aide & Custodian = Virginia Sprinkle
      Cafeteria = Edna Mae Smith
      Bus Drivers = John Eckerman, Robert Brunk (sub.), Leon Sprinkle, and Lee Weathermon

1972 – 1973

      Teachers = Margorie Pyatt (1-3) and Billy L. Dansby (4-6)

      Cafeteria = Edna Mae Smith

      Bus Drivers = Ada Eckerman, John Eckerman, Robert Brunk (sub.), and Lee Weathermon

1973 – 1974

      Teachers = Margorie Pyatt (K-3) and Billy L. Dansby (4-6)

      Teacher Aide = Marian Eggars

      Cafeteria = Edna Mae Smith

      Bus Drivers = Ada Eckerman, John Eckerman, Robert Brunk (sub.), and Lee Weathermon

1974 – 1975

      Teachers = Margorie Pyatt (K-3) and Bill Dansby (4-6)

      Cafeteria = Edna Mae Smith

      Bus Drivers = Ada Eckerman, John Eckerman, and Lee Weathermon

1975 – 1976

      Teachers = Cathy Fraser (K-3) and Billy L. Dansby (4-6)

      Cafeteria = Edna Mae Smith

      Bus Drivers = Ada Eckerman, Edna Smith (sub.), John Eckerman, and Lee Weathermon

1976 – 1977

      Teachers = Cathy Fraser (K-3) and E. Tom Martin (4-6)

      Teacher Aide = Carolyn Lou Gordon

      Cafeteria = Edna Mae Smith

      Bus Drivers = Ada Eckerman, Edna Smith (sub.), John Eckerman, and Lee Weathermon

1977 – 1978

      Teachers = Cathy Fraser (K-3) and Dennis D. Prewett (4-6)

      Teacher Aide = Phyllis H. Presgrove

      Cafeteria = Edna Mae Smith

      Sweeper = Sandra Faye Dill

      Bus Drivers = Ada M. Eckerman, Edna Smith (sub.), John G. Eckerman, and Lee Weathermon

1978 – 1979

      Teachers = Linda Learned (K-3) and Roger A. Price (4-6)

      Teacher Aide = Vera Hodges

      Cafeteria = Edna Mae Smith

      Sweeper = Pearl Thiel

      Bus Drivers = Ada M. Eckerman, John G. Eckerman, and Lee Weathermon

1979 – 1980

      Teachers = Susan D. Gibson (K-3) and LaVonne S. Lee (4-6)

      Teacher Aide = Vera Hodges

      Cafeteria = Edna Mae Smith

      Sweeper = Pearl Thiel

      Bus Drivers = Ada M. Eckerman, John G. Eckerman, and Lee Weathermon

1980 - 1981

      Teachers = Susan Dill (K-3) and Susan McDonald (4-6)

      Teacher Aide = Vera Hodges

      Cafeteria - Edna Mae Smith

      Sweeper = Deeda Slagle

      Bus Drivers = Ada M. Eckerman, John G. Eckerman, and Lee Weathermon

1981 - 1982

      Teachers = Deborah A. Baker (K-2) and Steven L. Baker (3-5)

      Teacher Aide = Robbie Gordon

      Cafeteria = Edna Mae Smith

      Bus Drivers = Ada M. Eckerman, John G. Eckerman, and Lee Weathermon

1982 - 1983

      Teachers = Deborah A. Baker (K-2) and Steven L. Baker (3-6)

      Teacher Aide = Roxann M. Lovell

      Cafeteria = Edna Mae Smith

      Bus Drivers = Ada M. Eckerman, Lee Weathermon, and Noralee Willis

1983 - 1984

      Teachers = Deborah A. Baker (K-2) and Steven L. Baker (3-5)

      Teacher Aide = Roxann M. Lovell

      Cafeteria = Barbara Wegner

      Bus Drivers = Ada M. Eckerman, Lee Weathermon, and Noralee Willis

1984 - 1985

      Teachers = Patricia A. Vincent (K-2) and Cody J. Vincent (3-5)

      Teacher Aide = Roxann M. Lovell

      Cafeteria = Barbara Wegner (until Jan 7), Carol L. Harshman (Jan 7 on)

      Bus Drivers = Ada M. Eckerman, Lee Weathermon, and Noralee Willis

1985 - 1986

      Teachers = Patricia A. Vincent (K-2) and Cody J. Vincent (3-5)

      Teacher Aide = Roxann M. Lovell

      Cafeteria = Carol L. Harshman

      Bus Drivers = Ada M. Eckerman, Delores R. Reichert, and Noralee Willis

1986 - 1987

      Teachers = Patricia A. Vincent (K-2) and Patricia Vincent (3-5)

      Cafeteria /Sweeper = Carol L. Harshman

      Bus Drivers = Ada M. Eckerman, Delores R. Reichert, and Noralee Willis

1987 - 1988

      Teachers = Trudy Workman (K-2) and Sonja D. Black (3-5)

      Teacher Aide/Cafeteria = Carol L. Harshman

      Bus Drivers = Ada M. Eckerman, Delores R. Reichert, and Noralee Willis

1988 - 1989

     Teachers = Diane R. Hensman (K-2) and Sonja D. Black (3-5)
     Teacher Aide = Carei L. Smith
     Cafeteria/Sweeper = Carol L. Harshman
     Bus Drivers = Ada M. Eckerman, Noralee Hoefer, and Delores R. Reichert

1989 - 1990

     Teachers = Diane R. Hensman (K-2) and Sonja D. Black (3-5)
     Teacher Aide = Carei L. Smith
     Cafeteria/Sweeper = Carol L. Harshman
     Bus Drivers = Marilee Brown, Noralee Hoefer, and Delores R. Reichert

1990 - 1991

     Teachers = Diane R. Hensman (K-2) and Brenda M. Wham (3-5)
     Teacher Aide = Carei L. Smith (until March 1), Carolyn L. Metz (March 1 on)
     Cafeteria/Sweeper = Carol L. Harshman
     Bus Drivers = Marilee Brown, Noralee Hoefer, and Delores R. Reichert

1991 - 1992

     Teachers = Brenda M. Wham (K-2) and Catherine M. Ringler (3-5 & Sp. Ed.)
     Teacher Aide = Carolyn L. Metz
     Aide/Special Education = Bonita A. Rouse (Jan 15 on)
     Cafeteria/Sweeper = Carol L. Harshman
     Bus Drivers = Marilee Brown Tolman, Noralee Hoefer, and Delores R. Reichert

1992 - 1993

     Teachers = Shawna L. Potter (K-2) and Catherine M. Ringler (3-5 & Sp. Ed.)
     Teacher Aide = Carolyn L. Metz
     Aide/Special Education = Bonita A. Rouse
     Head Cook/Sweeper = Carol L. Harshman
     Bus Drivers = Marilee Tolman (until Oct 30), Diane K. Bell (Nov 9 on), and Noralee Torczon

1993 - 1994

     Teachers = Catherine M. Ringler (K-2 & Sp. Ed.) and Laurie Vredenburg (3-5 & Sp. Ed.)
     Teacher Aide = Carolyn L. Metz (until Mar 11), Rita Lovell (after Mar 28)
     Aide/Special Education = Bonita A. Rouse
     Head Cook = Delores R. Reichert
     Sweeper = Diane K. Bell
     Bus Drivers = Delores P. Reichert, and Noralee Torczon

1994 - 1995

     Teachers = Catherine Ringler (K-2 & Sp. Ed.) and Laurie Vredenberg (3-5 & Sp. Ed.)
     Aides = Bonita A. Rouse and Collene M. Jackson (after Feb 3)
     Head Cook = Delores R. Reichert
     Sweeper = Diane K. Bell
     Bus Drivers = Diane K. Bell, Delores R. Reichert, and Noralee Torczon

1995 – 1996

    Teachers = Catherine Ringler (K-2 & Sp. Ed.) and Laurie Vredenburg (3-5 & Sp. Ed.)
    Aides = Collene M. Jackson and Bonita A. Rouse
    Head Cook = Delores R. Reichert
    Sweeper = Diane K. Bell
    Bus Drivers = Diane K. Bell, Delores R. Reichert, and Noralee Torczon

1996 – 1997

    Teachers = Catherine Ringler (1-3) and Bethanee Wipplinger (4-5 & Sp. Ed.)
    Aides = Collene M. Jackson and Bonita A. Rouse
    Head Cook = Delores R. Reichert
    Sweeper = Marilee Tolman
    Bus Drivers = Delores R. Reichert, Marilee Tolman, and Noralee Torczon

1997 – 1998

    Teachers = Catherine Ringler (K-3 & Sp. Ed.) and Bethanee Wipplinger (3-5 & Sp. Ed.)
    Aides = Colleen M. Jackson and Bonita A. Rouse
    Head Cook = Delores R. Reichert
    Sweeper = Marilee Tolman
    Bus Drivers = Noralee Hoefer, Delores R. Reichert, and Marilee Tolman

1998 – 1999

    Teachers = Catherine Ringler (K-3 & Sp. Ed.) and Bethanee Wipplinger (3-5 & Sp. Ed.)
    Aides = Sherry L. Hale, Collene M. Jackson, and Deborah K. Thomas
    Head Cook = Delores R. Reichert
    Sweeper = Marilee Tolman
    Bus Drivers = Noralee Hoefer, Lee Maxine Hohnhorst (after Mar 15),
        Delores R. Reichert (until April 14), and Marilee Tolman

1999 – 2000

    Teachers = Catherine Ringler (K-3) & Sp. Ed. and Bethanee Wipplinger (3-5 & Sp. Ed.)
    Aides = Sherry L. Hale, Collene M. Jackson, and Deborah K. Thomas
    Head Cook = Shirley A. Bentley
    Sweeper = Marilee Tolman
    Bus Drivers = Noralee Hoefer, Lee Maxine Hohnhorst, and Marilee Tolman

2000 – 2001

    Teachers = Catherine Ringler (K-3 & Sp. Ed.) and Bethanee Wipplinger (3-5 & Sp. Ed.)
    Aides = June R. Burling, Sherry L. Hale, and Collene M. Jackson
    Head Cook = Shirley A. Bentley
    Sweeper = Melanie R. Mollett
    Bus Drivers = Noralee Hoefer, Lee Maxine Hohnhorst, and Marilee Tolman

2001 – 2002

    Teachers = Catherine Ringler (K-2 & Sp. Ed.) and Bethanee Wipplinger (3-5 & Sp. Ed.)
    Aides = Sherry L. Hale and Collene M. Jackson
    Head Cook = Janice L. Kuntz

Sweeper = Laurie L. Denney
Bus Drivers = Noralee Hoefer, Lee Maxine Hohnhorst, and Marilee Tolman

2002 - 2003

Teachers = Catherine Ringler (K-2 & Sp. Ed.) and Bethanee Wipplinger (3-5 & Sp. Ed.)
Aides = Sherry L. Hale and Collene M. Jackson
Head Cook = Janice L. Kuntz
Custodian I = Laurie L. Denney (until April 11), James W. Kaszuba (after April 14)
Bus Drivers = Noralee Hoefer, Lee Maxine Hohnhorst, and Marilee Tolman

2003 - 2004

Teachers = Catherine Ringler (K-2 & Sp. Ed.) and Bethanee Wipplinger (3-5 & Sp. Ed.)
Aides = Collene M. Jackson and Linda D. Straub
Head Cook = Janice L. Kuntz
Custodian I = James W. Kaszuba
Bus Drivers = Noralee Hoefer, Lee Maxine Hohnhorst, and Marilee Tolman

Chapter 19 notes:
This list was compiled from a number of sources including: interviews with former teachers, students, and bus drivers; Janet Hanson's *Pioneer School 1904 to 1969* manuscript published in 1992; mentions of school teachers in newspaper articles found in the *Wyoming Stockgrower and Farmer*, (1903-1910), *Park County Enterprise*, (1910-1921), *The Cody Enterprise*, (1922-1924), *The Park County Herald*, (1924-1926), *The Cody Enterprise and Park County Herald*, (1926), *The Cody Enterprise*, (1927-1962), and numerous issues of *The Powell Tribune*. These were cross-checked against the school files found at the Wyoming State Archives which include: *Minutes of the Annual School Meeting Held in School District # 24* (1896, 1897, 1898, 1899, 1900, 1901, 1902, 1903, and 1904); "School Teachers," Wyoming State Archives records, Box 74; and "Teachers' Directory, Park County, 1911-1970", Wyoming State Archives, File 01.00.06. In cases of disagreement between Archives files and newspapers, I chose the newspaper to be correct, especially when a particular teacher was reported several times in newspaper accounts within the same year. After Clark District # 7 was consolidated with Powell District # 1 in 1970, information on teachers and staff from then until the current year was obtained from *Personnel Directories, Park County School District # 1, Powell, Wyoming* published yearly. Copies of these directories are filed in the Office of the District Superintendent, 160 N. Evarts Street, Powell. Information for some early years is incomplete because dates and names could not be verified from available records or family sources. This was particularly true for some of our bus drivers who served the schools before 1970. In those cases I have left the position blank rather than record in error.

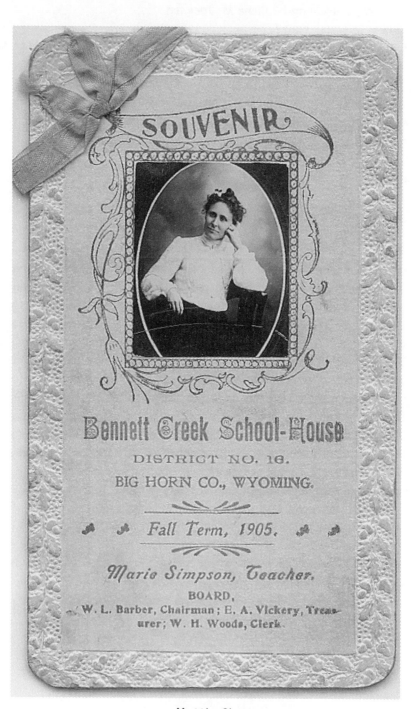

SOUVENIR

Bennett Creek School-House

DISTRICT NO. 16.

BIG HORN CO., WYOMING.

Fall Term, 1905.

Marie Simpson, Teacher.

BOARD,

W. L. Barber, Chairman; E. A. Vickery, Treasurer; W. H. Woods, Clerk.

Mattie Simpson
Sirrine School – 1896
Bennett Creek School 1905-1907

20
Remembering
School Days

"I was born in 1915 and they started me to school when I was five up at Cooke City at first. It was just a short time before we came out here in the fall. So I went that year to the Bennett Creek School. Our mother died the first of December (1921) so that's when my sister and I went to live with the Cards, our cousins.

"We went to the Paint Creek School up there. The one teacher that I remember here at Clark was Miss Ellingson. I had Mrs. Woods up there at Paint Creek. They're the only two teachers that I remember. There was a creek or maybe it was an irrigation ditch over there where we went to school at the Paint Creek School. We used to take our horse over there at noon to water him from the schoolhouse. We lived with Bert and Aunt Esther until the time we all left in July 1924 to go to Idaho." [1]

Mildred Petit Taylor
Paint Creek School student, 1920 - 1921
Paint Creek School student, 1922 - 1924

"I was born in 1911, and am the oldest. When I was old enough to go to school we moved out to Paint Creek in 1917. My father bought our land from Luce, and there was already a log cabin there.

"We walked or road a horse to school at Paint Creek. I don't think it was much over a half a mile. The schoolhouse was at the lower end of our place. It was up on the hill, and we lived down on the creek. There was a little schoolhouse across from where the newer schoolhouse was built. I remember some of the teachers I had – Lorraine Martin. She was born up on South Fork, and there was Vera Snyder. She was from Burlington.

"I milked cows and did things like that before I went to school. I herded sheep when we got a farm flock. My grandmother visited with us for a time, and she'd wake up in the morning and say, "Phyllis. It's getting daylight." And I'd get up and take the sheep out, and when it started getting hot in the day, why they'd come in. Around four o'clock in the afternoon I'd take them out again and keep them out 'till dark." [2]

Phyllis Bosley Lovercheck
Paint Creek School student, 1917 - 1925

"We liked those Vickery kids. Elsie left first when she finished the eighth grade, and then Jim and Jack went to school with us. Jim had a little gray donkey, and Jack had a big brown one. Jim would let us kids ride it around the school yard, and we rode very carefully around the sagebrush.

"Elsie and Fred walked to school, and Jim rode the little donkey, and Jack rode the big donkey. Of course, they had no saddles, no bridles - just a halter on them. At the school they used to turn them loose in the schoolyard. It was nicely fenced with barbed wire with lots of sagebrush down below.

"When it got cold, the animals would come up and stand on the south side of the schoolhouse. The little gray one would stick her head up to the window and bray, and the kids would just laugh, but Miss Cravens never scolded us. There was a horseshoe nailed to the side of the building, so they could tie a horse up to that.

"The Schmidt kids rode horse back, and they tied their horses, and they stood out there in the cold weather. There was Ethel and Alvin and Fred and Hazel Schmidt, and they had two horses so they rode double with the little kids.

"We walked to school all the time from home. If you went straight across, it was probably about 3/4ths of a mile - maybe a mile. We had to crawl through two fences and cross the creek. If you went around, it was a little further, but you had to go through gates. Sometimes in the spring when the water ran over the ice, it would be six inches deep at night.

"One time we got to the creek, and it had frozen over with a cone of ice up high, and we had just been walking across it all winter. Well, Della came across and she went right through it. She went down under the ice and came out a hole down below. Della was really crying because she was nearly frozen. My dad and mother were so thankful that nothing else happened. No one got scolded.

"When it was really cold my dad would take the team and put hay in the wagon, and my mother would put nice warm quilts in there. Then he would take us kids down to the school. Other kids just missed school when there was a blizzard or something, but my parents took us to school then. I've got certificates where I went to school each day.

"Once we were visiting some of my parents' friends in Bearcreek, and there was a blizzard and we couldn't come home. My mother said we cried that night because we were going to miss a day of school. So Monday morning when we got up and it was still snowing, we still went home.

"Our school was a one-room log building. It had a wood floor and it was just chinked inside and daubed outside. Every fall some of the men would come and check it out, and if it needed new dirt on the roof, they'd put a little more on it. Sometimes the ball would get stuck up there, and a boy would go up the corner where the logs stuck out and get the ball. We were warned not to go up there unless we had to, because it might kick the dirt. It was just dirt over slabs of wood. It never did leak.

"I remember the most about Miss Cravens - maybe because she was such a good teacher and she was older. She lived up Bennett Creek in a little tarpaper shack. She had a little brown horse named 'Billy' and a little chaise - a cart. Every morning that woman drove through the cold with Billy to school and back home again. It was hard to put the chaise on for one person, so Marian Eckloe and I would go out to help her.

"She wore long dresses and high laced flat shoes. Of course, she wore her hair up high. She was a good teacher. Her sister, Mrs. Miller and her husband moved in and lived with her. Then they all moved to Fromberg. I don't know if she kept on teaching after she moved there or not." [3]

Clytie Fuson Williams
Bennett Creek School student, 1915 - 1922
Clark School student, 1922 - 1924
Clark School teacher, 1929 - 1930

"Those were happy days at our Pioneer School. There were about ten kids when we went, but attendance varied from the first to the eighth grade. Some of the older ones attended the eighth grade a few times. We had fine teachers. I remember Mrs. Godfrey, who taught my older sister, Louise, and Fay Till, Margaret O'Donnell, Helen Peterson, and Fern Ashley.

"Some of us rode horses to school, and for a while we tied them up during school hours. That was pretty hard on them, so the school build a barn with four stalls I recall.

"My young brother, Richard, was kind of a 'cut up' when he started to school, and the teacher got after him. I told her that my mom said it was okay to spank him, so she got some good slaps on Richard. That was not the end of it, because the next day Mom came to school and both the teacher and I got a good scolding.

"We had a school program or play, and the community was invited to see it. Richard had a part to play and a few lines to recite, but when he got on stage to perform, all he did was laugh. Carl Carlson said that was the best part of the program!

"The teachers who came to teach were usually new to the community. And of course, the local bachelors always took special note and interest. They seemed to know when school got out. One was a cowboy who rode over quite frequently. There was also a very eligible bachelor who brought his alarm clock along to set it correctly by teacher's time. He always seemed to know when school was out at 4 p.m. The cowboy and the alarm clock bachelor never met, as far as I recall. Maybe, I thought, the bachelor's timing was off.

"Helen Peterson was a good teacher and was interested in manual training. So she started us building bluebird houses. The entrance had to be the size of a quarter. Dad said that was too small, so he would file it bigger with a wood rasp. We made birdhouses and gave them to the neighbors. I gave one to Carl and Emma Carlson.

"We enjoyed life and play. There was no football or basketball, but we played kick the can. We also played kick ball and the ball would occasionally get lodged back of the chimney. Then we would have to climb up in the belfry and crawl on onto the roof which as scary!

"One summer I got a contract with the school to poke the swallow nests down from under the schoolhouse eves. I'd drive up there in my two wheel cart pulled by Topsy, my horse. The contract was for $13.00. The nests had lots of bugs in them, so I had to be careful not to take them home on my clothes.

"Miss Peterson had the school district buy a coal oil stove. She had water in it and when it was heated, we'd put our food, which was placed in containers, in the water. Then we all could have a hot lunch. Cooked rice in a jar from home was a popular lunch item to be warmed up.

"Margaret O'Donnell told me not to jump my horse across the irrigation ditch in front of the school on the way home. But I did it anyway. On arriving home Mom said she wanted me to drive her up to the Lindquist store in the buckboard so she could do some shopping. It was a twenty mile round trip to the store. I was glad not to have to go to school the next day, but Miss O'Donnell did not forget that I had disobeyed her order. So I suffered from her lectures and discipline for quite a few days after this.

"Our teacher would also send us down to the basement to shovel coal into the furnace. Taking out the ashes was another school chore." [4]

Howard Sparhawk
Pioneer School student, 1922 - 1928

"It was May 5, 1929 and we thought it was past storming. Virgie, Iva and I wanted to go to school without gloves, so we put them under the Bennett Creek Bridge on the way to school. Roberta wasn't going to school then. Our folks got word that our little cousin had died, and they picked us up at school, and we were gone several days before the funeral.

"Well, it had turned cold, and of course, the creek froze. You know that it freezes from the bottom up and washed our gloves away. Our parents found out right away, because we didn't have them. We told them what we had done, and we'd gone back to look for them, but they were gone. There wasn't even one there. I will never forget them. They were horsehide, and we had gotten them for Christmas." [5]

Viola Bunn Gairrett
Clark School student, 1926 - 1934

"The school up there used to have a toilet on this side and a toilet on the other side. In the middle was a barn for horses. Well, some guys rigged up a slingshot, and I think it took four of them to work the thing. Well they get out there in that field to the west of it, and they'd shoot big rocks down on them. They had the whole bottom of that barn torn off, and the back of the outhouses. The Smith kids used to get me out there when I was in the toilet, and they kept me in there until I was late getting back into school." [6]

Lee Weathermon
Clark School student, 1929 - 1936

"When we got to school, it was cold! We were cold when we got there, if we had to walk or ride the horses. The school had this big old furnace. Of course, you could stand on it to get warm, but it was cold in there. Then we'd go and get our lunches and they were frozen. They were in those little cloakrooms. We usually kept them around the furnace in the wintertime.

"Then they had the noon hour, and I believe that that was the worst there ever was. It didn't make any difference how cold it was, we had to stay outside. In those days we didn't have warm clothes like the kids have now days. After standing out there in the wind, we were frozen when we got back inside."

"We always worked for perfect attendance, and I remember one time when Elmer and I were in school . Well the bus didn't run that morning, because the snow was so deep. So I begged Dad to take me in the car. Well, we got almost to where the Community Center is today, and I waded in snow over my knees to get to school. There were other kids at school, so the snow must have been deeper where the bus was. Dad came after me that afternoon. I think now how stupid that was to get to school. I don't believe in perfect attendance now.

"I was in seventh grade and Ann Collins taught that year (1936-37). She rang the school bell at one o'clock, and then locked the door. Marguerite Eckloe, Verla Brown and myself and others I can't remember were still outside, and she wouldn't let us in. She said, "You weren't there when the bell rang." So we sat outside on the doorstep for a while, and then we walked over to the Buttes and over to those graves. Then we came back just before the bus got there. Well, she wrote snotty notes home to our parents. I was counted absent for half a day, so that beat me out of that year's perfect attendance award.

"Ann Collins was the one who sat on the desk and told us about all of her dates over in Cody, and what she did over the weekend. Well this was great! We could ask a question, and she'd go ahead and tell everything. By then it was noon hour, so then we were outside until one, and then we came back in there. Once in awhile she assigned us something and she'd read it so fast that you could hardly write, and she wanted us to write it down. Sometimes we'd get her to talk the whole day." [7]

Roberta Bunn Gairrett
Clark School student, 1931 - 1939

"When I lived in Clark my closest friends were the Mardises. I remember walking to school and walking home. One night I had to stay after school for some reason, and I was crossing the ditch when I heard this noise. Here was this coyote with this trap on its foot. It just scared me to death 'cause I thought that thing was going to get me. So I whistled and carried on until I got past him quite a ways. Then I took off running all the way home.

"I had Mrs. Wogoman for a teacher too. I can always remember her because one time me and another kid – I can't remember who it was – but we cornered this rabbit under the culvert up there. We got some barbed wire and wound it up, and caught his hair and pulled him out. Well, Mrs. Wogoman came out there and caught us. The next thing I knew we were getting the back of our heads yanked. She said, "How do you like that?" And then she'd give us another one. "How's that one?" She let us know that we shouldn't have pulled the hair on that rabbit." [8]

Mark Weathermon
Clark School student, 1932 - 1936

"I started the first grade at Clark the fall of 1934. My first grade teacher was Constance Cubbage, who later was Constance Weiss. She taught grades 1 through 8, and was a very stern person, but a very good teacher.

"I was a little more fortunate than the earlier students for school transportation. My first year was riding an old mare that my dad had gotten from Jimmy Tough along with Iva and Roberta, my sisters. Iva rode the saddle with me behind, and then Roberta.

169

"Others such as Marguerite and Virginia Eckloe, Betty Lou Forsman on her part Shetland, and the Stidham kids - Lester and Marjorie - also rode horses. The horses were kept in a barn during the day. The building also served as a teacherage at one end. The Smiths, Weathermons, Briners, Lindquist and Johnson and others that I cannot remember, walked to school.

"Louise Simpson was driven to school in a vehicle. Her dad, John Simpson, worked for George Hopkins, who was a dentist, on his ranch on Lower Pat O'Hara. John had a little green Model-A pickup that he used, but Hopkins had this great big curtain car, make unknown that John used occasionally. We kids would just gloat over this car when he brought Louise to school.

"In 1935 Ray Bunn, my uncle, bought an International truck with a wooden school bus body on it, and contracted with the District to haul the kids. Three routes were established. So the first ones on were usually pretty early, but then the route was reversed in the evening. In 1936 the District bought a small suburban type bus, and Frank Thull was given the job as bus driver for many years.

"Ella Bunn, my aunt, was my second grade teacher. She returned in later years to teach again at Clark. The hardest was calling her Miss Bunn..

"The playground consisted of rock and gravel. Shoe soles didn't last long. Mom or Dad was always nailing soles on our shoes. Overalls all had patches at the knees due to the rocks and gravel. We were playing a game called follow the leader. Mary Ann Briner was the leader. She bent over and picked up a rock and threw it, and at the same time I bent over and got the rock in the mouth.

"Another time Bob Thull, Jimmy Johnson, and I were warned by Mrs. Wogoman, our teacher, to quit throwing rocks. Of course, we had to throw one more. She caught us and took us in the library, one by one and slapped the palms of our hands three times with a ruler. Well, my folks never knew about this until a few years before they died. I knew what I would have got if they had been told.

"I was fortunate to have good teachers. My eighth year started out with John Larmer, who quit at Christmas time to go into the service. Ethel Clark came from Paint Creek where she had been teaching, but students had moved, to finish out the year. Yes, I was in the cloakroom with Ervin Thull when Florence Stidham came in for a drink of water from the water bucket that had been packed in from the old cistern. Yes, Ervin made the remark, and of course, Florence ran and told the teacher. All hell broke loose.

"Ethel Clark was 24 years old and married to a one-eyed 83-year-old man. Someone went to the teacherage and told him, so here he came with a rubber hose and could hardly get up the steps. But he proceeded to give Ervin, a two hundred pound kid, a beating.

"All the kids were scared. Mildred Thull jumped up out of her seat and I thought she was going to hit the teacher. Well, this brought the School Board in. Ervin was expelled the rest of the year, and Ethel Clark quit, but came back to finish the year.

"Also during this year, the Thull kids had gone down to the old vacant George Berry house and found lots of live ammunition there. They brought it back to the school, and laid it on the old concrete base of the cistern. Then they dropped rocks on the shells to explode them. The saying was that we were shooting coyotes. George Brown and Richard

Thull each got a slug in their legs, and I got some powder burns. Mr. Larmer never did come out to see what was going on, but I can't blame him now.

"During Miss Mailander's term, she gave dances and used the money to buy playground equipment. She also went to Line Creek the following year and did the same there. Other teachers in later years, including Mrs. Lowe, gave dances to buy items for the school.

"We always had a big Christmas program, and I guess after I became a board member, I encouraged the teachers that this was a function for which the whole community always turned out - a program and then a dance afterward. Paint Creek, Line Creek and Pioneer all did the same. My family would always attend all of these programs, as others did also.

"The last day of school was another great day for the community. We had a picnic on the creek with games and fun for all. Some teachers had May Day programs too.

"Pioneer and Line Creek School Districts were family rich districts. Clark and Paint Creek were poor. Yet Clark always seemed to be ahead of the other ones with busses and a teacherage. Line Creek had the first high school bus driven by John Gairrett with his personal car until Line Creek and Clark consolidated in 1947.

"The Pledge of Allegiance and the Star Spangle Banner were sung on the opening of each school day.

"In 1956 I was elected to the School Board along with John Eckerman and Steve Torczon. I held this position until Clark consolidated with the Powell School District in 1970. I worked first to get bathrooms in the large schoolhouse, and later in the little school building. None of this was easy as money was hard to come by and still keeping the mill levy down to about 7 or 8 mills. People would not vote for a higher mill levy.

"I also worked hard to get the new school (excluding the gym) built. The community supported this project very well, except for one person. She said it was a waste of money, because people were going to quit having kids.

"Mrs. Sorensen and Mrs. Hill were, I believe, the two best teachers, to work together. They co-operated with the Board, were community-minded, and liked by all of the children. They continued to teach in Powell after consolidation.

"In closing there have been five generations of Bunns going to school at Clark. My great granddaughter, Nicole, is presently attending school there now."

Elmer Bunn
Clark School student 1934 – 1942
Clark School Board Member 1956-1969

"My first day of school! I jumped out of bed with that excited Christmas morning feeling, and quickly got into my new pink dress and mail-order shoes. I was too excited to eat breakfast, and was all-eyes to see what Mom had packed into the lunchbox that my brother, Harley would share with me. He grabbed the lunchbox in one hand and my hand in the other and away we went - just in time to see the school bus disappearing in a cloud of dust. I'd missed the very first day of school, and bawled all day.

"My elementary schooling began in the fall of '39 in an old white frame building with a full basement. It was also the community center. Meetings, voting, dances, and whatever all happened at the old Clark Schoolhouse.

"We had no running water there. There was a cistern and the older students were assigned the chore of carrying water by the bucket indoors for drinking and hand washing purposes. The bathrooms were two neat little white buildings at opposite sides of the schoolyard – left for the girls and right for the boys. The 'teacherage' sat in between them.

"All eight grades were taught in one big room by one teacher. That may sound a little nerve-wracking, but I doubt if we ever had more than 15 students total. Two or three teachers came and went during one school term, so maybe we were a little hard on their nerves!

"When I was a first grader wandering around the school ground at recess, I found myself at the bottom of a teaming mass of arms, legs and bodies. Half a dozen big kids, all pursuing the same ball, had run me down and trampled me under. My bottom lip was swollen, and my face looked like raw hamburger, as well as my elbows and knees. Mrs. Wogoman patched me up as best she could and sat me in front of the whole school during the next class period. I don't know to this day if she was punishing them.... or me.

"One memory I treasure is that we started each school morning with the Pledge to the Flag and followed that with a prayer. I don't think it hurt us a bit. One of the most honorable tasks that you could be assigned was raising the flag in the morning and lowering and putting it away at the end of the day. with windows, and our beautiful ridge of mountains was right out there, almost close enough to touch. They were both an inspiration and a detriment to me, because they did cause a lot of daydreaming on my part. Only the most responsible upper graders got that privilege. It was sacred.

"The whole west wall of the big classroom was banked with windows, and our beautiful ridge of mountains was right out there, almost close enough to touch. They were both an inspiration and a detriment to me, because they did cause a lot of daydreaming on my part.

"One day a group of older kids was playing softball at recess. While they were outside, Pop Thull, our janitor/bus driver, took the opportunity to do some repair work on the furnace. He had taken off the grill, a three-foot square piece of meshed metal, and was tinkering around inside the hole. About that time, the door burst open and in rushed Marjie Stidham, all flushed with excitement, yelling to Mrs. Wogoman, 'I just made a home ru... and down the furnace hole she went! She managed to hook her arms over the upper rim, and Pop Thull, from below, boosted her up and out, covered from head to toe with soot – badly shaken but unhurt.

"My very first teacher was Mrs. Florence Wogoman, and she was my very best teacher overall. She was wonderful and was one of those who put you on the right foot. Another one who stands out in my mind was Wilda Hoefer. She was a later one. She's still a sweet lady. We had a couple of men teachers through the years that were quite an experience for Clark. Clark had a quite a reputation, so I guess they thought they needed a man here.

"We had one teacher, Mary Jane Roney, who was barely older than the kids. I don't know how we fared academically, but we sure had fun! She wore her jeans, romped with us at recess, and it was hard to distinguish who was who. The older boys, especially, liked her, and each had his own secret 'crush' on her. One day, during a wild 'cowboys and Indians' game, they took a rope and tied her to the merry-go-round. She stayed there screaming and yelling all afternoon while we rode the swings, the slide, and the teeter-totter. We just had recess all day!

"Ervin Thull was a big, heavy boy, an 8th grader (for maybe the second or third year). He was a good kid, but full of mischief. Florence Stidham raised her hand and asked permission to get a drink of water which was drawn from the cistern and kept in a bucket in the cloak room. As she reached for her cup, Ervin, who was just exciting the room, whispered, 'Don't drink that water. I just p___d in the bucket.'

"Florence clapped a hand to her mouth, wheeled around, and ran straight to the teacher! Mrs. Clark was a skinny redhead with NO sense of humor. She accosted Ervin and bade him to bend over while she got her yardstick. Ervin, of course, pled innocent - he was just kidding Florence - and refused to obey.

"Mrs. Clark must have sent one of us - not ME - I was too scared to move! - to the teacherage to get her husband to come help. He was a doddery old fellow with only one eye, but here he came with a piece of rubber hose! Together, the two of them came at Ervin. He simply picked up his desk and used it to fend them off! Again, I don't remember the outcome, but I think the school board was called into the fray, and I think Ervin finished the year in peace, while it was the teacher and her husband who moved on.

"After leaving the eighth grade, the prospects of attending high school at that time meant boarding out in town as there was no means of daily transportation from Clark. Since I had been such a 'promising' student, the County Superintendent, Mrs. Patterson, offered to board me so that I could start high school in Cody

"If there ever was a county yokel, I was it! I had no conception of what 'town school' was all about, and I had never stayed away from home a night in my life. Changing classes by bells, a different teacher for every class, a different room for every class, and P.E. were all Greek to me, and I was so lost that I was just numb. I didn't comprehend anything; not even which of those many buses to board to get home at night.

"An older brother who had been through the same traumatic experience a few years earlier and knew the anguish that I was going through, came to Cody one evening and told me, 'Pack your suitcase. Mom needs you at home to help with the canning.' Arriving back home, I found Mom totally surprised to see me, and my brother, Darrel, had suddenly vanished.

"So I stayed home that winter, and went back through the 8th grade again, 'just to keep from getting rusty,' said Wilda Hoefer, the teacher I had graduated under. By then Clark had two teachers - one for the first four grades and a new one for the upper ones. She helped me a lot with math, my weak subject. And the next year the county was providing transportation to send us to Belfry, so that's where I went to high school." [9]

Juanita Smith Moore
Clark School student, 1939 - 1948

"When I came to Paint Creek to teach in '42, the school needed to be cleaned. It was in disrepair. They gave me a little bit more salary because I did have to clean. I had to clean the walls and the floor was in bad repair. I bought linseed oil and heated it on a little kerosene stove. I don't remember how I put it on the floor but I must have had a brush. I know I was down on my hands and knees working on that floor. I'm sure the walls were plastered, and I know that they were really dirty. There was a material called 'Dicadoo', a clay-like stuff that you made a ball out of, and then you rolled it like dough to clean the walls.

"Women didn't wear pants very much. We wore dresses. It took me quite awhile to decide that pants were more practical.

"There was a cistern at the Paint Creek School, and they filled it from the ditch that came out of Paint Creek. Kenneth Lundvall was on the school board, and it was his ditch. I suppose that he filled it before it got cold enough to freeze. The schoolhouse acre belonged to his place. Later on that was one of the places that we owned. Lundvalls lived down below the hill below the schoolhouse. They didn't have any school age children until the year I taught.

"I had three students that year, Wayne Lundvall, who had Wayne's Boot Shop in Cody was my first grader. I had Dwayne Black, a second grader, and his brother, Joe, an eighth grader.

"At Paint Creek I was out there by myself. You had no direction, and you didn't see your supervisors very often. The County Superintendent of Schools came out to our school, I think, only once or twice a year. So you really didn't know where you were. I liked teaching, but I really don't think that I was that good of a teacher. Knowing what I know now, I could have been a lot better, especially if I had had more materials to work with and someone to help and guide me." [10]

Georgia Frame Close
Paint Creek School teacher, 1942-43

"One of our first buses was an old Army ambulance, and it just had the seats down on both sides and not much for heaters. Once it started getting cold, there would be an ice build up on the floor. So you'd get in and skip and slide going to your seat. Terry Smith drove the bus, and he probably wasn't the best person to be driving. He thought it was great sport to get going real fast and then slam on the brakes. Everyone would then slide to the front of the bus, because there wasn't anything to hold onto. I can remember years later about the time I was in high school, that Buck Cox who was married to Mildred Clark, was driving the school bus. He got drunk one time and tipped the bus over.

"Line Creek consolidated with Clark when I was in the fifth grade so that must have been about 1946 or '47. They consolidated and then they had two teachers. Wilda taught the lower grades and Mildred Lowe taught the upper grades. Before Wilda came there was a guy who would just sit there and play tunes with the pointer on his desk and turn his eyelids inside out. He just left." [11]

Dorothy Cochrane Napier
Clark School student, 1942 - 1949

"I was born in Cheyenne, then I went to Billings to Eastern. They called it Eastern Normal School then, but they really didn't teach you what you're to know for the rural schools.

"School started in October about 8:30 because there was one bus. It was a big, old ambulance. I can remember one time that the bus broke down, Don and Ronald Williams and Dorothy Cochrane had to walk. They got so cold that their legs were just frozen. Del Gaines was the bus driver then, and he lived right there in the cabin at the school. So I took the kids in and put them in his bed to try and get warm.

"It was rugged. We had electricity, but we didn't have any water. The first year there was a man teaching there for a short time with me. He had bragged about teaching here and there, but he didn't teach the upper grades anything. One day around Easter he said, "I've got an appointment in town, can you cover for me?" Well he never came back.

"The second year I taught, they had another teacher, Mrs. Lowe, Elmer Bunn's mother-in-law. She had the upper grades and I had the lower grades. I was in the basement and she was upstairs for a while. We got along super fine.

"The next year they moved in the old Line Creek School building that was down by the river, and put it by the Clark School building. It was so much better for the little kids to have their own schoolhouse.

"In the fall of '48 I was not teaching at Clark. A woman was hired to teach the lower grades, who was a good enough teacher, but her husband caused problems with the Superintendent. So she was fired, and after Christmas they called me and said they were expecting me to come back. So I said, 'Okay.'

"Later after my husband and I lived up on the river, I substituted at the Pioneer School for Marjorie Cushman in '57 and '58. Later in the 60s I subbed for Dorothy La Follette there.

"I just had a wonderful time with all of the kids at both schools. We gave a benefit dance to buy library books, and we also saved a little money for the soup kettle that we warmed over the furnace register.

"At Christmas time we'd have our Christmas plays and programs on different days so that everybody could go. That way we could take in all three – Clark, Pioneer, and Belfry, because the older kids would go to the Belfry school. That was before we had to go to Powell.

"The last week of school was a busy one. Everyone in the community at Pioneer came for the last day school picnic. One year it was in our yard when we lived on the farm. One year we had it in the schoolyard. Three other picnics we had in three different cow pastures, because we had to have space to play baseball. At Clark, we had many picnics along the creek here and there, and also over at the Buttes." [12]

Wilda McLoughlin Hoefer
Clark School teacher, 1946 – 1948; 1949
Pioneer School substitute teacher, 1957-1958; 1962-1965

"I had never been out to Clark. I had never even been out in that direction at all. That windy, little old road that you went on took you forever to get there. Then when you got there, there was that building sitting in the middle of nowhere with rocks and dirt. It was like the end of the world to me after being over here where everything is so green. I was only nineteen years old.

"I had to teach the fifth, sixth, seventh and eighth grade, and I had no experience. The first and second grades were all that I was prepared for, but Mrs. Hetland taught the younger grades. So I just had to start, and I studied as hard as the kids did. I really worked hard.

"I can't remember who was there before me, but they must have had no discipline. You'd look up and the kids were crawling on their hands and knees to pick up things here and there, and they weren't used to discipline. So I really had to go hard on that. They had had a whole lot of teachers there, and none too long. So they weren't used to really working at school. I had the ones who really wanted to learn, and then the others. It took about a month, and then we got going. Then realized that I wasn't going to put up with that.

"Mrs. Hetland and I lived in the teacherage behind the school. She and her son, Joe, lived in one half and I lived in the other. We each had a big room with a kitchen and bathroom on the back. On the back there was a porch-like enclosed walkway, and I asked Mrs. Hetland, "Why did they build that?" And she said, "You'll find out in a while." So when the wind would start to blow, and the rocks started hitting the back of the building, then I knew whey they put that enclosed porch on there. It protected the back and you didn't feel the wind quite as bad.

"Mrs. Hetland was a really, wonderful lady. I wouldn't have made it without her. She was kind and caring, and we shared everything and did everything. Even after she quit teaching and moved into town, we remained really good friends

"The Clark kids didn't bring their lunches to school because we had a cafeteria. Mrs. Julia Garriett was the cook, and we had a hot meal every day. It was hard to work upstairs with that food cooking down in the basement.

"I never had any medical emergencies or anything strange. Mrs. Hetland was right next door in the other building and Mrs. Gairrett was there too. I knew they were there, and the kids knew it too.

"One of the things I remember was that I asked if there was a way to copy papers. In the city schools you were used to copying things, and there was a purple mimeograph machine there. Well they said they didn't think so, but I found one of those gelatin things. It was like Knox gelatin and you'd clean it off, and then write on it with one of those stylus-type pens. Then you rub it on there and it would make a copy. I could make five copies or so, then you could use it again. I didn't need more than four of five of anything, because I didn't have that many kids in each grade or on the same assignment.

"The Christmas program at Clark was a huge, huge undertaking, and the community expected the teachers to spend a great amount of time getting a fancy program ready. The month before it was exhausting. Everyone came. We had the program in the small school because more people could get in there, and it was packed. It was unreal how many people came. We did readings and plays, and we had a curtain. There was no stage. People sat on the desks, and there were a lot of chairs. Pioneer had its own Christmas play and program, but we didn't do as much as we did at Clark.

"Before I went to Pioneer, I made them promise me a copy machine, certain kind of books and paper. So when I got there I had everything that I wanted. They also hired a first and second grade teacher, so I didn't have to teach those grades. Nannie Walker taught those grades. I lived upstairs next to the classroom in the teacherage, and we shared the bathroom with the kids. She lived down in the furnace room in the basement.

"After Ervin and I got married around Christmas time in 1959, we still stayed there in the teacherage, but he left during the day while I was teaching. One of the things I remember was when Ervin got the mumps and the bathrooms were shared with the kids. So we did some careful cleaning and no one else got the mumps.

"I remember how cold it was in both schoolhouses with those huge, huge windows. The whole wall was windows, and when it was really cold, you had to dress warmly. At the time, ladies did not go to school with pants on, so I was cold a lot. At Clark the bathrooms were on either side of the front door, and they did freeze up a few times.

"At the Pioneer School the kids brought their own lunches, and parents drove them to school or they walked. The Denney kids walked sometimes, and the Fraker kids most always walked, because all they had to do was walk across the field from their house. They didn't go on the road.

"Looking back, it was a really good experience - both years that I taught out there. I always wished that I would have just kept on teaching out there, but after I got married Ervin didn't want me to work anymore. Later when I was over here in Powell, I even thought about going back, but I decided that I had better not, so I just stayed put and taught over here." [13]

Carol Brown Thull Christiansen
Clark School teacher, 1957 - 1958
Pioneer School teacher, 1959 - 1960

Chapter 20 notes:

---

[1] Mildred Petit Taylor, interview with author, Clark, Wyoming, June 01, 2001.

[2] Phyllis Bosley Lovercheck, interview with author, Powell, Wyoming, January 25, 2000.
    Note: Phyllis passed away on July 4, 2000 in Powell.

[3] Clytie Fuson Williams, interview with author, Cody, Wyoming, December 01 2003.

[4] Howard Sparhawk, letter to the author, January 20, 2004.

[5] Viola Bunn Gairrett and Roberta Bunn Gairrett, interview with author, Billings, Montana, August 28, 2000.

[6] Weathermon family, interview with author, Clark, Wyoming, July 03, 2001.

[7] Roberta Bunn Gairrett, interview with author, Billings, Montana, August 28, 2000.

[8] Weathermon family, interview with author, Clark, Wyoming, July 03, 2001.

[9] Juanita Smith Moore, 1995, and interview with author, Clark, Wyoming, on February 01, 1999; and Juanita Smith Moore, "Clark School Memories 1939 - 1948," written January 14, 2004.

[10] Georgia Frame Close, interviews with author, Clark, Wyoming, January 07, 1999, September 13, 2000, and December 17, 2000.

[11] Hazel Cochrane and Dorothy Cochrane Napier, interview with author, Clark, Wyoming, February 01, 2002.

[12] Wilda McLoughlin Hoefer, interviews with author, Clark, Wyoming, December 16, 1999 and January 19, 2000; and from her 2002 manuscript of her then 55 years in Clark.

[13] Carol Brown Christiansen, interview with author, Powell, Wyoming, January 23, 2004.

(No. 1011—New Series—July 1, 1889.)   (LOCATION PAPER.)

Post Office Department,

OFFICE OF THE FIRST ASSISTANT P. M. GENERAL,

Washington, D. C., _Feby 1 3_ 18_91_

Sir: Before the Postmaster General decides upon the application for the establishment of a post office at _Clark_ County of _Big Horn_ State of _Wyoming_, it will be necessary for you to carefully answer the subjoined questions, get a neighboring postmaster to certify to the correctness of the answers, and return the location paper to the Department, addressed to me. If the site selected for the proposed office should not be on any mail route now under contract, only a "Special Office" can be established there, to be supplied with mail from some convenient point on the nearest mail route by a special carrier (see section 733, Postal Laws and Regulations of 1887), for which service a sum equal to two-thirds of the amount of the salary of the postmaster at such office will be paid by the Department.

You should inform the contractor, or person performing service for him, of this application, and require him to execute the inclosed certificate as to the practicability of supplying the proposed office with mail, and return the same to the Department.

Very respectfully,

J. S. Clarkson

First Ass't Postmaster General.

To Mr. _Wm S Sirrine_

care of the Postmaster of _____, who will please forward to him.

STATEMENT.

The proposed office to be called _Clark_

☞ Select a short name for the proposed office, which, when written, ☜ will not resemble the name of any other post office in the State.

It will be situated in the _____ quarter of Section _____, Township _____ (North or South), _____

In case will not be acted upon.   _Applications for post offices_

Establishment of the first Clark Post Office at Sirrine Ranch

Mary Ellen Sirrine
Photo courtesy of Park County Historical Archives

21

Post Offices and Mail Service

For 76 years this community had a post office. In fact the Clark post office was located in four different places during those years until it was terminated on February 10, 1967.

The Post Office at the Sirrine Ranch

The first post office was located about one mile south of the Montana-Wyoming border along the Clarks Fork River in a then unsurveyed southwest quarter of Section 20 of T58N, R102W [1] of the Warren O. Sirrine ranch. After he and his family arrived here in 1889, [2] he saw the need for an area post office and made application to the Post Office Department in Washington, DC.

On February 13, 1891 the First Asst. Postmaster General replied to his application and requested that Mr. Sirrine provide the Department with additional information about the proposed post office location. In the letter Mr. Sirrine was told that if the site selected for the proposed office was not on an established mail route already under contract, than only a 'Special Office' could be established at his location with the mail coming there from some convenient point on the nearest mail route. And it would be necessary to have that contractor complete the attached paperwork "as to the practicability of supplying the proposed office with mail." [3]

Meeting the requirements specified in the Post Office Department letter was not a problem for Warren Sirrine, whose ranch was located just west of the Meeteetse Trail. Over this route stages traveled back and forth between Red Lodge and Meeteetse, not only carrying passengers but also the mail. Six miles north of the Sirrine ranch was the Dilworth ranch, which was one of established stops on the stage route. Here a post office had been established on October 17, 1884 with James R. Dilworth as postmaster. [4]

Included in the information requested by the Post Office Department's letter was the proposed name of the post office. Warren Sirrine was to "select a short name for the proposed office, which, when written, will not resemble the name of any other post office in the State." "The name of my Office is Clark," was his reply. [5] Sirrine's choice of a name on this document not only named a post office, but he unknowingly provided the name of the future community, which was to follow.

His application for the Clark post office near the banks of the Clarks Fork River was approved and officially established on February 27, 1891 with him as postmaster. [6] It was located "20 yards from said river on the south side of it."[7] The following year on November 22, 1892 Mary Coates Sirrine succeeded her husband as postmaster.

Six years later another post office was established just two miles down the Clarks Fork River at Chance, Montana with Lillie B. Chance as postmaster. [8]

On July 1, 1898 daily stage service from Red Lodge to Meeteetse went into effect, which also meant daily mail was delivered to Clark and to other offices along its route. [9] In November of that year the stage on its return trip from Meeteetse to Red Lodge was held up by two men a few miles north of Eagle's Nest. While one man covered the driver with a gun, the other cut the straps of the mail pouch and removed all of the registered envelopes. "The contents were pocketed and the envelopes were thrown on the ground. This done, the robbers ordered the coach to proceed." [10]

Mary Sirrine served as the Clark postmaster until July 1902 [11] when her husband's declining health forced her to give up the position. During her almost ten years serving as postmaster her salary was: $33.75 (1893), $46.85 (1895), $67.65 (1897), $62.99, (1899) and $87.60 (1901) [12]

The Post Office at the Barber and Parker Ranch

In late March 1902 as Mary Sirrine was serving her last two months as postmaster, David A. Berry put in the lowest bid for the contract to carry the mail between Red Lodge and Clark.[13]

On May 21, Alice M. Barber was appointed as the new Clark postmaster, and during the first week of July the Clark post office moved about ten miles away to the William Barber ranch south of Bennett Creek in the northeast quarter of Section 28. [14] Mail service by stage between Red Lodge and the new Clark post office was inaugurated that same week. While these events were taking place, there was an unsuccessful effort to get the post office location changed to the Berry ranch. [15]

Granville L "George" Berry, brother of David, was making the stage run from Red Lodge to the Clark post office at the Barber ranch by April of 1903. On one trip as he was about to leave the barn in Red Lodge, his horses took fright at the train, and took off completely demolishing his wagon and dashed through the fences at several residence lots. After they were finally captured, uninjured, George picked up the mail, secured a new wagon and resumed his trip to Clark.[16]

In June David Berry and his wife sold their ranch property to George, whose own property bordered theirs. [17] George Berry continued bringing the mail to Clark through 1903 and into 1904. In May of that year he was planning to have the first automobile mail route in Montana and establishing the service between Red Lodge and Clark.[18]

On April 14, 1909 William and Alice Barber sold their ranch to Daniel I Parker, [19] "and left with their daughters and son-in-laws for Buell, Oregon where they bought property. [20] Daniel Parker's son, David moved to the ranch and was appointed postmaster. [21]

In June Postmaster Parker posted a notice at the post office that hereafter the office would be closed on Sundays. [22] On his days off he often visited friends and family in Cody and left Chris Weathermon in charge of the post office during the times he was away. [23]

Starting October 1st, 1909 the post office offered money orders for purchases from mail order houses. [24]

In November there was a movement to get better mail service throughout the Clarks Fork Valley with mail coming to Belfry from Billings by train. If this was accomplished mail could come through Billings to Clark in one day, and mail leaving Clark in the morning would be in Billings that evening. [25] The following January mail service did improve dramatically when mail was brought to Belfry by train and there delivered to Clark by George Berry and his stage [26] Unfortunately the new plan was delayed for a couple of days when the stage was stopped by the worst snowfall that had been seen in eleven years. [27]

In February a petition was circulated to have the mail days changed so that mail would go to Belfry on Monday, Wednesday, and Friday and return on Tuesday, Thursday and Saturday. [28] and the following month the new schedule went into effect. [29]

Even though the mail was arriving and departing on a regular schedule, there were some postal customers who were complaining that the mail service was better before it was changed to a Belfry dispatch. Some mail postmarked in Bridger had taken 8 days to arrive in Clark, while a postcard mailed in Billings finally arrived here a month later. [30] No mention of what was causing the problem or if or how it was resolved appeared in future issues of the newspapers.

During the rest of 1910 Postmaster Parker made several trips to Cody, including one trip to serve as a delegate from Clark at the Democratic Convention there. While he was gone, his duties fell to Mrs. Harry Temple or to Chris Weathermon who took charge of the post office in his absence. [31]

Mark Weathermon became the new Star Route mailman in December 1910, but the mail carriers changed so often, it was noted that it was hard to keep track of who was filling the position. [32]

On April 12, 1911 Oscar Lindquist became the new postmaster of Clark, and the next month he petitioned the Post Office Department to move the post office from the Parker ranch to the Lindquist store a mile and a half away. [33] After his request was approved, the location of the Clark post office moved to the Lindquist store on June 1st. Charlie Snow, the "Clark Squib" noted that "it's a safe bet that ex-postmaster Parker is the happiest man in the valley, as he can now go to see his best girl without every patron at the post office cussing him." [34]

The second post office was at the Barber Ranch.
Photo courtesy of Marian Fricke Bainter

181

The Post Office at the Lindquist Store

Unlike his predecessor, Oscar Lindquist was very seldom away from his store where the post office was moved on June 1st, 1911. His dependability in this regard was noted in the newspaper when he made his first trip to Cody in 22 years. [35]

The Lindquist Brothers store was a perfect place to have the post office, because it was the social center for the Clark and surrounding areas. Here residents came to purchase food, clothing, ranch and farming supplies, to attend meetings, and to visit with neighbors when they came in to pick up or to send mail.

But not everyone got his or her mail here. Many residents who lived in the Pioneer area found it more convenient to receive their mail at the post office at Chance, two miles into Montana. After Lucinda Reno, the Chance postmaster, died in December 1915, there was agitation by some Pioneer residents to have that post office moved to Wyoming with a Wyoming citizen appointed as postmaster. Carbon County residents were vigorously opposed to moving this post office. They noted "that Wyoming already has a post office at Clark, 15 miles distant and that present location of the Chance office is nearly that distance from the Belfry office, with fewer residents on the Wyoming than on the Montana side." [36] Nothing resulted from the Wyoming suggestion, and the Chance post office was not moved. [37]

In August of 1917 a delegation of Clark residents including Chauncey Bever, Willard Hogan, James Hunter and Ed Fuson went to Cody to request better mail service for Clark and better communication with the county seat. Their complaint was that "our mail goes up into Montana and back into Wyoming, traveling two hundred miles by stage and train." They requested a tri-weekly stage from Belfry to Cody via the Clark post office with service to the ranchers on Paint Creek, Blaine Creek, Skull Creek and Cottonwood Creek. James Hunter thought that this route "would add greatly to Clark's commercial life as the ranchers here must of necessity transact a great deal of their business by mail. " The present mail contract was due to expire that June and a petition was being circulated to make the changes before that happened. [38]

The following year in October 1917 under new postal laws the Cody post office became the central post office for the other 17 offices in Park County - including Clark. All reports from the various post offices were to be made to the Cody postmaster, who was also responsible for the inspection of the offices under his jurisdiction. [39]

This change did nothing to address Clark complaints of their mail being delivered from Montana, and in March 1918 Logan Bostic was awarded the Belfry-Clark mail contract to begin in July. [40] Three years later while Mr. Bostic was cranking his jitney mail carrier, he received "a violent kick" that laid him up with a broken arm. [41] The next month he bought a truck to run a freight line in addition to his passenger and mail service. [42]

While mail was dispatched out of Cody to the Bald Ridge, Sunlight and Crandall areas, the contract for mail delivery from Belfry to Cody continued. A few of the other drivers or substitutes who traveled this route in the 1920's and are mentioned in newspaper articles included: O. W. Gould, Jody Brown, Roy Brown, Wilbur Bunn, Stanton Howard, and M. R. Smith. [43] After a snowstorm in late March 1936 cancelled a mail delivery, the stage driver "went from Belfry to Clark with a bobsled and team" the following day. The roads were later open to car traffic. [44]

Bennett Creek, Clark, Line Creek, Pat O'Hara, and Paint Creek residents continued to get their mail at the Lindquist store until January 31, 1940 when Oscar Lindquist retired as postmaster after serving 28 and a half years. [45] The following day the post office was moved out of the store to the Norris Gallentine ranch located in the northwest quarter of Section 26, and the postmaster position passed to Hulda Gallentine. [46]

The Post Office at the Gallentine Ranch

Hulda Sigveland Gallentine and her husband, Norris, were married in July of 1936 in Harlowton, Montana and had moved to Clark by 1938. They bought the old Gus Forsman ranch, and there in the small log cabin by the main house, she had the Clark post office starting February 1, 1940. Chet Bell currently owns the house and property.

In December of that year a post office was established for nearby Badger Basin and was located in the store there. Mrs. Leo Althoff was appointed postmaster. [47]

After some Clark residents requested that a Star route delivery be established in the area, a U. S. Postal Inspector visited Clark in November 1941 to look at the possible route, [48] but mail deliveries continued to be made to the Gallentine ranch post office.

In May of 1944 due to heavy rain, hail, and flood conditions, the mail delivery truck from Belfry was stopped near the old Marlin Bridge (now called Line Creek Bridge). The mail was brought the rest of the way to the Gallentine post office by saddle horse. [49]

New postal rules went into effect in May 1947 when mail delivery was stopped on holidays. "The first holiday being effected at Clark post office was Memorial Day." [50]

The Last Location of the Clark Post Office

In mid-September, 1950 the Clark Post Office was moved back to the Lindquist Ranch. Mrs. Gallentine resigned as postmaster, and Mrs. Florence Lindquist became postmaster. [51] The post office remained here until the U. S. Postal Service discontinued it on February 10, 1967, and effective that day all mail in the Clark area was "delivered by route carrier out of Belfry. [52] Paul Travis had the mail route until 1976 when Earl and Louis Black took over the mail route until October 1991. [53] In 1969, two years after the post office at the Lindquist ranch was discontinued, Florence sold the property to Ada and John Eckerman and her brother, Lee Weathermon. [54]

On October 30, 1991 rural mail delivery from Belfry was terminated, and the following day, mail was dispatched from the Powell post office and carried by Ken Mees. He has been our rural contract mail carrier ever since and has delivered the mail to Pioneer, Clark. Line Creek and Paint Creek residents six days a week through snow and ice as well as in good weather. Starting 22 years ago with about 100 mailboxes, Ken has seen Clark's population growth reflected in the 220 boxes he now delivers to along his route. [55] . He has continued the personal service that area residents have received since the first post office was established at the Sirrine ranch in 1891.

Chapter 21 notes:

[1] Big Horn County Book 1, p. 63.

[2] "W. O. Sirrine is the pioneer ranchman of the valley, and located there 14 years ago, being called a fool for doing so. He is now a wealthy man, nevertheless, having 640 acres of the finest land all under ditch; lots of sheep and other stock and several houses, the last one erected being two stories high, its white paint contrasting beautifully with the dark green alfalfa which covers hundreds of acres surrounding it..." (*Wyoming Stockgrower and Farmer*, June 09, 1903, p. 1).

[3] Letter with application from the Office of the First Assistant Post Master General to Mr. Warren O. Sirrine, dated February 13, 1891.

[4] Letter from Jane F. Smith, Acting Director, Social and Economic Records Div., General Services Administration, National Archives and Records Service, Washington, DC to Bronson D. Tolman, Clark, Wyoming, dated October 17, 1966; In 1885 Eva J. Armstrong came out from Pennsylvania to work for Mr. Dilworth and run the post office. (See her obituary in *Carbon County Journal*, September 6, 1912, p. 1) Dilworth was killed in July 1891, and the Dilworth post office was discontinued on December 15, 1891 less than a year after the post office at Clark was established. ("On Trial for Murder," *The Livingston Post*, October 29, 1891, p. 2; "What the Verdict Means," *The Livingston Post*, November 5, 1891; Don Tolman, *Talk on Dilworth Cattle Company*, Red Lodge, MT, April 27, 1995).

[5] Application of Warrant Sirrine to the Office of the First Assistant Post Master General, dated February 13, 1891.

[6] John S. Gallagher and Alan H. Patera, *Wyoming Post Offices 1850 – 1980*, (The Depot, 1980), p. 99.

[7] Post Office Department, Topographer's Office document dated April 29, 1891 filled out and signed by Warren O. Sirrine on May 21, 1891.

[8] The next year on October 12, 1899, her husband, Nathan Chance, was appointed as Chance postmaster. (Ltr. from Jane Smith to Bronson Tolman, 1966; Dennis and Meryl Lutz, "Montana Post Offices: 1864- 1974," Montana Postal Cache, Vol. 1 #1, Feb. 1975, p. M-17, Montana Postal History Society, Havre, MT 59501.

[9] Red Lodge Picket, July 2, 1898, p. 3 and Carbon County Sentinel, July 8, 1898, p. 5.

[10] "Meeteetse News," Carbon County Sentinel, November 11 1898, p. 4.

[11] Post Office Department, Topographer's Office, Washington, D.C. document signed by Mary E. Sirrine on April 09, 1900; Ltr. from Rita L. Moroney, Research Administrator/Historian, Office of the Postmaster General, Washington, DC 20260-0011, to Ms. Debra J. Eddy, Charlotte, MI, dated July 21, 1988.

[12] Ibid.

[13] *Carbon County Chronicle*, April 1, 1902, p. 5.

[14] Letter with document from the Topographer's Office, Post Office Department, to Postmaster at Clark, dated June 30th, 1902 and signed by Alice M. Barber, July 11, 1902.

[15] *Carbon County Chronicle*, July 11, 1902, p. 5.

[16] *Red Lodge Picket,* April 24, 1903.

[17] Warranty deed #10252 from David T. Berry and his wife, Mahala Jane Berry to Granville L. Berry for the amount of $1025 for 160 acres. W ½ SW ¼ and SE ¼ SW ¼ , Section 13 and NW ¼ NW ¼ of Section 24 in Township 57, Range 102W dated June 02, 1903. Witnessed by Carrie Vickery and Justice of the Peace, Eli Vickery on 03 June 1903. Recorded in Big Horn County Book 2, p. 20 on June 12, 1903.

[18] *Red Lodge Picket,* August 21, 1903, p.5; April 14, 1904, p. 5; and May 19, 1904, p. 8.

[19] Warranty deed #37335 dated 14 Apr 1909 from William L. Barber et ux. to Daniel I. Parker. Filed in Park County, Wyoming records, Book 3, p. 250 and filed on May 7, 1909.

[20] "Clark Items," *Powell Tribune,* May 1, 1909, p. 4; "Clark's Fork Squibs," *Wyoming Stockgrower and Farmer,* June 11, 1909; "Clark's Fork Squibs," *Wyoming Stockgrower and Farmer,* July 02, 1909, p. 2; and "Clark Squibs," *Wyoming Stockgrower and Farmer,* December 10, 1909, p. 8.

[21] "Local News," *Wyoming Stockgrower and Farmer,* April 8, 1909, p. 5.

[22] "Clark Fork Squibs," *Wyoming Stockgrower and Farmer,* June 4, 1909, p. 7.

[23] *Wyoming Stockgrower and Farmer,* June 18, 1909, p. 8; July 16, 1909, p.2; September 10, 1909, p. 2; October 1909, p. 8.

[24] *Wyoming Stockgrower and Farmer,* October 1, 1909, p. 8.

[25] "Clark Squibs," *Wyoming Stockgrower and Farmer,* November 05, 1909, p. 8.

[26] "Clark Squibs," *Wyoming Stockgrower and Farmer,* January 14, 1910, p. 5.

[27] Ibid.

[28] "Clark Squibs," *Park County Enterprise,* February 11, 1910, p. 10.

[29] "Clark Squibs," *Park County Enterprise,* March 5, 1910, p. 2.

[30] "Clark Squibs," *Park County Enterprise,* April 16, 1910, p. 8.

[31] *Park County Enterprise,* July 16, 1910, p. 8; October 12, 1910, p. 5; December 24, 1910, p. 8.

[32] "Clark Squibs," *Park County Enterprise,* December 24, 1910, p. 8 and December 31, 1910, p. 7.

[33] "Proposed Location of Post Office, Post Office Department, First Asst. Postmaster General, Washington, Oscar F. Lindquist, candidate, May 25, 1911.

[34] *Park County Enterprise,* June 7, 1911, p. 4.

[35] *The Cody Enterprise,* December 20, 1922, p. 8 and January 31, 1923, p. 8.

[36] "Would Move Chance Post Office to Wyoming," *Park County Enterprise,* March 22, 1916, p. 8; "Wyoming Covets the Chance Post Office," *Carbon County Journal,* January 12, 1916, p. 1.

[37] Ludlow Reno, temporarily took over as postmaster after the death of his wife. On March 1, 1916 Durwood B. Moore was appointed postmaster. He was succeeded by Allen Campbell who was appointed on August 24, 1918. Then Bertha R. Pitt succeeded him on April 8, 1920. When the position became vacant again and was declined on March 10, 1921 by Ida M. Elze , postal authorities disestablished the Chance post office on June 15, 1921.. (Jane F. Smith Ltr., 1966).

[38] "Belfry Items," *Carbon County Journal,* August 15, 1917, p. 2.

[39] *Park County Enterprise,* October 24, 1917, p. 8.

[40] "Belfry," *Carbon County Journal,* March 20, 1918, p. 6.

[41] *The Picket-Journal,* February 9, 1921, p. 8.

[42] *The Picket-Journal,* March 30, 1921, p. 2.

[43] *Park County Enterprise,* October 12, 1921, p. 4; *Park County Herald,* April 2, 1924, p. 6; April 15, 1925, p. 6; January 27, 1926, p. 3; March 10, 1926, p. 3; *The Cody Enterprise and the Park County Herald, July 7, 1926, p. 3;* and *The Cody Enterprise,* February 12, 1930, p. 5.

[44] "Lower Clarks Fork," *The Cody Enterprise,* April 08, 1936, p. 7.

[45] *The Cody Enterprise,* January 31, 1940, p. 3 and p. 6.

[46] Letter and Application for Proposed Location of Post Office from First Assistant Postmaster General to Postmaster Hulda Gallentine dated January 26,1940 and her returned filled-in application dated February 12, 1940.

[47] "Lower Clarks Fork," *The Cody Enterprise,* December 25, 1940, p. 3.

[48] "Clarks Fork," *The Cody Enterprise,* November 05, 1941, p. 3.

[49] "Clarks Fork," *The Cody Enterprise,* May 24, 1944, p. 5.

[50] "Clarks Fork," *The Cody Enterprise,* June 04, 1947, p. 3.

[51] "Clarks Fork," *The Cody Enterprise,* September 22, 1950, p. 6.

[52] "Post Office Closes at Clark," *The Powell Tribune,* February 7, 1967, p. 1; also John S. Gallagher and Alan H. Patera, *Wyoming Post Offices 1850 - 1980,* 1980, p. 99.

[53] Earl and Louise Black, phone conversation with the author, April 9, 2004.

[54] Mortgage Document with Release of Homestead, Park County Book 334, p. 245, signed February 27, 1969.

[55] Ken Mees, conversation with the author, Clark, Wyoming, January 15, 2004.

Ken Mees

Since October 31st, 1981, our rural contract mail carrier, has been bringing mail from the Powell post office to Clark – six days a week, through snow and ice as well as good weather. Starting 22 ½ years ago with about 100 mailboxes, Ken has seen Clark's population growth reflected in the more than 225 boxes he now delivers to along his route. He has continued the personal service that area residents have received since the first post office was established at the Sirrine ranch in 1891.

22
Lindquist Brothers Store

"A look into the Lindquist Brothers store will prove to anyone that we have the nicest and best stocked country store in this part of the state."
Park County Enterprise, December 14, 1910

Oscar and Charles Lindquist came to the Helena area in the early 1890's. The two single men had moved there from Red Wing, Minnesota where they were born and where they grew up working as potters for their father, John Lindquist, a crockery merchant. [1]

After their younger sister, Martena Howard's husband died in Canada, she moved to Helena in 1895 to join her brothers. It was about this time that Charles Lindquist opened a mercantile business in Austin, Montana, a little town located in the Greenhorn Mining District of Lewis and Clark County, about thirteen miles northwest of Helena. Martena, moved to Austin to help her brother operate the store, [2] and by 1900 their brother, Oscar was also working with them. [3]

Oscar and Charles Lindquist were looking for public land to purchase, and in 1901 they traveled south to Clark and filed on adjoining 320-acre parcels in Sections 15, 21 and 22. Then they returned to their homes and business in Austin. [4]

Charles made a return trip to Clark in November to visit his ranch property, and on his return to Austin discovered that his girlfriend had been seeing a local miner while he was away. After having two heated arguments with her about her unfaithfulness, Charles shot and wounded her, then took his own life. He died on November 27th, 1901, and his funeral was held at Oscar's house in Austin the following day. [5] His body was then brought to Helena for burial in Forestvale Cemetery. [6]

Oscar was appointed administrator of his brother's estate. Charles' property in Sections 21 and 22 of T57N, R102W of Clark had been left to six heirs: Gustafia, his mother, to Oscar, Martena, and Andrew, and to Andrew's teenage children Goldie and Edward Lindquist.

Oscar, with help from Martena and their mother, Gustafia, took over the operation of Lindquist store in Austin. Oscar made at least one trip a year in 1902 to check on his and Charles' land claims here in Clark. [7] He came again in March 1903, along with Dr. Bishop B. Kelly who had filed to purchase the 320 acres directly north of the Lindquist acres. [8]

Meanwhile, Martena married Charles J. Burt, a former printer and railway mail clerk, on April 12, 1902 in Helena. [9] Their brother, Andrew had also died in Minneapolis. Oscar was appointed Administrator of Andrew's estate, and his widow, Emma Munson Lindquist and her two children, Goldie and Edward, moved to Austin. [10]

In November of 1903 Charles Burt leased Dr. Bishop Kelly's ranch property,[11] and Oscar and his brother-in-law made plans to establish a store on Oscar's property. [12]

A front-page story in the Red Lodge Picket newspaper described their planned enterprise: "Mr. Burt and his brothers-in-law own and control over 900 acres of land in one bunch. They are erecting a number of buildings on the ranch, including a store and a blacksmith shop, and next spring they will open a general merchandise store establishment under the name of Lindquist Brothers. It will be located about a mile and a half this side of the Clark post office. Mr. Burt was in Red Lodge the first of the week and leased one of the Nutting residences, where Mrs. Burt, who is still in Helena, will make her home for the winter, or until suitable quarters are prepared on the ranch." [13]

While Oscar ran the store in Austin, Charles Burt oversaw his own property and those of Oscar's and the Charles' heirs in Clark. Area newspapers mention one trip by Oscar in May 1905 to Clark to visit his ranch property. [14]

Later that summer on July 26, 1905 Oscar married Emma Munson Lindquist, Andrew's widow and his sister-in-law. [15]

On September 8, 1906 Oscar's Clark ranch began drawing water from Little Rocky Creek to begin irrigation of 75 acres of his property. [16] This was to fulfill part of the requirements necessary to acquire final title to his acreage.

Water was also appropriated on the same date from Little Rocky Creek to irrigate 225 acres of his deceased brother Charles' claim. [17] Evidently he was splitting his time between Austin and Clark, with his brother-in-law, Charles Burt, continuing to oversee operations here.

In the summer of 1909 he had arrived back on his Clark ranch intending "to close out his interests in Austin and put in a store here in September. He will then be able to personally superintend the ranch." [18]

By September the new store on the Lindquist ranch was being stocked up, and "a carload each of groceries and lumber" was expected that week. The Meeteetse stage was already making deliveries and pickups at the ranch. [19]

His brother-in-law, Charles Burt was again overseeing these operations, as Oscar was sick in Austin. He did return before the end of the month recovered from his illness and "looking forward to the time when he could like here permanently." [20] A dance was held at the Lindquist ranch on Christmas night. [21]

While Burt was overseeing the Clark operations, he also had opened his own livery business in Belfry. Frank Simmons was running that business for him. [22]

By March of 1910 the stage bringing the mail was arriving in Clark on Monday, Wednesday and Friday at 1 p.m. and leaving Tuesday, Thursday, and Saturday at 6 a.m. Oscar had completed the moving of his store from Austin to Clark by the middle of June and was "now able to serve his customers." [23] In July the "Silvertip Nine" and the "Clark Outlaws" played a baseball game on the grounds of the store with the "Silvertip Nine" winning 9 to 8. [24]

On November 9th, 1910 Oscar completed the homestead requirements for the Government land office in Lander to transfer title of his 320 acres to his ownership. [25] The following April 27th, the homestead requirements on his brother, Charles' property were fulfilled. [26]

By year's end the road between the Lindquist store and the post office at the Parker ranch to the south had been improved. One resident gave his impression of the new enterprise: "A look into the Lindquist Brothers store will prove to anyone that we have the nicest and best stocked country store in this part of the state." [27]

Chris Weathermon was kept busy hauling freight for the store, and by April of 1911 a second larger warehouse and bunkhouse had just been completed. On June 1st the Clark post office at the Parker ranch was moved to the Lindquist store. [28]

The Lindquist Brothers store quickly became the focal point and social center for the Clark community. Here area residents came to purchase food, clothing, ranch and farming supplies, and to send and receive mail. In February of 1913 Oscar Lindquist sent out teams to haul ice to be stored for summer use. "This means lots of ice cream and lemonade for their patrons next summer." [29]

By December the store was moved into a new building, which made for "a roomy, up to date establishment. The post office will be located to the right, as you enter the new part, with the groceries in the rear." [30]

Lee Weathermon, who spent much of his childhood in Clark with his family, vividly remembered the interior of the Lindquist store: "When you walked in the door, there straight ahead was the post office right there in the middle of the room. It had cubbyholes with the mail in them. Off to the left there was kind of a round circle thing with clothes, and on that side of the store there was candy too. Then you kind of went down an aisle to the back and there were groceries on each side. There also had a refrigerator back there with pop. I don't remember if they sold meat or not." [31]

His sister, Ada Eckerman, remembered an experience with their younger brother at the hand pump out behind the store where store patrons could get water. Mark, who was six or seven years old at the time, and she were getting a drink. "Mark had his hand up there, and I pulled the handle and took off part of his little finger. It's still shorter today." [32]

The Lindquist Brothers store was the focal point for the area communities serving not only as a grocery store and post office, but also as a place for meetings and social gatherings. Here members of the Clarence Pearson family and their guests purchase supplies before a trip up into the Beartooth Mountains in 1915. Photo courtesy of Carol Briggs Joy and Dorothy Pearson Williams.

The Lindquist Brothers Store with horse hitched outside with snow on ground.
Photo taken in late teens or early 1920's, courtesy of Joise Denney Wolchesky

Although he never knew how it happened and never asked, Lee also remembered that Oscar Lindquist was missing his right hand and always covered the stump with a black sock held on by rubber bands. "He'd put that old pencil in there, and he could write like everything." [33]

Clytie Fuson Williams, who grew up in Clark and returned to teach at the Clark School in 1929 – 1930, had her own memories of Mr. Lindquist and the store. "Mr. Lindquist had a big store. He sold everything, and he had three little buildings. One had sugar and flour in it. Another one had supplies for cattle like stock salt. Another one had outdoor supplies like big nails. In that store he had a grocery store, post office, clothes, shoes, overalls, and rubber boots. He had everything. He had slab bacon, big round cheese, and carbide lights. He never left the place or went to anything.

"He was a little short man with no fingers on one hand. He wore a black sock over that with a big elastic band, and he'd stick that pencil through that elastic. He was a good writer and smart. He did a lot for the community. He carried people because there were only a few moneyed people in the community. The rest were mostly poor dirt farmers with no income to amount to anything. We always got a treat when the folks paid their bill – sack candy. He was a wonderful old merchant." [34]

On April 23, 1914 Mrs. Gustafia Lindquist, who had been living for some time with her son, Oscar, died at his and Emma's home in Clark. [35] She is buried in our cemetery.

Oscar and Emma donated a tract of land to School District 8 for the new site of the Bennett Creek School on September 8, 1921. The 200' by 220' parcel in Section 21 had been part of Charles Lindquist's property. By terms of their contract with the School District, if the site was ever abandoned for school purposes it was to "revert to the owner

Emma Lindquist
Flash's Studio portrait taken December 1941.
Copyrighted photo used by permission of Tom Egenes.

of the tract of land from which it is taken." [36]

Beginning in 1906, Oscar and Emma had gradually extended their ranch holdings through the purchase of four of the family heirs' interests in the Charles Lindquist property in Section 21 and 22, including deceased brother Andrew's share. By May 1926 they owned all but Edward's share. [37]

Most of Oscar Lindquist's store purchases were made from sources in Red Lodge. When he made a trip to Cody in mid-December 1922, it was reported in the newspaper that it was first trip to that city in 22 years. [38]

In September 1924 Oscar and John Simpson drove over to Cody to accept delivery of several cans of baby trout from the Bozeman hatchery to be planted in some of the small streams of the Clarks Fork. [39] In November Oscar and Emma left for a one-month trip back to Minnesota and a side-trip to Wisconsin where they visited former Clark residents and their long-time friends, Mrs. James Hunter and her sons. [40]

Many community and organizational gatherings were held at the Lindquist store, including the annual meetings of the Bennett Buttes Cemetery Association [41] as well as those of the local stock association. [42]

The Lindquists employed a number of community members to work in their store including: Mrs. Harry Temple,[43] Emma Hasselstrom, (Emma Lindquist's niece and later the wife of John Simpson), [44] Mrs. Alice Trumbo, [45] and Ed Vine. [46] John and Emma Simpson looked after the store when the Lindquists took a vacation. [47] Fred Schmidt and Alex Wells cut winter ice to put up for use in summer. [48] Lambert Holthuse, Dick Oglesby and M. R. Smith hauled salt, [49] so did Fred Myers, Stanton Howard, Willard Hogan, Orloff

Simpson, E. T. Fuson, and John Simpson. [50]

Chris Weathermon and Bill Cooper erected new fences on the ranch, [51] and Bert Stidham also worked at the store. [52] When Oscar became ill, John and Emma Simpson moved from their ranch to the Lindquist ranch to help there, as well as to work in the store. [53]

Kids often accompanied their parents to the store when they bought groceries or other supplies or paid their bills. Often Emma or Oscar treated the kids to candy at such times. [54] Ada Eckerman also remembered, "Of course when we went in the store, we were told to behave ourselves. We never got out of line in there, because Mom and Dad would have never stood for that." [55]

Occasionally such parental admonitions were not followed. "I remember one time that Terry and Darrell Smith walked down to the store and went in the back and got us a pop. Old man Lindquist was up there at the front. One of them got a can of pop, shook it up, and then pulled his finger off the top. About that time old man Lindquist was coming to the back, and he shot him with that pop. All three of us ran out the back." [56]

On January 31, 1940 Oscar Lindquist retired as postmaster after serving in that position since 1911. [57] The following day the post office was moved from the Lindquist store to the Norris Gallentine ranch, and the position of postmaster passed to Hulda Gallentine. [58]

During the next two years Oscar's health began to decline, and on February 18, 1943 while enroute for a medical appointment, Oscar Lindquist died of a heart attack in Laurel, Montana. [59] Emma continued to operate the store with help from the Emma Simpson, [60] as well as with intermittent help from son Ed and daughter-in-law, Florence who were then living in Bearcreek, and Julius (Bill) Radius who was living at the ranch during 1944.

While Emma was away in Laurel visiting her daughter, Goldie Rockvam, Florence came over from Bearcreek to take care of the store. When Ed came over on the weekend to check on Florence, he became alarmed at the absence of Bill Radius from the ranch. Radius' body was soon discovered at the Harry Temple place where he had died of a heart attack. [61]

As mining work continued to decline in Bearcreek as a result of the Smith Mining disaster, Ed and Florence decided to move back to Clark in 1945 to take over full-time operation of the Lindquist ranch and the store. Ed also drove the local school bus. [62]

In September Emma sold most of her ranch to Edward and the remainder of Charles' former property to her daughter, Goldie Rockvam the following year. [63] She divided her time between living in Clark with Ed and Florence and with Goldie and her family in Laurel, Montana. Emma died in Laurel on April 8th, 1948 and was buried next to Oscar in Mountview Cemetery, Billings. [64]

In September 1950 the post office was moved back to the Lindquist Store, after Hulda Gallentine resigned as postmaster and Florence Lindquist became the acting postmaster. [65]

Ed and Florence continued to operate the Lindquist Brothers store, post office, and ranch until the fall of 1960 when Ed underwent surgery in Billings. He died in the Coe Hospital in Cody on December 11th. [66]

When the U. S. Postal Service discontinued the Clark Post Office on February 10, 1967, [67] Florence made the decision to close the store, sell its inventory, and then sell the property.

Long-time resident, Georgia Close, remembered one humorous incident when the store's inventory was being sold. "They were selling out things from the store, and my husband, Harold, came home with a bunch of what looked like malt balls candy, but they were laxatives. My kids got a hold of them and what a mess!" [68]

On February 27th, 1969 Florence sold the property and buildings to Ada and John Eckerman and her brother, Lee Weathermon. [69] Five months later in she sold the mineral rights to the oil and gas on the 880 acres to James R. Beasley of Casper. [70]

Florence moved to Billings, where she lived alone in her home on Yale Avenue until 1989 when she became a resident of Parkview Convalescent Center. She died on October 10, 1991, and was buried in the Nealis family plot at Holy Cross Cemetery, Butte, Montana. [71]

Lee Weathermon, a third generation member of the Clark community, continues to live in the former Lindquist house on the ranch that for more than sixty years was the social center of the Clark community. While many of the original ranch buildings are still there, the old store building burned down in 1976 due an accidental fire. [72]

Chapter 22 Notes:

[1] U.S. Census, 1870 and 1880, Town of Red Wing, Goodhue County, Minnesota, pages 355 and p. 494B.

[2] Letter from Shirley Jawort, granddaughter of Martena Howard Burt, dated December 2, 1999.

[3] U. S. Census, 1900, Lewis and Clark County, Montana, 10N, R5 West, page 7B.

[4] BLM Land Serial # WYL 0003211 and # WYL 0001321; "Pioneer Merchant Dies at Laurel," *The Cody Enterprise,* February 24, 1943, p. 3.

[5] "Charles E. Lindquist Shoots Julia Tostevin, and Then Takes His Own Life," *Helena Independent Record,* November 28, 1901. Note: Julia was the daughter of Peter Tostevin appointed postmaster of Austin when the post office opened in 1901 in a place formerly known as Butler.

[6] Correspondence from Helena researcher, Patti Yedlicka, to the author on January 10, 2004.

[7] *Carbon County Chronicle,* April 8, 1902, p. 5.

[8] *Carbon County Chronicle,* April 8, 1902, p. 5; and March 24 1903, p. 3.

[9] The 34-year-old Burt was born in Omaha, Nebraska in 1868, the son of Richard and Elizabeth Davis Burt. (Lewis and Clark County, Montana marriage license #3396 dated April 10, 1902, and marriage certificate dated April 12, 1902; and Letter from Shirley Jawort, December 2, 1999).

[10] Administrator's Deed between Oscar Lindquist, Administrator, Estate of Andrew Lindquist, and Goldie M. Rockvam, Park County Book 54, p. 230-231.

[11] The northwest corner of this property is where the Project Telephone building is located today. Clark old-timers know this as "Kelly's Corner."

[12] "Store for Clark – Lindquist Brothers and C. J. Burt Will Engage in Business," *Red Lodge Picket,* November 12, 1903, p. 1.

[13] Ibid.

[14] *Carbon County Gazette,* May 11, 1905, p. 5.

[15] Marriage License # 4190, State of Montana, County of Lewis and Clark, dated July 26, 1905; Marriage Certificate, State of Montana, County of Lewis and Clark, filed July 27, 1905.

[16] Certificate of Appropriation of Water, State of Wyoming, Certificate Record 36, p. 23; filed on April 11, 1914, Order Record #5, p. 12.

[17] Certificate of Appropriation of Water, State of Wyoming, Certificate Record 36, p. 24; filed on April 14, 1914.

[18] "Clark's Fork Squibs," *Wyoming Stockgrower and Farmer,* July 16, 1909, p. 2.

[19] "Clark Squibs," *Wyoming Stockgrower and Farmer,* September 10, 1909, p. 2.

[20] "Clark Squib," *Wyoming Stockgrower and Farmer,* October 01, 1909, p. 8.

[21] "Clark Squib," *Wyoming Stockgrower and Farmer,* January 14, 1910, p. 5.

[22] "Clark Squibs," *Wyoming Stockgrower & Farmer,* January 28, 1910, p. 8.

[23] "Clark Squib," *Park County Enterprise,* June 18, 1910, p. 8.

[24] "Clark Squib," *Park County Enterprise,* July 30, 1910, p. 4.

[25] Land Office Title Transfer, 11/9/1910, 320 acres, to Oscar F. Lindquist, Document # 021, Accession/Serial # 161150 and BLM Serial # WYL 0000021 under authority of Desert Land Act of March 3, 1877.

[26] Sale Cash Entry Title Transfer, 4/27/1911 to Heirs of Charles E. Lindquist, 320 acres, Document # 03211, Accession/Serial # 193939, BLM Serial # WYL 0003211.

[27] "Clark Squib," *Park County Enterprise,* December 14, 1910, p. 8.

[28] *Park County Enterprise,* 4 March 1911, p. 2; and 19 April 1911, p. 3; "It is now 'Uncle Sam' Lindquist, the post office having been moved from the Parker ranch to the Lindquist store on the 1st. And it's a safe bet that ex-postmaster Parker is the happiest man in the valley, as he can not go to see his best girl without every patron at the post office cussing him," (*Park County Enterprise,* June 7, 1911, p. 4).

[29] *Park County Enterprise,* February 19, 1913, p. 4.

[30] "Clark," *Park County Enterprise,* December 17, 1913, p. 5.

[31] Lee Weathermon, interview with author, Clark, Wyoming, November 04, 2003.

[32] Ada Weathermon Eckerman, interview with author, Clark, Wyoming, November 04, 2003.

[33] Lee Weathermon, interview.

[34] Clytie Fuson Williams, interview with author, Cody, Wyoming, October 07, 1998.

[35] "On April 23 the pall of death settled over the home of our popular and esteemed merchant, Oscar F. Lindquist in the death of his mother Mrs. Gustafia Lindquist, who died as she had lived, a true Christian woman. Mrs. Lindquist was 79 years of age at the time of her demise, and leaves surviving her one son, Oscar F. Lindquist, a daughter, Mrs. Charles Burt of Belfry, Montana. She lost her husband many years ago, who was buried at Red Wing, Minnesota and since that time she has made her home with her only surviving son." (*Powell Tribune,* May 8, 1914, p. 1; "Clark," *Park County Enterprise,* May 6, 1914, p. 7)

[36] Contract for Warranty Deed, Park County Book 50, p. 159.

[37] Quitclaim Deed, Gustafia C. Lindquist to Oscar F. Lindquist, dated 12 December 1909, Book 82, p. 392-93; Administrator's Deed, Oscar Lindquist, Admin. Of Estate of Andrew M. Lindquist to Goldie M. Rockvam, dated February 28, 1923, Book 54, p. 230-31; Warranty Deed, Goldie M. Rockvam to Oscar F. Lindquist, dated May 25, 1926, Book 82, p. 390-92; Warranty Deed, Martena C. Burt to Oscar Lindquist, dated May no day, 1926, Book 90, p. 112-13.

[38] *Cody Enterprise,* December 20, 1922, p. 8 and January 31, 1923, p. 8.

[39] "Buffalo Bill Town Doings," *The Park County Herald,* October 01, 1924, p. 8.

[40] "Clark," *The Park County Herald,* November 5, 1924, p. 6 and December 3, 1923, p. 6.

[41] *Park County Herald,* May 21, 1924, p. 8.

[42] "BEAR TOOTH STOCKMEN HAVE MEETING AT CLARK – The members of the Bear Tooth stock association met at the Lindquist store on Tuesday, and talked over the many problems which are confronting them in the handling of their stock during the ensuing season. "Many ideas of handling stock on the range were discussed and some very fine points were brought out through the talks made." (*The Park County Herald,* March 10, 1926, p. 1).

[43] *Park County Enterprise,* December 17, 1913, p. 5.

[44] *Bridger Times,* December 15, 1921.

[45] *Cody Enterprise and Park County Herald,* October 13, 1926, p. 8.

[46] *Cody Enterprise and Park County Herald,* November 17, 1926, p. 11.

[47] *The Cody Enterprise,* January 12, 1927, p. 10.

[48] *Cody Enterprise and Park County Herald,* February 9, 1927, p. 9; *Cody Enterprise,* January 27, 1932, p. 6.

[49] *Cody Enterprise and Park County Herald,* March 23, 1927, p. 8.

[50] Park County Herald, October 01, 1924, p. 7.

[51] *Cody Enterprise and Park County Herald,* April 13, 1927, p. 8.

[52] *Cody Enterprise and Park County Herald,* September 21, 1927, p. 8.

[53] *The Cody Enterprise,* May 02, 1928, p. 6 and June 06, 1928, p. 5.

[54] Ada Weathermon Eckerman, interview with author, November 30, 1998.

[55] Ada Weathermon Eckerman, interview with author, November 04, 2003.

[56] Lee Weathermon, interview with author, November 04, 2003.

[57] *The Cody Enterprise,* January 31, 1940, p. 3.

[58] Letter and Application for Proposed Change of Location of Post Office from First Assistant Postmaster General To Postmaster Hulda Gallentine dated January 26, 1940 and her returned filled-in application dated February 12, 1940.

[59] *The Cody Enterprise,* February 24, 1943, p. 3.

[60] *The Cody Enterprise,* March 31, 1943, p. 7.

[61] *The Cody Enterprise,* May 31, 1944, p. 7.

[62] *The Cody Enterprise,* September 19, 1945, p. 8; and December 15, 1960, p. 1.

[63] Warranty Deed with Release of Homestead, Emma C. Lindquist to Edward O. Lindquist, dated September 15, 1945, Book 136, p. 283 and 284; Warranty Deed with Release of Homestead, Emma C. Lindquist to Goldie May Rockvam, dated January 11, 1946, Book 136, p. 544.

[64] *The Cody Enterprise,* 14 April 1948, p. 5 and *The Billings Gazette,* April 09, 1948, p. 10. She is buried in Section 2, Lot 1, Mountview Cemetery, Billings.

[65] *The Cody Enterprise,* September 22, 1950, p. 6.

[66] *The Billings Gazette,* December 12, 1960, p. 17; *The Cody Enterprise,* December 15, 1960, p. 1. He is buried next to his mother and Uncle Oscar in Mountview Cemetery, Billings.

[67] John S. Gallagher and Alan H. Patera, *Wyoming Post Offices 1850 – 1980,* (The Depot, 1980), p. 99.

[68] Georgia Close, interview with author, Clark, Wyoming, December 01, 1999.

[69] The sale included Sec. 15, and NW $\frac{1}{4}$ and N $\frac{1}{2}$ NE $\frac{1}{4}$ Section 22, T. 57N, R. 102W. Mortgage Deed with Release of Homestead Document No. 129336, Park County Book 334, p. 245 signed on February 27, 1969 and filed March 10, 1969.

[70] Park County Book 339, p. 524.

[71] *The Billings Gazette,* October 13, 1991, p 14A.

[72] Rose Cox, conversation with author, Powell, December 4, 2003.

23

Circuit Ministers and Churches

The first Sunday school and church services were held at area schoolhouses with ministers coming from out of the area to conduct the gatherings.   As early as 1903 mention is made of such services being held at the Bennett Creek schoolhouse which had an organ to assist with church music: "The new school house organ is a beauty, and our Sunday school should be a success this summer with good music to assist in keeping up interest. Rev. Torrence of Laurel, Montana will hold religious services in the schoolhouse next Friday evening, June 5th." [1]

In October 1909 Bennett Creek area residents were putting forth efforts to increase attendance at the services of their Bennett Creek Sunday school. Charles A. C. Snow, who for many years served as our Justice of the Peace and as a Trustee for the Clark School District, composed words and music entitled, "My Father's Business," which he dedicated to the Wyoming Sunday schools. [2]

Later in the month the Sunday school was reorganized with Mrs. Carrie Vickery, Miss Lucy Barnhart (later Mrs. Wilbur Bunn), and Charles B. Hubbard serving as teachers. [3] Mrs. Carrie Vickery, was also named superintendent, with Charles B. Hubbard, serving as asst. superintendent. David Parker filled the secretary and treasurer's position. [4]

New literature and music had been acquired, and area residents were encouraged to "come out and help swell the crowd and add your voice whether you can sing or not." [5] With Lucy Barnhart and Mrs. John E. (Everetta) Ricketts were praised as accomplished organists and as a result, "the singing is better than ever before." [6]

Paint Creek church group outside schoolhouse, August 21, 1915.
Photo taken Josephine Brown, courtesy of Elmer Bunn.

The Circuit Ministers

While local teachers taught regular Sunday school services, Belfry ministers who traveled here conducted the early church services. In 1910 Rev. Finch A. Clarke traveled to the Bennett Creek School house to conduct church services on Saturday evening. [7]

Three months Rev. Claudy, a new minister who had recently moved to the area from New Jersey, began conducting church services at the Sirrine schoolhouse every Sunday afternoon, and then at the Bennett Creek schoolhouse later in the evening. [8] His Clark services were "well attended," and he was "preaching to a crowded house every Sunday evening." [9] At one Sunday evening service, he conducted a funeral at the schoolhouse "for the late Mrs. Stanley who had died about a month" earlier "on the McKeever place of spotted fever." [10]

In February 1911 Rev. T. M. Patterson organized the Sheldon Jackson Memorial Presbyterian Church at Bennett Creek with eighteen charter members. [11] The following October the Clark Sunday school members reorganized and elected Mrs. Lucy Barnhart, superintendent, Mrs. Ben Eckloe, assistant superintendent, and Charles B. Hubbard, secretary-treasurer. [12]

Other ministers who traveled south from Belfry to conduct services here, and who are mentioned in newspaper articles, include: Rev. W. W. Warne, who preached on Wednesdays in 1911, and Rev. Blaney, who was here in July and August 1914. Rev. Blaney services were well attended, and at one service, he "preached on the theme of how to be better, and we all listened." [13]

By this time church services were also being held regularly at the Paint Creek schoolhouse on Sunday evenings. [14]

Rev. Daniel Spencer McCorkle arrives

In 1916 Harry Simpson and Gilford E. Youst contacted the Board of Home Missions to request that a permanent minister be sent to the Clark and Chance areas. Rev. Daniel McCorkle, a Presbyterian minister serving at Sunrise, Wyoming, was selected. His planned arrival in February was delayed two months until a minister could be selected to replace him in Sunrise. [15]

Daniel Spencer McCorkle was born in March 1880 in Ridge Prairie, Missouri, the son of Archibald and Hepsabeth McCorkle. He received his early education while working on his father's farm.

In 1903 he entered Missouri Valley College, a Presbyterian-sponsored school at Marshall, Missouri. During the summers, he worked as a farm hand. After his graduation in 1909 he joined the Socialist Party and organized a chapter of the Intercollegiate Socialist Society on the Missouri Valley campus.

While studying for a master's degree in sociology at Columbia University in 1910, he was also enrolled at Union Theological Seminary in New York. During the summer of 1911 he worked in Bearcreek, Montana, and used this experience in his master's thesis, entitled: "An Agricultural Community, or the Social Phenomena of a Rural District,"

After he graduated from Union Theological Seminary in 1913, he met Panayiota Alexandrakis, a native of Greece who had graduated from Springfield International

College. They married the following year and moved to Sunrise, Wyoming where Rev. McCorkle served as a Presbyterian minister. One of his goals was to improve the life of the miners and their families in the Colorado Fuel and Iron Company-controlled town. As a result in 1915, he testified before the United States Commission on Industrial Relations.

Rev. McCorkle met success at his post in Sunrise and was elected as moderator of the Cheyenne Presbytery in 1916. The following year his wife was pregnant, and he thought it was time to seek a new position elsewhere. He applied to the Board of Home Missions of the Presbyterian Church, headquartered in New York City for a position. They offered him a missionary position at the Congregation of the Sheldon Jackson Memorial Church with stations at Bennett Creek, Chance, Paint Creek and Pioneer, with a yearly salary of $480, to begin on July 1, 1917. He gladly accepted their offer and arrived early at Chance on April 1, 1917. His wife remained in Wheatland until after the birth of their son. [16]

The newly-arrived minister held services at the Bennett Creek and Paint Creek schoolhouses on May 6th, and it was reported that his "services are worth attending as Rev. McCorkle has a forceful message to deliver and a forceful manner of delivering it." [17] The following Sunday there was a gathering at the Pioneer schoolhouse with preaching in the morning and afternoon with a basket dinner. [18]

Three weeks later "a goodly gathering of the members of the Sunday schools of Chance, Pioneer, Bennett and Paint Creek met at Otis Gould's grove on Bennett Creek on Sunday, June 10th, 1917 for a children's day program and picnic dinner." [19]

There were 150 in attendance including people from Cody, Powell, Chance and Belfry who enjoyed the "bountiful basket dinner" which was eaten "under the beautiful shade trees." Following the dinner a program of songs and recitations by the children was given under the direction of Rev. McCorkle and local church superintendent, Dave Parker. "The exercises were entertaining and the weather being favorable, a thoroughly enjoyable afternoon was spent by all present." Also in attendance at the activities were Rev. Carlson and his wife of Powell, who "delivered an earnest and helpful message to the people of the Clarks Fork Valley." [20]

Mrs. Panayiota McCorkle and her new son, Antonio, arrived to join her husband at their Chance ranch home on June 21st. [21]

Being a circuit minister was not without its perils. The following month while Rev. McCorkle and his wagon team were crossing Clarks Fork River on the Sirrine Bridge near Ira Toothacher's, the bridge started to collapse. Only fast action on his part and the strength of his horses pulled the wagon to safety just as the bridge went into the river. Only the wagon's rear wheels went into the river. [22]

On September 4, 1917 pledge sheets were circulated from the communities of Pioneer, Chance, Clark, and Paint Creek who felt "that our churches should have more help from our Pastor and that one of the best ways to help him in his work is for the churches to own an automobile for his use; therefore we pledge the amount set opposite our names for the purpose of buying a church automobile (a Ford 5-passenger) and agree to pay this amount at once or within thirty days to Mr. Harry Simpson or some member of the Committee. This car is to remain the property of the church and to be used by whoever is the resident pastor." Fifty individuals signed the pledge for a total amount of $420.50. [23] There were also undated pledge sheets for donations towards Rev. McCorkle's salary in the amount of $488. [24]

On January 15, 1918 the Sheridan Presbytery held a special session at the Belfry Presbyterian Church to examine Mr. Joseph E. Tope for licensure and ordination into the Christian ministry. The moderator, Rev. Walter G. Pitkin of Cody, appointed Rev. McCorkle of Chance as the clerk pro temp, while Rev. Samuel C. Ryland of Powell was the third minister in attendance. The three clergymen examined Mr. Tope with questions in religion, church history, theology, church government and constitutional questions required to become licensed, as well as with questions on the English Bible for ordination. Others present were Delegate Dave Parker and Alternate Delegate Harry G. Simpson, who represented the Sheldon Jackson Memorial Presbyterian Church of Clark. As a result of the questioning, the ordination of Joseph E. Tope was unanimously approved. Rev. Tope served throughout the Clarks Fork Valley until the mid-1920's when he and his family moved to Casper.[25]

In April 1918 Rev. McCorkle and his family moved from Chance to the former Pioneer School building on the Ed Simpson ranch, and later that month attended the Sheridan Presbytery annual meeting at Greybull. [26] By 1922 he and his family had relocated to Bearcreek, where he was teaching at the Bearcreek High School, as well as continuing to perform his regular ministerial duties at the Bennett Creek and Paint Creek churches. [27]

He was the speaker along with Professor Hamilton of Belfry at the Memorial Day services held at the Clark schoolhouse in May 1924 where "a fine program had been arranged for the occasion and people of Clarks Fork valley observed the day in a truly appropriate manner. After the services those present gathered at the Parker grove for a picnic and social gathering." [28] In August he made arrangements to have an old-fashioned picnic for Paint Creek residents in the Natural Corral, and he wanted "everyone to come with well-filled baskets." [29]

In September he announced that starting October 12th, he would also be holding church services at the Pat O'Hara schoolhouse on the Two-Dot Ranch, and inviting "every man, woman and child to come and help make this a rousing meeting. Bring your best singing voices." [30]

Rev. McCorkle alternated his well-attended services each week between Clark, Chance, Pat O'Hara and Paint Creek. He was "well pleased with the fine turnout last Sunday, as the majority of the Paint Creeks were there to listen to his splendid sermon, which he is kind enough to give us once a month." [31]

Although he made the trip from Bearcreek to Paint Creek during one fierce December 1924 snowstorm, he cancelled the service due to the bad weather.[32]

During 1925 Rev. McCorkle, sometimes accompanied by his wife and two sons, continued holding services in Clark, Paint Creek and Pat O'Hara Creek.[33] In late May he was busy calling on friends in Clark and Paint Creek to solicit church memberships, and on Memorial Day he again held services at the Bennett Buttes Cemetery, after which a basket dinner was served.[34]

His church membership drive was successful in getting about thirty members in his valley church organization. "He has been a patient and faithful worker for the good of mankind, and we are glad to see that the community is waking up to the fact and responding to the call for the uplift of better brotherhood." [35]

By then the membership of Sheldon Jackson Memorial Presbyterian Church of Chance and Clark including the earlier charter members consisted of: [36]

Dorothy Vickery Buck (Mrs. Roy)
Jody Brown (Mr.)
Ethel Bunn (Mrs. Wilbur)
Olivia Earle (Mrs. E. J.)
Maggie Fouse (Mrs. W. H.)
Anna Sophie Harkin (Mrs. Edward E.) - Rec'd Feb. 10th, 1918 (Confession)
Mattie Johnson (Mrs. George W.)
Clifford Johnson (Mr.)
Iona Johnson (Miss)
Marion Johnson (Miss)
Ella Johnson (Miss) – Rec'd Feb. 10, 1918 (Confession)
Anna Lindsay (Mrs.)
Jeannette Lindsay (Miss)
Panayiota A. McCorkle (Mrs. Daniel S.) – Rec'd Feb. 10, 1918 (Letter)
Rebecca Mandeville (Mrs. Robert) – Rec'd June 10, 1918 (Letter)
Hannah Pearson (Mrs. C. A.)
Edward Pearson (Mr.)
Dorothy Pearson (Miss)
Harry G. Simpson (Mr.)
Edith Simpson (Mrs. Harry G.)
Nannie Simpson (Miss)
Ella Simpson (Miss)
Amelia Sirrine (Mrs. Orton)
David Parker (Mr.)
Emma Parker (Mrs. David)
Charles Elmer Townsend (Mr.)- Rec'd Feb. 10, 1918 (Letter)
Elsie Mable Townsend (Mrs. Charles E.) – Rec'd Feb. 10, 1918 (Letter)
Carrie B. Vickery (Mrs.)
Elizabeth Vickery (Miss)
Elsie Vickery (Miss)
Teddy Vickery (Mr.)
Hazel Walters (Miss)
Esther Weathermon (Mrs. Mark)
George E. Youst (Mr.) Dismissed Dec 1917 to Belfry Presbyterian Church

For the next five years both Rev. and Mrs. McCorkle were active with their church activities at Clark and Paint Creek. While they continued to live at Bearcreek, they were frequent dinner and houseguests of the Peter Johnson family of Line Creek, who also came to Bearcreek to visit them. [37] In March 1926 he delivered a sermon in the Line Creek schoolhouse "to a small but attentive audience." [38]

In 1930 the McCorkles said goodbye to their many friends and moved with their two sons to Conrad, Montana where he served the town and surrounding agricultural area as their Presbyterian minister. For the rest of his life until his death in July 1956, he continued the good work that was characteristic of his thirteen years in the Clarks Fork Valley.[39]

A Number of Circuit Ministers Serve

With the leaving of the McCorkles, Belfry, and Powell ministers once again came to Clark and Paint Creek to deliver church services, while area residents conducted the local Sunday school classes.

In August 1930 the Clark Sunday school reorganized and Mrs. William Cochrane was elected superintendent, Mrs. Wilbur Bunn, assistant superintendent, Mrs. Gus Forsman, president of the adult class and Mrs. John K. Large, teacher of the primary class.[40] Mr. Michelmore, the District Sunday school Missionary, organized a Sunday school at the Pioneer School the following March, and in July a minister from Belfry began conducting services there every other Sunday at 3:45 p.m.[41] Rev. G. Scott Porter of Belfry also began holding services at the Clark Schoolhouse on evenings during the week.[42]

During July 1933 vacation church school was held at the Pioneer School. Rev. Porter assisted by Frances Madison, Florence Simpson and Minnie Johnston conducted the school, which had 30 children in attendance during the daily afternoon meetings. At the end of the two-week school, the Clark children joined another group from Belfry and had a lawn picnic at the John Fouse home. There were fifty-five children present at this celebration.[43]

Through the rest of the 1930's several ministers from nearby areas churches conducted services at the Clark, Pioneer and Paint Creek schoolhouses and oversaw church activities here. These included Rev. Wills of the Powell Presbyterian Church, Rev. G. Scott Porter from Belfry, and Rev. Prouty of Miles City.[44] Sunday school classes were once again reorganized at Paint Creek, Pioneer and Clark.[45] Area residents were delighted when Rev. and Mrs. Daniel McCorkle returned in November 1939 for a week's visit with old time friends.[46]

Our Lady of the Valley Catholic Church

As early as 1942 Catholic services were held at the Line Creek School conducted by Father Frederick Kimmet who had come to St. Barbara's Catholic Church in Powell in the fall of 1935.[47] The Clark area was under the administration of the St. Barbara's Parish, as was Cody at that time.

During World War II while Father Kimmet was serving as a chaplain with the armed services, Father Francis T. Penny continued his work at Clark, as well as served as the administrator of St. Barbara's until Father Kimmet's return in January 1944.[48]

It was during these years that the Catholic services moved from the Line Creek School to the old abandoned Ballard house on one of the Badura family ranch properties. Here Father Penny began conducting the services until Father Kimmet's return to Powell in January 1944.[49]

Father Daniel Carroll succeeded Father Kimmet in 1948, and later on one of his many trips to conduct services at the old abandoned ranch house, he looked at the poor condition of the building with its "sagging floor and the failing rafters" and suggested to his congregation there that if they "valued their lives, they'd better build a church." [50]

Area families pledged money and labor towards building the new church. Some of these included: Don and Margaret Fraker, Mick and Delores Fraker, David and Elmarie Denney and their sons, Frank Thull, Francis (Pat) Thull, Michael Thull, Frank Getzfried, Frank Badura, Pete Badura, Joanne Badura, Dominic, Joanne and John Badura, Robert Badura, P. J. Montang, Stephen and Agnes Torczon, and Dennis and Margaret Torczon. The Badura brothers had heavy equipment whose use they also donated to the project. [51]

Under Father Carroll's direction work began. Lumber was obtained in Montana and brought to the site. Others scooped out a basement from the rocky soil, poured concrete, and erected the 28' x 50' church building, which they named Our Lady of the Valley Church. [52]

St. Anthony's Catholic Church in Cody, which was in the process of erecting a new church building to replace their smaller one, donated the pews and the altar. [53] Total cash outlay was $6,600 "due to the unselfish labor by the people of the Clarksfork area." [54]

Father Carroll celebrated the first mass in the new church on Christmas day, 1953. Six months later in June the Badura Brothers, a family corporation consisting of John, Dominic, and Robert and Ina Badura, donated 2 separate pieces of land "south of the new Badger Ditch" in Section 7, T.57N, R102W consisting of 4.25 acres on which the new church was located. [55]

On October 6th Bishop Herbert M. Newell of Cheyenne came to officiate at the dedication and blessing of the new mission chapel before "a large attendance of members and friends." Twenty visiting priests attended the dedication, which was followed by a solemn high mass. After the services the ladies of the chapel served a luncheon, and that evening Bishop Newell conferred the sacrament of confirmation upon 50 parishioners. [56]

Our Lady of the Valley Church

Father Daniel Carroll continued to conduct services at Our Lady of the Valley Church until he left St. Barbara's Parish in 1975. He was followed by Father Charles Taylor from 1975 until 1982 when Monsignor John F. Meyer came. [57]

On October 25, 1987 thirty-nine members of the Powell and Cody Catholic congregations began walking from Powell to Clark on a pilgrimage to promote world peace. They carried a shrine honoring Our Lady of Fatima along on their journey. By the time they arrived at Our Lady of the Valley Church, the group had grown to nearly 350 with representatives from the Worland, Thermopolis, Lovell and Greybull congregations. Only certain churches in Wyoming had been designated pilgrimage sites, and "Our Lady of the Valley is one of only a handful of sites chosen in the state." [58]

Msgr. Meyer left Powell on May 27, 1988 to assume duties as pastor of Sacred Heart's pastor in Greybull. [59] He was succeeded by Rev. Fred Wendel who served St. Barbara's Parish and the Clark congregation from May 1988 to July 1990 when he left to take over Saints Cryril and Methodius Parish in Rock Spring. That month Rev. John Wright came from St. Joseph's in Cheyenne to become the new pastor in Powell and Clark. [60]

On January 16, 1991 Robert B. Badura and his wife, Ina, granted to the Church of St. Barbara, a remainder interest in an additional 8.5 acres of property including a house which was located next to other Our Lady of the Valley Church property. [61] After Robert Badura's death on April 1, 1996, ownership of the property transferred to the Church of St. Barbara as surviving life tenant. [62]

Father Wright retired in September 1999 and was followed by Father Tom Ogg who served the parish until June 30, 2002. From then until the present time Father Peter Johnson has served as pastor of St. Barbara's and Our Lady of the Valley Church. [63]

On August 10, 2000 a corrective Warranty Deed was issued by the Most Rev. Hubert J. Hart, D.D., Bishop of Cheyenne, President of the Catholic Diocese of Cheyenne and President of the Church of St. Barbara, consolidating into one parcel totaling 11 acres all of the previous Badura family property gifts to the Church of St. Barbara. [64]

The Bennett Creek Church

Even after the establishment of a Catholic church in the Pioneer area, there still wasn't a church for the Protestant community members. During the 1940's Sunday church services conducted by visiting ministers continued to be held at the Clark schoolhouse, while Bible study groups were meeting at the Guy Pointer, John Simpson and other residents' homes,[65] and from time to time there would be a mention in local newspapers that the Sunday school was reorganizing again at the Clark School with a good turnout. [66]

During 1958 until mid-June 1959 Rev. Ward Barter was making a weekly trip from Powell to deliver sermons to the appreciative Clark Protestant residents. [67] After he moved to Newcastle, there must have been a void on Sundays because it was noted once again that: " Residents of Clark community met at school house Sunday morning to organize Sunday school and a great deal of interest was shown." [68] Through the 1960's and into the early 1970's there still wasn't a dedicated church with a full-time resident minister.

This was to change with the arrival in September 1970 of Juanita and Roy Gordon and their family from Imperial Beach, California. Son Ernie Gordon and his wife, Carol and their family came first and settled on a ranch on the Clarks Fork River, which at one time had been owned by the Harold Close family and others.

Roy and Juanita came up to visit several times that first year, and by June of the next year, they also decided to move here. They bought the old Pate Pointer ranch from John and Ada Eckerman, and moved here in August 1971.[69]

Juanita loved the area but thought, "Gee, they don't even have a church out there." This really bothered her. She said they were having Sunday services at the Clark schoolhouse, which were being given by Rev. John Cunningham from Powell. [70]

One evening on the way to Powell, their son Ernie said to his father, "Dad, why don't you and Mom donate an care of land here to build a church? And we'll build a church." [71]

With help from Reverend Cunningham in Powell, and with permission from the Eckermans who still held the mortgage to their entire ranch property, [72] the Gordons donated one acre of their land to the First Southern Baptist Church of Powell on January 31, 1972. [73] Their son Ernie had previously selected the site for the future church, which had a clear view of the entrance to the Clarks Fork Canyon. Soon after, the Gordons established a church building fund with a large donation from Pate Pointer.[73]

On April 8th 1972, while cleaning out an irrigation ditch on his Clarks Fork River property, Ernie Gordon was killed in a tractor rollover. A memorial fund was established in his name and donated to the building fund of the Bennett Creek Baptist Church, whose name had been suggested by Rev. Cunningham. [74]

In December Wilbur Bunn located the site for the well to be drilled later on the church property. That same month Lloyd and Larry Thiel leveled the area for building. [75]

While on a trip through Belfry, the Gordons saw a former classroom building at the Belfry School, which was slated for removal. After some negotiations, members of the future church congregation purchased the building from Rex Jackson for $1500 on February 6th, 1973. They contracted with Bill Underzuber to move it to the church site for $1,000. [76]

Lloyd and Larry Thiel dug the trench for the building as a donation, and on February 26, 1973 the concrete was poured for the foundation. The next afternoon the old pink classroom building arrived from Belfry with help from Montana Power who donated their services. Duane Wiltse, pastor of the Reorganized Church of the Latter Day Saints, laid the concrete blocks, as a donation. Others who worked those days included Leon and Virginia Sprinkle, Roy and Juanita Gordon, Carol Gordon, Ernie's widow, Ray and Emma Marney, and Burger Bolin from Powell. [77]

The remodeling of the building began two months later in April 1973 using a floor plan that Juanita Gordon had drawn based on her former church in California. Her grandson, Shane Gordon who was seven at the time, drew a picture of how he wanted it to look. Harley Neuenschwander was hired as a carpenter to remodel the building, and everything was removed from the old building except the light fixtures and furnace. Von and Elizabeth Holton donated a year of their tithes as the funds to finish up the inside. [78]

Returning from a trip to Cooke City, the Gordons saw a church in Sunlight, which had a window that they liked. Because the church was locked, they took a picture through the front door of the church and gave it to Harley to pattern for the back window of the

Bennett Creek Church. On May 3rd, 1973 the well was drilled which produced an abundance of water.[79]

Three months later in August Leon Miller, a member of the Powell Baptist Church, hired another carpenter, Harvey Adams to help finish the building. Others from the Powell church also stepped in to help. Sonny Ratcliff, Louie Parnell, Allen Dugger, Gene Montgomery, Frank Schanafelt, Keith Johnson, and Frank Blevins came out to Clark and poured the front concrete steps. Frank Blevins also wired the building for electricity. [80]

Enough pews to fill the church were purchased from the Cody Baptist Church for $50 and were refinished by Gene and Wilma Montgomery. Phyllis Alanko donated an old piano, which had once been used at the old Bearcreek School, and her sister, Helen Arner furnished an antique piano stool. A beautiful hand-carved pulpit over one hundred years old, which had been made by a relative Mrs. Leon Miller, was donated by a Liberty, Missouri Baptist church. It matched the pews perfectly.[81]

Von and Elizabeth Holton, Earl and Louise Black and Charlene Black painted the woodwork and the windowsills, Roy Gordon serviced the furnace, and Mr. and Mrs. Keith Brown cleaned the light fixtures. Carol and Juanita Gordon found the perfect green carpet in Lovell, which was installed by the volunteers. These and other gifts helped with the final completion of the church. [82]

A former school bell was given to the church by Tillie Badura, [83] which was installed the day before the dedication. On November 25, 1973 the Bennett Creek Baptist Church was dedicated. Rev. Cunningham, who was then living in southern Wyoming, returned to speak at the dedication services attended by 123 people. [84]

Rev. Ralph L. Bowen came over from Powell to conduct weekly services. He conducted Ray Marney's funeral there on March 21, 1975,[85] which was the first funeral to be held in the new church. The funeral of ten-year-old Shane Gordon, who was killed by lightning four months later in July, was the second one. His father donated money from a life insurance policy to purchase the trees that were planted on the church property. [86] A few days later the first wedding was held there when Sonny Ratcliff's son, Rusty, married Tammy River. [87]

Rev. Otha Martin arrived from Somerville, Alabama on April 11, 1976 and became the church's first permanent pastor. Rev. Mickey Wells followed him in 1986, and served until September 6, 1992. After he left, Rev. Kurt McNabb became interim pastor. Three years later in October 1995 the church membership asked him to become the church's permanent pastor. On December 14, 1995 the church began its monthly 55-Plus Dinner program which continues to this date. [88]

Through the late 1990's it was apparent that Rev. Kurt McNabb's growing congregation had outgrown its original church building. Plans were formulated and with gifts of labor, money and furnishings, a new larger church was built on the south side of the original one. Atnip Construction, LLC, was the general contractor for the project with the following local subcontractors accomplishing specific construction tasks: Prospector Engineering, Architect Keith Pryor, Nicholson Dirt Works, Thiel Excavation, F & R Insulation, McNeil Concrete, United Building Center, Cody Lumber, J & J Sheetrock, T. J. Electric, Absaroka Water Systems, Beartooth Marble, Big Horn Redi-Mix, Smith Masonry, and Kenco

Security. Both residents and out-of-area friends provided financial support for the project, while many local residents also pitched in to assist the contractors with many of the building details. [89]

The new church was dedicated at 2 p.m. on March 9th, 2003 in the presence of 251 members, Clark residents, and well-wishers. Those attending services in the new Bennett Creek Church can be equally inspired by the same view of the Clarks Fork Canyon that was the impetus for the Gordon's gift of land more than thirty years ago. [90]

In a newspaper interview about the history of the church a few days earlier, Juanita Gordon said, "It was a blessing to our family to have been part of this." [91]

The new Bennett Creek Church was dedicated on March 9th, 2003

Carmel of the Immaculate Heart of Mary Monastery

On October 15, 2003 Bishop David Ricken officiated at a Mass at St. Barbara's Catholic Church to dedicate the new Carmelite monastery located on the grounds of Our Lady of the Valley Catholic Church. More than four hundred people filled the church for the dedication services during which Michael Wright was installed and received his habit.

St. Barbara's loaned the former rectory and Badura house for use as the monastery, and it required extensive cleanup to remove mold that had accumulated after years of sitting empty. Then workmen began remodeling work to remove walls, reshape rooms, and repair electrical wiring and fixtures. Three Cody residents - Dennis Beaudrie, Jerry Boyston, and Chris Maslak - spent more than 400 hours building an elaborate Carmelite altar featuring statues of saints, marble top and intricate hand-crafted details which were based on ancient designs.

Brother Michael Mary joined Father Daniel Mary, a native of Clark, in the monastery, and after a blessing led by Bishop Ricken, the gates were closed and the two monks began their cloistered life - one that included silence, Spartan living conditions, eight hours of daily prayer, and limited contact with the outside world. The two monks don't eat meat and rely on food donations from area residents who ring a bell outside and leave their gifts at the six -foot wooden gate. They hope to eventually have livestock for milk and a garden to raise their own food.   Father Daniel Mary envisions about 30 additional monks in the future. [92]

Chapter 23 notes:

[1] "Bennett Creek Briefs," *Wyoming Stockgrower and Farmer*, June 9, 1903, p. 1.

[2] "More Local News," *The Wyoming Stockgrower and Farmer*, October 08, 1909, p. 4

[3] "Clark Squibs," *Wyoming Stockgrower and Farmer*, November 05, 1909, p. 8.

[4] "Clark Squibs," *Wyoming Stockgrower and Farmer*, November 19, 1909, p. 8.

[5] Ibid.

[6] "Clark Squibs," *Wyoming Stockgrower and Farmer*, December 10, 1909, p. 8.

[7] "Clark Squibs," *Park County Enterprise*, March 26, 1910, p. 8.

[8] "Clark Squibs," *Park County Enterprise*, June 11, 1910, p. 8.

[9] "Clark Squibs," *Park County Enterprise*, June 18, 1910, p. 8.

[10] Ibid.

[11] The 18 charter members were: Dorothy Vickery, Jody Brown, Ethel Brown, Olivia Earle, Mary Lindsay, Anna Lindsay, Jeannette Lindsay, Harry G. Simpson, Amelia Pugh, David Parker, Emma Vickery, Carrie B. Vickery, Elizabeth Vickery, Elsie Vickery, Ted Vickery, Hazel Walter, Esther Weathermon, and George E. Youst. (Membership, Sheldon Jackson Memorial Presbyterian Church of Chance, Montana and Clark, Wyoming, as gathered by Daniel S. McCorkle," found in Daniel S. McCorkle Papers, Manuscript Collection 59, Box 6, Montana Historical Society, Helena.   The Sheldon Jackson Memorial Presbyterian Church held services at the Bennett Creek, Paint Creek, Pioneer and Chance schoolhouses and was organized under the auspices of the Presbyterian Church authority. The Church was named for the early Rocky Mountain area Presbyterian missionary who had died in May 1909. Born into a staunch Presbyterian family in Minaville, New York on May 18, 1834, Sheldon Jackson graduated from Union College in 1855, and from Princeton Theological Seminary in 1858. Soon after he became an ordained Presbyterian minister. Church officials rejected his request to serve overseas, but instead assigned him to an extensive missionary career, which began in western Wisconsin and southern Minnesota. From 1869 to 1882 he traveled to Nebraska, Iowa, Arizona, New Mexico, Utah, Colorado, Wyoming and Montana where he established more than a hundred churches and missions. In 1870 he became superintendent of missions for the Rocky Mountain territories. In 1877 his interested switch to Alaska where he founded numerous schools and training centers to serve native Alaskans. Sheldon Jackson College in Sitka was one of these schools, which he started as a training school in 1878. The college, which is co-educational today, is Alaska's oldest continuous operating school having celebrated its 125th year in April 2003. He also found the Sheldon Jackson Museum in 1887, Alaska's oldest museum. He died on 02 May 1909. For more information on this extraordinary man see: Norman J. Bender, *Winning the West for Christ: Sheldon Jackson and Presbyterianism on the Rocky Mountain Frontier, 1869-1880*, University of New Mexico Press, 1996 and Elizabeth A. Tower, *Reading, Religion and Reindeer: Sheldon Jackson's Legacy to Alaska*, Anchorage, Alaska, 1988.

[12] "Clark Squibs," *Park County Enterprise*, October 22, 1910, p. 5.

[13] *Park County Enterprise,* May 17, 1911, p. 7; "Clark," 1 July – Special to the Enterprise," *Park County Enterprise,* July 4, 1914, p. 2.

[14] "Paint Creek," *Park County Enterprise,* August 15, 1914, p. 4 and December 5, 1914, p. 4.

[15] Ltr. From Daniel S. McCorkle to Miss Nannie Simpson, dated January 12, 1917; ltr. from Daniel S. McCorkle to Harry Simpson, dated January 26, 1917; ltr from Daniel S. McCorkle to Gilford E. Youst, dated January 26, 1917; Ltrs. found in Daniel S. McCorkle Papers, Manuscript Collection 59, Box 3, Folder 12, Montana Historical Society, Helena.

[16] Signed agreement between the Board of Home Missions of the Presbyterian Church, No. 156 Fifth Avenue, New York, New York and Rev. Daniel S. McCorkle signed on August 6th, 1917; Rules for Missionaries and other biographical material found in Daniel S. McCorkle Papers, Montana Historical Society, Helena; and "Belfry Items," *Carbon County Journal,* June 13, 1917, p. 4.

[17] "Clark," *Park County Enterprise,* May 16, 1917, p. 7.

[18] "Clark, May 11, 1917," *Park County Enterprise,* May 16, 1917, p. 7.

[19] "Belfry Items," *Carbon County Journal,* June 13, 1917, p. 4.

[20] *Park County Enterprise,* June 20, 1917, p. 5; also July 4, 1917, p. 5.

[21] "Belfry Items," *Carbon County Journal,* June 27, 1917, p. 6; and "Clark," *Park County Enterprise,* June 27, 1917, p. 6.

[22] "Belfry Items," *Carbon County Journal,* July 4, 1917, p. 3); Note: This former wooden bridge crossed over the Clarks Forks River to the west of today's Sunlight Feed Lot in Pioneer. Nearby is Allen and Laura Denney's ranch. Ira Toothacher's former place was on the northwest side of that bridge. Today the bridge at this location is concrete, having replaced the former one in fall of 1972.

[23] Pledge sheets (3) for the purpose of buying a church automobile, dated September 4, 1917. Found in Daniel S. McCorkle Papers, Collection No. 59, Montana Historical Society, Helena.

[24] Names on the list included: Mrs. C.A. Pearson, H. G. Simpson, Edgar Simpson, F. L. Clark, Orton Sirrine, Walter Cochrane, Mrs. Mary Lindsay, Mrs. E. J. Earl, Edith Simpson, Nannie Simpson, Ella Simpson, Ladies' Aid, G. E. Youst, J. C. Brown, Mrs. M. S. Weathermon, T. C. Parker, Mrs. Vickery, Guy Earl, Hazel Walter, Anna Lindsay, David Parker, Mattie Johnson, E. M. Clark, Peter Rockvam, Mr. and Mrs. O. F. Lindquist and Mrs. Rebecca Mandeville. (Ibid.)

[25] Presbytery of Sheridan – Minutes of Special Session Held in Belfry Presbyterian Church, Belfry, Montana, January 15, 1918," Document in Daniel S. McCorkle Papers, Collection No. 59, Box 6, Folder 5, Montana Historical Society, Helena; Rev. Joseph Tope and his wife, Flora and three children: Charles, Mary, and George moved to Casper in the mid-1920's where they lived in town and maintained a homestead on Hat Six Road. (Obituary of eldest son, Charles Joseph Tope, who died in Casper on February 23, 2004 – *The Cody Enterprise,* March 1, 2004, p. A-3)

[26] "Belfry," *Carbon County Journal,* April 3, 1918, p. 6; "Belfry Items," *Carbon County Journal,* April 17, 1918, p. 4; Mrs. Augusta Brough remembered that during the influenza epidemic in 1918 Rev. McCorkle stopped at their Paint Creek ranch where she had a number of sick people in bed. While she was busy washing linens and taking care of the sick, he helped her feed their cattle. He helped her with some of her other work, then he was on his way. She remembered, "He couldn't stop to rest. He had heard that there were others in distress." ("Mrs. Augusta Brough Tells Story of the Early Days of Paint Creek," *The Cody Enterprise,* November 28, 1950, p. 2)

[27] "Paint Creek and Clarks Fork," *Cody Enterprise,* June 7, 1922, p. 4; McCorkle Papers, Helena.; "Paint Creek," *The Park County Herald,* May 14, 1924, p. 2

[28] *The Park County Herald,* June 4, 1934, p. 1.

[29] "Paint Creek," *The Park County Herald,* July 30, 1924, p. 4; "Clark," *The Park County Herald,* August 6, 1924, p. 6.

[30] "Pat O'Hara," *The Park County Herald*, September 24, 1924, p. 6.

[31] "Paint Creek," *The Park County Herald*, November 12, 1924, p. 3; also October 08, 1924, p. 6; November 05, 1924, p. 6; and "Pat O'Hara," *The Park County Herald*, November 19, 1924, p. 6.

[32] "Paint Creek," *The Park County Herald*, December 3, 1924, p. 3.

[33] "Paint Creek," *The Park County Herald*, February 18, 1925, p. 6; "Clark," *The Park County Herald*, April 1, 1925, p. 3; "Paint Creek," *The Park County Herald*, April 8, 1925, p. 7"; and "Clark," *The Park County Herald*, April 22, 1925, p. 7.

[34] "Paint Creek," *The Park County Herald*, May 27, 1925, p. 7 and "Clark," *The Park County Herald*, June 03, 1925, p. 7.

[35] "Paint Creek," *The Park County Herald*, June 17, 1925, p. 3.

[36] Exact copy of "Names of members of Sheldon Jackson Memorial Presbyterian Church, of Chance, Montana and Clark, Wyoming as gathered by Daniel S. McCorkle," in McCorkle Papers, Collection # 59, Montana Historical Society, Helena.

[37] "Clark," *The Park County Herald*, June 24, 1925, p. 3; July 8, 1925, p. 9; December 30, 1925, p. 6; "Clark," *The Cody Enterprise and Park County Herald*, September 01, 1926, p. 6; December 01, 1926, p. 4; and November 23, 1927, p. 8.

[38] "Paint Creek," *The Park County Herald*, March 10, 1926, p. 3.

[39] He was appointed to the Board of Public Welfare by Montana Governor Sam Ford, and he used his position to publicize the plight of the retarded and mentally ill. Encouraged my much public support, Rev. McCorkle established the Montana Welfare Association in 1947 to extend the work of the Public Welfare Board. Throughout his life he maintained his membership in the Socialist Party, which often caused some difficulty in his ministerial career. (Daniel S. McCorkle Papers, Collection No. 59, Montana Historical Society, Helena.)

While Rev. McCorkle was busy with his ministerial duties in Clark and Paint Creek, he was also active in the promotion of personal civil liberties - activities which were probably not known in this area, and if so, weren't publicized in Cody newspapers. In December 2001 at the 30th anniversary of the ACLU in Montana, it's Executive Director, Scott Crichton, hailed Rev. McCorkle as one of the early field organizers who first worked the coal fields in Carbon County in 1918. He was also cited for his outspoken opposition to mob rule by the 'Liberty Committee' against Finlanders in Red Lodge and German farmers in the Belfry area. "It was natural for McCorkle to lead the ACLU over the coming decades." ("ACLU Celebrates 30 Years of Defending Montanans' Rights," *The Billings Outpost*, December 5, 2001, p. 1)

[40] "Clarks Fork," *The Cody Enterprise*, August 27, 1930, p. 3.

[41] "Lower Clarks Fork," *The Cody Enterprise*, March 25, 1931, p. 6; and July 08, 1931, p. 6.

[42] *The Cody Enterprise*, September 23, 1931, p. 8 and December 09, 1931, p. 9.

[43] "Lower Clark Fork," *The Cody Enterprise*, July 26, 1933, p. 8 and August 09, 1933, p. 6.

[44] "Lower Clark Fork, *The Cody Enterprise*, June 27 1934, p. 3; November 14, 1934, p. 10; May 08, 1935, p. 6; May 29, 1935, p. 6; July 10, 1935, p. 3; January 01, 1936, p. 4; June 24, 1936, p. 3; January 26, 1938, p. 7, May 04, 1938, p. 7; June 08, 1938, p. 6.

[45] "Clarks Fork," *The Cody Enterprise, June 15, 1938, p. 2;* July 13, 1938, p. 6; and July 20, 1938, p. 6.

[46] "Clarks Fork," *The Cody Enterprise*, November 29, 1939, p. 6.

[47] "Clarks Fork," *The Cody Enterprise*, March 11, 1942, p. 3; "First Catholic Services Held in Robinson Home in 1908," *The Powell Tribune*, March 09, 1954, p. 4.

[48] Ibid, *The Powell Tribune*.

[49] Agnes Thull Torczon and Linda Roselia Torczon, interview with the author, Cody, Wyoming,

February 02, 2004; In January 1944 Rev. Francis T. Penney went back to Cody and became the first resident pastor of St. Anthony's Catholic Church. For a history of St. Anthony's Catholic Church see: Msgr. Francis T. Penney, Rev. Charles Brady, Mrs. Marie Manorgan and Mrs. Florence Livingston, "St. Anthony's Church, Cody, Wyoming," Manuscript in Park County Archives, Cody.

[50] "15 Families Build Our Lady of the Valley," *Catholic Rural Life,* March-April 1959, p. 11.

[51] Agnes Thull Torczon and Linda Roselia Torczon, interview.

[52] *Catholic Rural Life,* March-April 1959, p. 11.

[53] Agnes Thull Torczon and Linda Roselia Torczon, interview.

[54] Ibid.

[55] Warranty Deed and Release of Homestead from the Baduras to Hubert Newell, Bishop of Cheyenne, signed June 26, 1954 and filed in Park County Book 191, p. 507 on July 29, 1954.

[56] "To Dedicate New Chapel at Clark, *Powell Tribune,* October 5, 1954, p. 1; "Clark's Fork, by Emma V. Simpson," *The Cody Enterprise,* October 21, 1954, p. 3; Linda Thull was one of the 50 parishioners who participated in the sacrament of confirmation conducted by Bishop Newell that evening. (Agnes Thull Torczon and Linda Roselia Torczon, interview.)

[57] Judy Buckingham, Secretary of St. Barbara's Parish, information provided to the author, Powell, Wyoming, February 9, 2004.

[58] *Powell Tribune,* October 22, 1987, p. 1 and October 27, 1987, p. 1 & 2.

[59] *Powell Tribune,* May 19, 1988.

[60] *Powell Tribune,* July 12, 1990, p. 1.

[61] Grant Deed, signed by Robert B. Badura and R. Ina Badura, husband and wife, dated January 16, 1991, and recorded in Park County M.F. Book 188, page 773.

[62] Affidavit of Survivorship, signed by Rev. John Wright, May 21, 1996 and filed on May 24, 1996 as Park County Doc. 1996-2946.

[63] Judy Buckingham, information provided to author.

[64] Warranty Deed was filed on September 5, 2000 as Park County Document 2000-5152. This corrected previous W.D. filed on April 26, 2000 as Document 2000-2196, which listed the three separate parcels. A new survey map of the combined parcels was filed as Instrument 2000-2918 in Book G, p. 28.

[65] "Clarks Fork," *The Cody Enterprise,* March 05, 1947, p. 5 and March 26, 1947, p. 7.

[66] "Badger Basin, by Mrs. Everett Kelsey," *The Cody Enterprise,* April 23, 1953, p. 9.

[67] "Clarks Fork by Emma V. Simpson," *The Cody Enterprise,* August 21, 1958, p. 6; November 09, 1958, Sec. 2, p. 6; March 19, Sec. 2, p. 10; April 16, 1959, Sec. 2, p. 9; and June 11, 1959, p. 13)

[68] "Clarks Fork by Emma V. Simpson," *The Cody Enterprise,* February 25, 1960, p. 6.

[69] Juanita Gordon, interview with the author, Cody, Wyoming, December 09, 2003.

[70] Ibid.

[71] Ibid.

[72] Ibid.

[73] In "T. 57N. R. 102 W., a tract of land two hundred and nine (209) feet in width north and south and two hundred and nine (209) feet east and west, containing one acre more or less and located as the northeast corner of a tract of land forty (40) rods in width north and south, one hundred (100) rods in length east and west, located in the southeast corner of $S\frac{1}{2}$ $SW\frac{1}{4}$, Section 23. Expressed provided that the property herein described shall be used only for church purposes, and in the event of such nonuse or dissolution of this corporation, the grantee hereby covenants and agrees to reconvey said premises to grantors, their heirs, successors, or assigns." (Warranty Deed, Park County Book 379, p. 348).

[73a] Juanita Gordon interview.

[74] Ibid.

[75] Ibid.

[76] Ibid.

[77] Ibid.

[78] Ibid.

[79] Ibid.

[80] Ibid.

[81] Ibid.

[82] Ibid.

[83] Juanita Gordon, letter to the author, December 13, 2003.

[84] "A Lot of Faith Makes Rural Church a Clark Reality," *Looking at Agriculture*, April 27, 1976, p. 9.

[85] *The Billings Gazette*, 20 March 1975.

[86] "New Clark Church Has Nostalgic Past," *The Cody Enterprise*, March 5, 2003, p. 2.

[87] Juanita Gordon interview.

[88] Rev. Kurt McNabb, conversation with the author, Clark, Wyoming, February 10, 2004; and Janice Kuntz, conversation with the author, February 10, 2004 from information she took from church business meeting records. On February 5, 1995 Janice was elected treasurer of the church, a position she continues to hold today.

[89] Bennett Creek Church dedication announcement, *The Cody Enterprise*, March 5, 2003.

[90] Art Kidwell, personal notes on March 9, 2003 dedication.

[91] *The Cody Enterprise*, March 5, 2003, p. 1.

[92] "Monks Seek Joy of Praying for Others in New Carmelite Monastery at Clark," *The Powell Tribune*, October 9, 2003, p. 17; "Monastery near Clark Will Be Consecrated," *The Cody Enterprise*, October 15, 2003, p. A-5; "Former Summer Home Now a Haven of Holiness," *The Billings Gazette*, October 15, 2003, (internet copy); "Monastery Dedicated in Joyful Mass," *The Powell Tribune*, October 21, 2003, p. 1 & 3.

Sunday school group standing in front of the Pioneer School house in 1916

24
Bennett Buttes Cemetery

The Bennett Buttes Cemetery is located in the SE ¼ SW ¼, Section 22, Township 57 N., Range 102 W. It is just west of the Bennett Buttes, which gave its name to the cemetery site. This location is in the vicinity of the Bennett Creek campsite where Colonel Nelson Miles and his U.S. Army troops camped before and after their confrontation with the Bannock Indians in September 1878.

The first burial on the land that would be later designated as a cemetery is believed to be Miranda Weathermon, [1] the wife of early homesteader Solomon F. Weathermon. She suffered a stroke and died four days later on August 15, 1909. [2]

Although the oldest headstone date in the cemetery belongs to Glen A. Beaton, 2 year-old son of Archie and Grace Palmer Beaton, who died on May 18, 1901, it is believed that he was not buried there at the time of his death. This was also the case of the second oldest stone belonging to James T. Rickards who died a year later in 1902. He was first buried on his ranch and was later moved to the cemetery, [3] as was Henry Parker who died in March 1913. [4]

In 1910 it was suggested by a local resident in the *Cody Enterprise* that it would "not be a bad idea to fence the graveyard... and not allow stock to trample over the graves." It was also suggested that "it would be an easy matter to acquire the land from the Government." [5]

Three months later the question of fencing the cemetery was brought up again and "one party offers to give $10 and a load of posts and another will give a load of posts and help with the job." [6]

Work on the cemetery continued off and on during the next three years. During that time the Bennett Buttes Cemetery Association was formed. The cemetery was also surveyed and plotted into 20-foot square lots with aisle 8-feet wide between the lots. A driveway 27 feet wide was constructed through the center of the cemetery. Those wishing to select lots could see the plat at the Lindquist Brothers store, where everyone in the community came to get supplies and their mail. An article in the *Park County Enterprise* documented these cemetery improvements, and also mentioned that area residents were "taking great pride in this last resting place, and it is a credit to the community." [7]

On November 18, 1913 fourteen residents signed the Articles of Incorporation of the Bennett Buttes Cemetery Association. The articles stated that the corporation would exist for fifty years from that date, and the place where its principal business would be transacted would be at the Snow Ranch on Little Rocky Creek with Charles A.C. Snow, as its agent. It also stated that it would have 14 Directors. Those appointed for the first year were the 14 residents who had signed the document: Oscar Lindquist, Elisha M. Clark, Clara Hunter, Emma Lindquist, Carrie Vickery, Harry Temple, C. B. Hubbard, Emerson Bunn, Solomon F. Weathermon, Daniel I. Parker, Ben Eckloe, Ed Card, Albert A. Owens, and

Joseph C. Brown . [8]

In November 1914 Charles A. C. Snow, the Secretary of the Cemetery Association filed notice that on the 9th day of January 1915, the Association was intending to make final proof to establish claim to the cemetery land. Witnesses to attest to the validity of the claim were: Walter T. Barber, Gordon J. Parker, Edgar Vickery and David Parker. The patent for the 40-acre Bennett Buttes Cemetery was issued by the government on May 3rd, 1916. [9]

The Cemetery Association's annual meetings were held at the Lindquist Brothers store. Residents were invited to attend these meetings at which time board members were elected or reelected. [10] At the March 1916 meeting it was announced that the income tax against the cemetery "had just been assessed against it in the amount of one cent."

A newspaper article the following week questioned the logic of this government move as it "costs an average of one dollar each to collect these small assessments" by the internal revenue collectors. [11]

To raise money for the cemetery, lots were sold, while others were given in exchange for work and for donated materials to the cemetery. One of these work projects was erecting a fence to keep stock off the graves. On May 16th, 1914 a box social and dance were held at the Clark schoolhouse with the proceeds going to erect a summerhouse in the cemetery. [12]

Volunteers helped with the building of the small round wooden building. It was approximately 20 feet to 24 feet in circumference and partially open for ventilation. Seats lined the inside walls, and there was a pulpit in the interior center. Here were held funerals, as well as church, and yearly Memorial Day services. Elmer Bunn had been told as a child that the Lindquist Brothers store donated the material for the building, [13] which was located approximately where the flagpole is today.

Clytie Fuson Williams remembered being christened there by Rev. Daniel McCorkle when she was ten years old. During that Sunday church service in 1919 he also christened her sister, Evalyn and Mrs. Lena Forsman. [14]

Dances and socials were other means by which funds were raised in the early years of the community. In 1923 a dance was held at the Bennett Creek School house for the benefit of the cemetery. This was because "the Bennett Creek grave yard has been considerably neglected and is in need of funds to repair and beautify it, so all those who have, or expect to have a personal interest in this community property, are urged to turn out and show their public spirit." The next year in September the residents of Paint Creek observed Flower day at the cemetery." [15]

In 1925 when the Bennett Buttes Cemetery Association held its annual meeting at the Oscar Lindquist home, O. C. Bevelhymer was re-elected president, Oscar F. Lindquist was re-elected secretary and Mrs. Augustine Brough was elected as treasurer. [16]

A month later in May the Paint Creek, Line Creek and Clark schools combined at the Clark schoolhouse and "gave an entertainment, supper, and dance to raise funds for the Cemetery Association." [17]

Prior to Memorial Day that year several Paint Creek residents, Mr. and Mrs. Joseph

Brown, Mr. and Mrs. William Brough and Mrs. Grace Bevelhymer spent a day at the cemetery "getting it in order for Memorial Day." They reset some of the monuments and cleaned up the grounds. [18]

On Memorial Day services and a basket dinner were held at the schoolhouse as well as placing of flowers on the cemetery graves. By 1928 regular Memorial Day services were being held at the cemetery. [19]

From the 1930's through the 1960's there is no mention in local newspapers of the cemetery or of the Association. Elmer Bunn's history reports that the Association dissolved and all work on the cemetery was abandoned even though residents were still buried there whether they owned a lot or not. Some non-residents were also buried there. The round summerhouse fell into disrepair and as a result, was torn down by Andy Marler in the 1950's. [20]

By the 1960's the cemetery grounds were taken over by sagebrush and cactus, and the planted trees were long dead. Over these years Memorial Day was always a gathering day for Bunn family members. They would take care of their family graves raking and filling in those that needed it. They put flowers on their graves and on those who had no family left. Other families took care of their members in the same way. Elmer remembered that relatives of Edgar Vickery, who was killed during World War I and buried in France – came each year to place an American flag by the marker over his empty gravesite. Family members and others in the community expressed the desire that the cemetery needed to be cleaned up, but nothing happened. [21]

In 1974 Ethel Bunn and her daughter, Virginia Teichert circulated a petition to establish a cemetery district, and in the election held April 14th, 1976 it failed to pass by a majority. Several other attempts to form a district also narrowly missed passing by Clark voters [22] until January 22, 1985 when another petition for the establishment of a Clark cemetery district was circulated by Barbara Bunn and Walt Teichert and present to the Board of County Commissioners. [23]

A public hearing was conducted at the Pioneer Community Hall on March 19th, and there were no protests lodged by any interested or disinterested parties at the hearing nor were written protests received within the thirty days period after the hearing. As a result, on April 19th the Board of County Commissioners ordered that an election be held a month later on May 20th for the organization and establishment of the cemetery district. A majority of the property owners and non-property owners in the proposed district voted for the establishment of the cemetery. As a result the Bennett Buttes Cemetery District was established. [24]

Two days later a Cemetery District Trustee Election was held and 39 votes were cast. The following Trustees were elected: Barbara J. Bunn, Dave Hoffert, Leland Settel, Wilbur E. Bunn Jr., Dona Settell, and Walter Teichert. On August 29th the Commissioners approved the Cemetery's Election Procedure, which would be followed in future elections to elect or re-elect Trustees to the Cemetery Board. [25]

It was a year after the District was formed before any tax money would be available to start work. The Board went to work transforming the long-neglected cemetery. The first project was to resurvey the cemetery, and to relocate the corner markers, which had disappeared. In the following years Elmer and Walter drilled a well and hit water at 68 feet. Lloyd Thiel was hired to level and clean the brush from the west side of the cemetery where few graves were then located. The Bunns, Juanita Moore, Rose Cox and Walt Teichert worked to remove the sagebrush and rocks in the rest of the cemetery so that it could be leveled so that grass could eventually be planted. [26]

Until a permanent irrigation system could be installed Barbara and Elmer Bunn hauled their 3" x 30' irrigation pipes from their ranch and began watering. The next year in 1989 Three Seasons Trenching of Cody was hired to put in an automatic 4-line sprinkler system. Gary and Carol Bunn, who were working for this company, did that actual system installation. In 1990 a 4-foot chain length fence was installed with two drive-thru and one walk-thru gates. [27]

Each year more improvements took place. A memorial area with concrete walks bordered with planted bushes was established in the northwest corner of the cemetery. Spruce and ash trees were planted along the fence. Ed Denney built and installed the flagpole, poured concrete and helped with hauling fertilizer for the lawn. [28]

One of the first projects board members had undertaken was identifying unmarked graves. Using records kept by Ethel Bunn and other family's members as well as newspaper obituaries at the Cody library, every grave in the cemetery except one was identified. Relatives were contacted who helped pay for the small markers placed on each grave. Those with no family had their marker purchased by the District. Today every grave in the cemetery is marked. [29]

Since 1985 the cemetery's caretaker position has been filled in turn by: Mickey Wells, June Burling, Mary Lee Tolman and currently Susan Hoffert.

Today in 2004 current board members include: Elmer Bunn, president; Ed Denney, vice president; Rose Cox, secretary, and Barbara Bunn, Juanita Moore, and Art Kidwell.

Like past board members, Donna and Lee Settel, Dave Hoffert, Walter Teichert and Don Tolman, the current ones are ensuring that the Bennett Buttes Cemetery continues to be a beautiful community asset and a fitting memorial to those who have lived here before us.

Chapter 24 notes:

[1] Elmer Bunn, *History of Bennett Buttes Cemetery*, manuscript, 1998.

[2] "Clark Squibs," *Wyoming Stockgrower and Farmer*, August 27, 1909, p. 2.

[3] Bunn, 1998.

[4] "Clark," *Park County Enterprise*, March 19, 1913, p. 4.

[5] "Clark Squib," *Park County Enterprise*, August 24, 1910, p. 1.

[6] "Clark Squib," *Park County Enterprise*, November 19, 1910, p. 5.

[7] "Clark," *Park County Enterprise*, May 31, 1913, p. 4.

[8] Articles of Incorporation, Bennett Buttes Cemetery Association, signed November 18, 1913, notarized by Charles A. C. Snow, Justice of the Peace on November 18, 1913 and filed in Park County Courthouse on December 12, 1913. Recorded in Articles of Incorporation, Book 1, p. 75.

[9] Application Serial number 06713, *Park County Enterprise*, December 02, 1914, p. 3; Patent #527321for the cemetery property was issued under the Act of Congress of March 01, 1907 entitled "an act to authorize the sale of public lands for cemetery purposes." (Recorded in Park County Book 25, p. 192).

[10] "Clark, Wyoming," *Park County Enterprise*, March 22, 1916, p. 8.

[11] "Clark," *Park County Enterprise*, April 12, 1916, p. 8.

[12] *Cody Enterprise*, Wednesday, April 25, 1923, p. 1; and "Paint Creek," *Park County Herald*, September 17, 1924, p. 6.

[13] Bunn, 1998.

[14] Clytie Williams interview with author, Cody, Wyoming, December 01, 2003.

[15] *Cody Enterprise*, Wednesday, April 25, 1923, p. 1; and "Paint Creek," *Park County Herald*, September 17, 1924, p. 6.

[16] "Paint Creek," *Park County Herald*, April 15, 1925, p. 6.

[17] "Paint Creek," *Park County Herald*, May 13, 1925, p. 7; "Clark," *Park County Herald*, May 20, 1925, p. 7.

[18] "Paint Creek," *Park County Herald*, June 03, 1925, p. 5 and p. 7.

[19] "Paint Creek," *Park County Herald*, May 27, 1925, p. 5; Rev. Daniel S. McCorkle of Bearcreek delivered the sermon for the Memorial Days service. ("Clarks Fork," *Cody Enterprise*, June 06, 1928, p. 11.

[20] Bunn, 1998.

[21] Ibid.

[22] In the election held on April 14, 1976 thirty votes were cast. The vote count was: Property Owners – 16 For, 10 Against; Non-property Owners: 1 For, 3 Against. There was no majority so the election failed to establish the cemetery district. (Commissioners' Record, Book 9, p. 126; Bunn, 1998.

[23] Park County, Wyoming Commissioners' Record, Book 12, p. 297 – 299.

[24] Park County, Wyoming Commissioners' Record, Book 12, p. 303.

[25] Park County, Wyoming Commissioners' Record, Book 12, p. 741 – 744.

[26] Bunn, 1998.

[27] Ibid.

[28] Ibid.

[29] Ibid.

25

Clark Fire District

"The fire was started in a lightning storm near the mouth of the Clarks
Fork last Wednesday and fishermen near the area saw the blaze get started.
Last weekend the fire was well under control, due to the promptness in
reporting the fire, but high winds and the extremely dry conditions in the
area saw the blaze erupt into an inferno that is now out of control." (1955) [1]

The Establishment of the District

Since the earliest settlers moved here, combating natural or man-caused fires was mostly accomplished by individuals protecting their own property, or trying to help a neighbor protect theirs. An organization dedicated to this purpose did not exist in Clark until the 1970's when the Clark Fire District was established.

After a majority of the property owners and non-property owners voted for its establishment, the Park County Board of County Commissioners was petitioned to create the new fire district for the Clark area. At their meeting on October 10, 1973 they created the Clark Fire District, [2] and ordered that another election be held on November 1st by the voters in the new district for the purpose of electing a three-member Board of Directors.

As a result, Paul Worst, an employee of the Wyoming Game and Fish stationed at the Clarks Fork Fish Hatchery, Dennis Wegner, an area farmer and mechanic, and Richard Coburn, then owner of the Edelweiss, were elected to serve as the Clark Fire District's first Directors with 3, 2, and 1- year terms respectively. The findings of the election were entered into the Commissioner's Records at their meeting on November 6th, 1973. [3]

The first meeting of the Clarks Fork Fire District was held on January 16, 1974 at the Clarks Fork Fish Hatchery to organize volunteer firemen, to elect a fire chief, an assistant fire chief and a secretary/treasurer. Twenty-seven men signed up to be volunteer firemen at the meeting. It was decided that two assistant chiefs were needed - one for the north end of the district, and one for the south end. Officers would serve for two years. Then nominations and elections were taken for the open positions with the following results. Miles Bennett, was elected fire chief, Bill Dansby, was elected Assistant Chief for the south end of the District, while Leonard Torczon was elected Assistant Chief for the north end. Elmer Bunn, was elected secretary/treasurer. After the group looked over the fire truck, their present equipment and what was needed, it was decided that the next meeting would be held a month later on February 13th. [4]

At the February monthly meeting it was decided to elect another director for the middle area of Clark, and Wilbur Bunn was nominated and elected. Everyone agreed that Bylaws for the District were needed and volunteers were appointed to write and present them at the next meeting. Members were asked to consider what equipment was needed so that it could be placed in the June budget request. It was also decided to hold regular meetings on the first Tuesday of the month. [5]

During the remainder of 1974 the Fire District was given its first fire truck and some equipment by the Park County Commissioners, and Mick Fraker donated his barn for temporary housing. The District signed a mutual fire aid agreement with the Belfry Fire District, and held two fund-raising dances - one in March, the other at Halloween to buy needed fire equipment. Fire drills were held in April and October, and a system was set up for fire calls where one fireman called another, who in turn called another until everyone was alerted. Because the community still had party lines, it was important to know who was on which line. Bylaws were written that year which required that two officers be elected yearly in December for a term of two years, and all firemen would have a physical examination every three years. At the December meeting an election was held to replace the Secretary/Treasurer and the South-end Captain. Joe Satake from the Fish Hatchery succeeded Elmer Bunn, who did not wish to run again, and Dennis Wegner was elected as South-end Captain.

During that first year for the District, thirty-two individuals served as volunteer firemen: [6]

Harold Aggers	Tony Gordon	Buster Tolman
Mike Bennett	Mike Jackson	Bob Torczon
Miles Bennett (Chief)	Jerry Krenning	Leonard Torczon
E. B. Bohlin	Jerry Linsdau	Dennis Wegner (Board)
Earl Black	Paul Miller	Gus Worm
W. E. Bunn (Sec/Treas.)	Mike Nottingham	Paul Worst (Board)
Rich Coburn (Board)	Joe Roach	Bobby Walters
Craig Cooper	Joe Satake	Kenny Walters
Bill Dansby	Lee Settel	Harvey Willis
Larry Denney	Don Terry	Duane Wiltze
Mick Fraker	Melvin Tilley	

Events during 1975 - 1979

The second year for the District in 1975 began with the same Board Members and with renewed concerns about the need for a permanent place to house the fire engine. In June Game and Fish granted the District a long-term lease for a location near the Fish Hatchery and gave permission to erect a building on the site. After estimates of different types of building construction were considered, it was decided to proceed with one made with concrete blocks. A 32' x 32' block fire hall with a 12' ceiling was constructed during September and October at an estimated cost of $3,000. Larry Thiel did the leveling, while Bill Dansby poured the footings and did the cement for the floor. Others in the community helped with the construction, which was accomplished on weekends. By the December meeting it was reported that the fire truck was now located in the new firehouse, the heaters there were working, but insulation was still needed. In June Rick Colburn was re-elected as a Director to a three-year term. Other elections scheduled for December were postponed until January 1976. [7]

At those elections Miles Bennett was re-elected Fire Chief, Leonard Torczon as Asst. Fire Chief, and Larry Thiel as Captain. Three men attended the fire school in Cody on May

1st and 2nd. There were no fire meetings during the summer, when Rick Coburn resigned as Secy/Treasurer. Elmer Bunn was appointed to take his place. At the December meeting elections were held for 1977 and the following were elected: Jerry Linsdau as Captain, Lee Settel as Assistant Chief and Harvey Willis as Sec/Treasurer. [8]

During 1977 Dennis Wegner, Elmer Bunn and Leonard Torczon served on the Board of Directors. Leonard Torczon replaced Paul Worst who was transferred by the Wyoming Game and Fish. Bob Torczon was elected Fire Chief after Miles Bennett was also transferred by Wyoming Game and Fish. Monthly meetings were held in the firehouse, and in November Larry Denney was elected as Sec./Treasurer after Harvey Willis resigned. Cards listing all firemen and their telephone numbers were to be distributed to all residents in the district. [9]

In 1978 the Board consisted of Dennis Wegner, Leonard Torczon and Wilbur E. Bunn, Jr. Dennis Wegner served until June 20th, when he resigned and Walter Teichert was appointed to fill his vacancy. In September the monthly meetings date changed to the second Tuesday of each month. [10]

During 1979 the Board consisted of Walter Teichert, Leonard Torczon and W. E. Bunn, Jr. In September the District received permission from Game and Fish to plan addition for the firehouse. [11]

Significant Events During the 1980's

Board members during 1980 were Walter Teichert, Leonard Torczon and W. E. Bunn, Jr. Dave Hoffert was elected Fire Chief. In March a special meeting was held to discuss plans for the firehouse, and what the volunteers would like to see in it. A 10' x 18' drive through metal door was installed in the fire hall, and a fire truck was purchased from the Cody Fire District. A phone system was also set up to alert firemen. The By-laws were amended to make residency in the Clark District a requirement for membership, and all references to males were removed. Bob Torczon, Larry Denny and Leonard Torczon were elected to the positions of Assistant Chiefs. [12]

In 1981 Walter Teichert, Leonard Torczon and Wilbur E. Bunn, Jr. served on the Board of Directors. Dave Hoffert served as Fire Chief. A new telephone system was set up to alert firemen to fire calls. Six fire extinguishers were purchased for used in six firemen's personal vehicles, and six pagers were purchased for firemen use. A first-aid class was given to the firemen who also received more equipment for their first-aid kids. [13]

The Fire District Board included Walter Teichert, Leonard Torczon, and Wilbur E. Bunn, Jr. in 1982. Dave Hoffert continued as Fire Chief. During the year the firehouse was repainted and re-roofed. Mutual aid was begun with the Sheriff's Department and with Search and Rescue. Discussions of enlarging the fire hall continued. [14]

During 1983 the same Board members continued to serve, and Dave Hoffert remained as Fire Chief. Significant events this year included the enlargement of the fire hall. Dave Hoffert did the dirt work, and Bob Torczon worked on the fire hall roof with assistance from others firemen. Elmer Bunn resigned from the Board when his job required him to move to Thermopolis. In June Paul Ranschau was appointed to fill the vacancy. In September the District's first medical unit, Truck #4, was purchased from the Powell

Hospital. A First Responder Class held at the Pioneer Community Center marked the beginning of medical response personnel in the District. Dave Hoffert, Lee McDonald and Dave Ranschau spearheaded the creation of the group, and Lee became its first president. Lavonne McNabb, Virginia Ranschau, Darleen Sirrine, Donna Settle, and Olinda Nottingham were the charter members of this First Responder Group, who answered medical calls with the other Clark Fire personnel. [15]

Board members Walter Teichert, Leonard Torczon and Paul Ranschau directed operations of the Fire District during 1984. Fire Chief Dave Hoffert continued to oversee operations with the firemen and equipment. The most significant improvement, which was realized this year, was changes in the phone system, which allowed emergency calls to be received in the firemen's homes. In April Kay Torczon was hired to do secretarial work for the Board, and then in July, she was asked to keep the ledgers and books for the Fire Department. [16]

In 1985 Board members remained the same, who in May approved the use of fire equipment by local residents for fire protection during ditch burning or for protecting valuable property. It was agreed that residents would be held responsible personally and financially for the equipment that was borrowed. The Fire Department planned to give another CPR course that was open to the public, and new radios were purchased for some of the fire trucks. [17]

Walter Teichert, Leonard Torczon, and Paul Ranschau continued as Board members in 1986, as did the Fire Chief, Dave Hoffert. Five members of the First Responder Group took an EMT course in Powell during the summer – Kay Torczon, Bob Torczon, Virginia Ranschau, Evie Donaldson, and Lavonne McNabb. Also that year the First Responder Emergency Medical Technicians were incorporated in the Clark Fire Department, and after Lee McDonald was transferred out of the area, Lavonne McNabb was elected to take his place as president. She was also made training officer of the group. In October Kay Torczon took her place on the Board to replace Paul Ranschau. [18]

In 1987 Walter Teichert, Leonard Torczon and Kay Torczon continued on the Board, and Dave Hoffert continued as Fire Chief. The events of the year included repairs on fire truck pumps and tanks, radios, and necessary vehicle maintenance. [19]

Walter Teichert resigned from the Board in May 1988, and in June Wilbur E. Bunn, Jr. was appointed to temporarily fill the vacancy left. His son, Gary Bunn, was elected to fill the former Teichert position, and he took his seat on the Board in August. The following year in November 1989, Gary Bunn resigned and Kurt McNabb was appointed to finish his term. Lavonne McNabb inquired why the Clark ambulance could not meet the Powell or Cody ambulances enroute to save time in transporting medical cases, and was told that when the District bought the ambulance they made an agreement with the Powell Hospital that the Clark ambulance would only be used in Clark and would not transport. [20]

The 1990's through Present

During 1990 Leonard Torczon, Kay Torczon, and Kurt McNabb continued on the Board while Dave Hoffert continued as Fire Chief. In late August bids were advertised for two weeks to buy a new fire truck with a 1000-gallon steel tank and steel boxes. The lowest bid of $104,692 was received and accepted from Pierce trucks who met the required specs.[21]

At the business meeting of the Clark Volunteer Fire Department held on January 1st, 1991 elections were held and Dave Hoffert was re-elected Fire Chief. Lavonne McNabb was elected President of the EMS, and Bob Torczon, Leonard Torczon and Larry Denney were elected Asst. Fire Chiefs. Kay Torczon was re-elected Secretary/treasurer. Regular Board Members Leonard Torczon, Kay Torczon and Kurt McNabb continued during the year. In August it was decided that Dave Hoffert, Leonard Torczon, Paul Burling and Earl Martin would fly to Appleton, Wisconsin to inspect and accept up the new fire truck at Pierce Manufactures. Leonard and Earl would drive the truck back, while Dave and Paul would fly back with Pierce Manufactures paying for one roundtrip airline ticket. During September the firehouse was painted. [22]

During April 1992 a household fire extinguisher check was done for the community. The Fire District also agreed to pay half the cost for one additional extinguisher per household if it was wanted. Elections were held in October for a new Board, which resulted in Earl Martin, becoming President, Leonard Torczon serving as Budget Officer and Kay Torczon serving as Secretary. In December elections were held to elect a new Fire Chief, secretary and four Captains. Bob Torczon was elected Fire Chief, Larry Denney was elected Captain for # 2, Leonard Torczon was elected Captain for #3, and Lavonne McNabb was elected Captain of #4, and Kay Torczon was elected secretary/treasurer of the Clark Volunteer Fire Department. Half of the profits from the Firemens Ball that year were donated to a needy family in the community for Christmas.[23]

During 1993 and most of 1994 the Board included Earl Martin, Leonard Torczon and Kay Torczon. Bob Torczon was Fire Chief. Early in the summer of 1994 Earl Martin died, and when elections were held that August, Kay Torczon was re-elected and Kurt McNabb was elected back onto the Board. Leonard Torczon was asked to complete the remaining two years of Earl Martin's term. He was elected Board chairman. Kurt McNabb was elected Budget Officer and Kay Torczon was made Secretary/Treasurer. The Board requested that the Fire Chief give a monthly status report on training and time frames when new training was needed. They also researched a cost estimate of adding a new addition to the fire hall. [24]

During 1995 the three Board members remained the same, and Bob Torczon continued as Fire Chief. The District joined the Wyoming State Firemens Association in February, and in March it was decided that the District would pay for the cost of fire school for those signing up to go, but if the individuals later changed their mind and did not go, then they would reimburse the District for the cost of the class. The revised By-laws of the Clark Fire Department were approved in April. In August it was decided to rent out the old fire truck # 2 to the County when they wanted it. [25]

During 1996 the three Board members remained the same, and Bob Torczon continued as Fire Chief. Most of the activities that year were concerned with repairs of fire equipment and the purchase of a new pump and tires for some of the fire trucks. At the January meeting, Leonard Torczon resigned from the Board due to his move out of the District. Lee McDonald was appointed at his replacement to complete his term. In

February it was decided to sell the Dodge fire truck. Lee McDonald resigned at the May meeting due to being transferred. Dave Hoffert was appointed to the Board to fill his vacancy. Larry Denney was elected to the Board later in the year replacing Kay Torczon. The Board has remained the same into 2004. [26]

Summary of Volunteers 1974 – 2004 [27]

Board Members

Rich Colburn 1973 – 1976
Paul Worst 1973 – 1977
Dennis Wegner 1973 – 1978
Elmer Bunn 1977 – 1983, 1988
Leonard Torczon 1977 – 1997
Walter Teichert 1978 – 1988
Paul Ranschau 1983 – 1986

Kay Torczon 1986 - 1997
Gary Bunn 1988 - 1989
Kurt McNabb 1989 – 1992; 1994 - Present
Earl Martin 1992 - 1994
Lee McDonald Feb - May 1997
David Hoffert 1997 - Present
Larry Denney 1997 - Present

Fire Chiefs

Miles Bennett 1974 – 1977
Bob Torczon 1977 – 1979
Dave Hoffert 1980 - 1992

Bob Torczon 1993 - 1997
Paul Burling 1997 - Present

Volunteers

Harold Aggers
Mark Badura
Shane Baughman
Randy Bauwens
Jean Beauchamp
Jim Beauchamp
Mike Bennett
Miles Bennett
Chester Bettger
E. B. Bohlin
Earl Black
Ken Brown
Elmer Bunn
Gary Bunn
Paul Burling
Than Christman
Bob Clark
Rick Colburn
Brian Condrey
Woody Connett
Craig Cooper
Jim Cox

Rose Cox
Jim Cybert
Bill Dansby
Ed Denney
Jerry Denney
Joann Denney
Larry Denney
Tina Denney
Jim Dill
Barbara Dodge
Donna Dodge
Kodi Dodge
Kyle Dodge
Larry Dodge
Evie Donaldson
Dirk Everett
Brad Ferguson
Mick Fraker
Steve Fraker
Tony Gordon
Frank Hagemeister
Richard Hare

Kirk Harshman
Noralee Hoefer
Dave Hoffert
Emilie Hoffert
Kristie Hoffert
Nate Hoffert
Susan Hoffert
Maxine Hohnhorst
Ron Hohnhorst
Mike Jackson
Phil James
John Johnson
Mike Jones
Martin Kimmet
Bret Kolacney
Jerry Krenning
Bill Kuntz
Dale Laboucane
Jerry Linsdau
Rollin Marney
Scott Marney
Earl Martin

Lee McDonald
Bill McGregor
Corey McGregor
William McGregor
Carol McNabb
Jeff McNabb
Kurt Mcnabb
Lavonne McNabb
Slim Metcalf
Paul Miller
Mike Nottingham
Tim Nottingham
Dave Nunley
Dewanna Nunley
Rob Poncelet
Ken Purdum
Dave Ranschau
Paul Ranschau
Virginia Ranschau
Joe Roach
Joe Satake
Greg Savagian

Jerry Schneider	Mark Snyder	Bob Torczon	Ken Walters
Luke Schneider	Walt Teichert	Clara Torczon	Dennis Wegner
Matt Schneider	Don Terry	Doug Torczon	Mickey Wells
Donna Settel	Larry Thiel	Kay Torczon	Harvey Willis
Lee Settel	Lloyd Thiel	Leonard Torczon	Duane Wiltze
Tommy Severude	Steve Thull	Robert Tucker	Gus Worm
Darlene Sirrine	Melvin Tilley	Jim Verplancke	Paul Worst
Gordon Sirrine	J. B. Tolman	Jim Walker	Sam Zug
Roy Slagle	Rocky Tolman	Bob Walters	

Current Clark Fire Volunteers

Volunteer	Since	First Medical Training First Responder/BEC	EMT Since
Larry Denney	1974	1983	
Dave Hoffert	1977	1968 PA ambulance attendant 1972 EMT Class, Cody 1983 First Responder Class	
Kurt McNabb	1981		
Lavonne McNabb	1986	1983 First Responder Class 1983 First Responder Group	1986
Paul Burling	1987	1986	1992
Susan Hoffert	1991	1983 First Responder Class	1993
Nate Hoffert	1995	1999	
Tina Denney	1995	1997	2001
Kristie Hoffert	1998	1991	1993
Kodi Dodge	1998	1999	
Lloyd Thiel	2001		
Emilie Hoffert	2002		
Chester Bettger	2002		
Don Smith	2003		
Bob Jacobs	2003		

Chapter 25 notes:

[1] *The Cody Enterprise,* September 15, 1955, p. 1.

[2] At the preliminary election held prior to petitioning, the vote in favor of establishment was 16-0 by non-property owners and 51-12 by property owners for a total of 79 votes cast. The legal boundaries of the newly-created Clark Fire District were designated as: "Beginning at the northwest corner, T.58 N., R. 103 W (unsurveyed); thence south to the southwest corner of T. 57 N., R. 103 W. (unsurveyed); thence east to the northwest corner of T. 56 N., R. 103 W.; thence

south to the southwest corner of Sec. 18, T. 56 N., R. 103 W.; thence east to the southeast corner of Sec. 16, T. 56 N., R. 103 W.; thence north along the section line for about ¾ of a mile; thence east on a line projected west from the south lines of Tracts 54, 55, 184, 183 and 182 to the west line of T. 56 N., R. 102 W.; thence north to the north line of Tract 155, T. 56., R. 102 W.; thence west along said north line of Tract 155 to the Clark's Fork River; thence north and east along said river to the west line of T. 56 N., R. 102 W.; thence north to the midsection line of Sec. 6, T. 56 N., R. 102 W.; thence east on the midsection lines to the east line of T. 56 N., R. 102 W.; thence south to the southeast corner of Sec. 12, T. 56 N., R. 102 W.; thence east to the southeast corner, Sec. 12, T. 56 N., R. 100 W.; thence north to the northeast corner of said township; thence west to the southeast corner of T. 57 N., R. 100 W.; thence north to the northeast corner of said township; thence west to the northwest corner of Sec. 3 of said township; thence north to the north boundary of Wyoming; thence west along said boundary to the point of beginning." (Park County, Wyoming Commissioners' Record, Book 8, pgs. 472 – 473); These same boundaries would be established for the Bennett Buttes Cemetery District 12 years later. (Commissioners' Record, Book 12, p. 297;) Another election was called to be held in the district on November 1st, at which time Paul Worst, an employee of the Wyoming Game and Fish stationed at the Clarks Fork Fish Hatchery, Dennis Wegner, an area farmer and mechanic, and Richard Coburn, then owner of the Edelweiss. were elected to serve as the Fire Districts first Directors serving 3, 2, and 1 year terms respectively. The actual vote was: Paul Worst (28), Dennis Wegner (22), Richard Coburn (13), Gene Gardner (13), and Anthony Gordon (13). Richard Coburn was selected by a draw from the three candidates who had tie votes. (Park County Commissioners Record, Book 8, pg. 484).

[3] The actual vote was: Paul Worst (28), Dennis Wegner (22), Richard Coburn (13), Gene Gardner (13), and Anthony Gordon (13). Richard Coburn was selected by a draw from the three runner-up candidates who each received the same number of votes. (Commissioners Record, Book 8, pg. 484).

[4] Minutes of the Fire Meeting held on January 16, 1974, W. E. Bunn, Secretary.

[5] Minutes of the February 13, 1974 meeting, W. E. Bunn, Secretary.

[6] Minutes of the Fire Meetings held on March 5, April 2, May 7, June 4, August 6, September 11, October 1, November 4, and December 3, 1974.

[7] Minutes of the Fire Meetings held on February 4, March 4, June 3, July 1, August (no day), September 2, and December 2, 1975.

[8] Minutes of the Fire Meetings held on January 6, March 2, April 2, May 4, June 1, September 7, October 5, and December 7, 1976.

[9] Minutes of the Fire Meetings held on March 1, June 8, November 1, and December 5, 1977 and Clark Fire Protection Board Meetings held in July and on August 2, September 6, October 4, November 1, and December 6, 1977, and Clark Fire Protection Board Meetings held in July, on August 2, September 6, October 4, November 1, and December 6, 1977.

[10] Minutes of the Fire Meetings held on June 6, September 11, October 2, November 5 and December (no date), 1978, and the Clark Fire Protection Board Meetings held on January 3, in February (no date), in March (no date), on April 10, June 6, July 13, August 1, September 5, September 19, October 7, November (no date), and December 5, 1978.

[11] Minutes of the Fire Meetings held in January (no date), on February 16, March 5, April 2, June 4, September (no date), and December 18, 1979, and Clark Fire District Board Meetings held in January (no date), February 16, March (no date), April 2, May 1, June 5, July 5, August 9, September 3, October 1, November 6, and December 17, 1979.

[12] Minutes of the Fire Meetings held on January 8, February 3 and 5, and March 31, 1980 and the Clark Fire District Board Meetings held on January 8, February (no date), March 3, April 1, May 1,

June 3, June 13 (special meeting), June 18 (special meeting), July 1, August 5, September 16, September 25 (special meeting), October 7, October 10 (special meeting), November 10, and December 2, 1980.

[13] Minutes of Clark Fire District Board Meetings held on January 6, July 7, August (no date), and September 8, 1981.

[14] Minutes of Clark Fire District Board Meetings held on January 12, April 13, May 11, July (no date), September 22, and December 8, 1982.

[15] Susan Hoffert, "1983 Significant Events," *History of Clark Fire District and Clark Volunteer Fire Department in Honor of Those Who Have Served,* 2003.

[16] Minutes of Clark Fire District Board Meetings held on April 10, May 9, July 5, and December 11, 1984.

[17] Minutes of Clark Fire District Board Meetings held on May 15, July (no date), and December 10, 1985.

[18] Minutes of Clark Fire District Board Meetings held on April 9, July 8, and October 14, 1986; also Susan Hoffert, "1986 Significant Events," *History of Clark Fire District.*

[19] Minutes of Clark Fire District Board Meetings held on February 10, April 13, June 8, June 30, October 12, November 10, and December 8, 1987.

[20] Minutes of Clark Fire District Board Meetings held on April 12, May 10, June 14, August 23, December 13, 1988, and April 11, 1989, November 14, 1989.

[21] Minutes of the monthly meetings of the Clark Fire District held on January 9, February 13, March 13, April 10, May 8, June 12, July 10, August 14, September 11, October 9, November 13, and December 11, 1990.

[22] Minutes of the Business Meeting of the Clark Volunteer Fire Department held on January 1, 1991; Minutes of the regular monthly meetings of the Clark Fire District held on January 8, February 14, March 12, April 16, May 7, June 18, July (no date), July 9, August (no date), September (no date), October 8, November (no date), December (no date), 1991.

[23] Minutes of the regular monthly meetings of the Clark Fire District held on January 14, February 11, March 10, April 15, May 21, June 9, July 14, August 11, September 8, October 13, November 10, and December 1, 1992.

[24] Minutes of the monthly meetings of the Clark Fire District Board held on January 12, February 9, March 9, April 13, May 11, June 8, July (no date), August 17, September 15, October 12, November 18, and December 22, 1993; and Minutes of the monthly meetings of the Clark Fire District Board held on January 12, February 15, March 15, April 12, May 10, June 14, July 12, August 16, September 13, October 11, November 8, and December (no date), 1994.

[25] Minutes of the monthly meetings of the Clark Fire District Board held on January 10, February 7, March 14, April 19, May 9, June 13, July 12, August 22, September 12, October 10, November 14, and December 12, 1995.

[26] Minutes of the monthly meetings of the Clark Fire District Board held on January 9, February (no date), March (no date), April 9, May 14, June 11, July 9, August 13, September 17, October 8, and November 12, 1996; and minutes of the monthly meetings of the Clark Fire District Board held on January 14, February 11, March 18, April 8, May 13, and June 17, 1997.

[27] This summary of Board Members, Fire Chiefs, Volunteers and Current Fire Personnel was researched and compiled by Susan Hoffert from Fire District Records, and was given to the author to include here with her permission.

26
Clark's Fork Fish Hatchery

Construction of the Wyoming Game and Fish Department's largest fish hatchery began in the spring of 1969 and was completed prior to March 1, 1970 when fish production began at its new location on the west bank of the Clarks Fork River just upstream from the Line Creek Bridge in Clark. [1]

A crowd of over three hundred people[2] were present three months later on June 5th when Wyoming Governor Stan Hathaway dedicated the new $1.2 million facility to "better fishing in Wyoming." He also added, "There is fishing today in many streams in Wyoming where there was none years ago."

The Governor praised the efforts of the Wyoming Game and Fish Commission and noted that the hatchery "would be a keystone in its plans to re-stock lakes and streams through the state as well as to rehabilitate others." [3] This facility replaced the former one, which was located seven miles north of Cody on the east side of Highway 120.

The new Clarks Fork facility, located on 195 acres of deeded land, also includes many public fishing access points. Its main purpose is the hatching and rearing of fish for stocking into state waters that allow public fishing. This site was chosen because of the presence of 12 natural underground springs, which supply cold, disease-free water year round to the hatchery. The volume of water from the springs varies with the season from 5,000 gallons per minute in April to 7,000 gallons per minute in October. When the flow is the heaviest it averages 11.5 million gallons per day at an average temperature of 52 degrees F.

Water from the springs flows by gravity through pipes into a large collection box at the hatchery where it is aerated and then flows onward into and passes through the 12 fish raceways before it is returned to the Clarks Fork River. Because the water is constantly flowing it never freezes even in winter on its coldest days.

Five staff biologists who live in the homes on the grassy knolls overlooking the raceways are responsible for the production, care and transport of approximately one to two million trout annually.

The biologists oversee the collection and fertilization of trout eggs, which are sorted for the highest quality and incubating inside the hatchery. After the eggs hatch into "swim-up fry", they develop utilizing their yolk sac as food. When it is depleted, they "swim-up" to the water's surface in search of food. Then they are fed a commercial grade of trout food to promote size growth. Later they are moved outside to the raceways where they continue to develop into larger fish.

The 12 raceways, each divided into three 10' x 100' sections, provide the rearing areas for the young Eagle Lake rainbow, Fall rainbow, Firehole rainbow, Brown, Snake River cutthroat and Yellowstone cutthroat trout. When the need arises, grayling are also raised here for stocking.

As the fish are maturing, other biologists are surveying Wyoming watercourses to determine which ones need to be stocked, and with what species, how many, and what size.

After the fish have matured to the size required for stocking, they are usually transported in trucks to the lake, river or stream where they are to be released. When delivery is required to high mountain lakes or other locations where trucking is not possible, special helicopters fitted with side tanks are used. In either case the tanks are insulated to keep the temperature of the tank water constant. Oxygen bottles, air stones and aerators provide the fish with oxygen during transport. In the year 2000, the staff of the Clark's Fork Fish Hatchery moved 106,000 pounds of fish by land and air.

The Clark's Fork Fish Hatchery is open daily from 8 a.m. to 5 p.m. and visitors are welcome. Interpretative displays in the hallway explain the State's fisheries management program there.[4]

Chapter 26 notes:

[1] "Construction of State's Larges Fish Hatchery Slated for Clark," *The Cody Enterprise,* March 12, 1969, p. 1; "The Clark's Fork Fish Hatchery," Wyoming Game and Fish brochure, no date.

[2] The signed Guest Book kept in the archives of the Clark's Fork Fish Hatchery indicates there were 306 individuals present at the June 5, 1970 dedication ceremonies.

[3] "Hatchery Dedicated," *The Powell Tribune,* June 9, 1970, p. 1 and "Hathaway Dedicates Clark Fish Hatchery," *The Cody Enterprise,* June 10, 1970, p. 13.

[4] The operational details about this facility used in this chapter were found in the following: "Why Not Visit Fish Hatchery," Wyoming Game and Fish Department brochure, n.d.; "Life Cycle: Ideal Conditions Boost Clark Hatchery's Trout Development," *The Cody Enterprise,* August 27, 2001, p B-8; "Clarks Fork Fish Hatchery," Wyoming Game and Fish Department brochure, 2003; Clark's Fork Fish Hatchery Superintendent Dave Miller, conversations with the author, Clark, Wyoming, October 30, 2003 and March 30, 2004. John Chaffey and John Burns, conversations with the author, Clark, Wyoming, April 12, 2004.

2004 Staff: (L to R): Superintendent Dave Miller,
Brian Blutt, John Chaffey, and Chester Bettger.
Not present for photo: John Burns and Wayne Holm.

27

Clark-Pioneer Recreation Center

The creation of the Clark-Pioneer Recreation Center was a magnificent example of the same community spirit of neighbors helping one another to accomplish a common goal that was the hallmark of the areas earliest residents.

Throughout the area's history, residents gathered at the Pioneer, Clark, Paint Creek, and Line Creek school houses to have church services, meetings, dances, and other social events. Some meetings were also held at the Lindquist store. There had always been a need and a desire to have a central facility, which would be used exclusively for community activities, and be large enough to accommodate all who wished to attend. As the area became more populated, the need was even more evident.

One of the earliest efforts was in 1910 when some residents were talking about building a dance hall near the Lindquist store. [1] Twenty-five years later in March of 1935 a group of Pioneer area residents went to Cody, Ishawooa, and Powell in search of ideas in order to build a community center. Members of the group included: William H. Fouse, Ed Simpson, Clarence Pearson, Carol Carlson, Fred Myers, Joe Williams and Ralph Fouse.[2]

Later that month at a community meeting they "decided to go ahead with plans for a community hall," and members of the same group with the addition of Ben Madison "went to Cody and Powell to look at buildings and get prices on material." [3] Whatever their plans, the project never fully developed and soon died. The schoolhouses continued their auxiliary role as community meeting places. Even this was to change in the late 1980's.

In August 1989 a group of Clark residents came before the Powell School Board and angrily questioned why they had not been allowed to use the Clark school building for a dance at the Clark Reunion weekend earlier in the summer. They had been told their request had been denied because it was not a school function. During this meeting the Board was told about an agreement which had been made in December of 1969 when the Clark School was about to become part of Powell School District #1. At that time Clark area residents had been guaranteed that the building could continue to be used for community activities with a decision by the State Attorney General, who had ruled that "school-owned buildings in small communities could utilize the facilities for community functions." Don Tolman speaking at the meeting said, "that the buildings should be available for the community's use because the people of this community are the ones who got the bond passed. We helped to build it." [4]

School Board President Bill Metzler said it had not been their intent to close the building down," and that it sounded "like a misunderstanding." He wanted the district attorney to review the 20-year old document.[5] As a result of this incident, many area residents saw an urgent need for a community center.

Two years later Linda Lindsdau of Powell who knew of need for a community recreation center in Clark mentioned to Barbara Bunn that Ed Stratman of the Park County Rec Board had money available for recreation purposes. Because area resident, Evie Donaldson was a friend of Stratman, she invited him to come to her house here in Clark to discus the community needs for a recreation facility. At that meeting in late September or early October 1991 were Barbara Bunn, Linda Lindsdau, Ed Stratman, Evie Donaldson and Don Tolman, who because of his interest in a rec center, had been invited to attend the meeting. Stratman told the group that if the community could come up with some matching funds that the County Rec Board would give some help for the building. "People working and volunteering their time toward the project also counting as matching funds." This meeting became the first one, which eventually resulted in the Clark-Pioneer Recreation Center.[6]

The second meeting was held on November 10th at Don and Jackie Tolman's home attended by representatives from the area's communities to further discuss the possibilities of building a community center.

At that Sunday evening meeting Elmer and Barbara Bunn, Evie Donaldson, and Don Tolman discussed the center idea, the need for a site, and organization to begin the project. The enthusiastic response of those at that meeting resulted in the calling of a community meeting within two weeks to see if other residents would support such a project.[7]

The community meeting thirteen days later at the Clark school was attended by about 70 Clark-Pioneer residents and conducted by Don Tolman to develop a plan for constructing a community center for social and recreational purposes. He explained the idea of a community recreation center and how part of their property taxes supported Park County's Recreation District, as well as Powell's Recreation District. If a suitable building was available, programs sponsored by the Powell Recreation District could be made available here, as well as other government-assisted programs.

In addition many social and recreation activities could take place here that could no longer be held using the local school facilities because of insurance requirements, and of local, state or federal regulations. Getting a center in Clark required a building, land on which it would be located, and the forming of a non-profit corporation with by-laws to oversees its operation. A basic set of bylaws for the Clark Area Recreation Project, had been set up previous to this meeting.

Those in attendance were enthusiastic about the project and suggested what types of activities they would like to see take place here. They then voted to form a non-profit corporation, and passed the proposed by-laws. A motion was made that five directors be elected with staggered terms to oversee the operation of the corporation.

This motion passed and the following directors were elected: Evie Donaldson, Don Tolman, Elmer Bunn, Cathy McGregor and Bill Dansby. It was further decided that area residents would control the proposed facility, it must be accessible to the public, and an annual meeting would be held on the first Saturday in November, At that time community members would elect the Board of Directors, who would in turn elect their own officers. Larry Denney made a motion that the name of the project be the Clark-Pioneer Area Recreation Project, which was seconded and approved by the attendees.

After the public meeting was adjourned the Board met for the first time and elected its first officers: Don Tolman, president, Evie Donaldson, Vice President, Cathy McGregor, Secretary, and Elmer Bunn, Treasurer. [8]

At the December 5th board meeting, Evie Donaldson brought definite ideas about the building to the rest of the members. "The structure should be built in the most functional manner possible. Traffic flow should be considered. It should be fireproof and as maintenance free as possible with all exits both in size and number according to Code." She also thought that after the design of the building was agreed upon that bids should be accepted from a number of contractors, especially those willing to work with local volunteer labor. [9]

Ed Stratman and his wife also attended the meeting and reported that he had already discussed the community center project with the Park County Recreation Board. He provided a sample agreement form and voucher and suggested that the Clark Board's proposal list matching funds including cost and donations of labor, goods and money.[10]

On December 10th Articles of Incorporation for the Clark Pioneer Recreation Project were filed with the Wyoming Secretary of State. [11]

The next six months a great deal of time and effort were expended by area residents to raise money for the building. A $60,000 grant was received from Park County Parks and Recreation, as well as $45,000 from the Children's Recreation Society of Philadelphia, and donations from local residents. Cash and material donations were also contributed from the Cody and Powell business communities.[12]

On April 1, 1992 the Board contracted with AgriStructures, Inc. & Steel Structures to construct the building according to the plans and specifications that they submitted. The all-metal building was to contain a 60' x 80' x 24' gym attached to a 40' x 75' x 10' meeting room. The contractor was paid $59,610 for the work which was to be completed on or before the June 1st deadline. [13]

On April 6, 1992 Evie Donaldson and her Rock Creek Ranch donated a parcel of land containing 5.06 acres in the NE ¼ SW ¼ of Section 22, T. 57 N., R. 102 W. to the Clark Pioneer Recreation Project. [14] Five years later in June 1997 Freeman A. Fowler donated 6.18 acres of land which was located directly to the west of the Donaldson gift. [15]

Eight months after the initial meeting the community had its long-awaited Recreation Center. Today thirteen years later this facility is used on a daily basis for meetings, dinners, social events and athletics. A fine rodeo arena was built by volunteer labor and with donated materials to the northwest of the building.

The community center is not supported by County, State or Federal funds, but instead continues to be maintained by donations and fundraisers. The Powell Recreation District contributes a small amount yearly to help with providing recreational programs. This amount is dependent upon the county tax revenue and the District's budget. One of our board members serves on the Powell Rec Board.

The Clark-Pioneer Recreation Center played an important role during the summer of 2003. On July 16th a lightning strike near Deep Lake ignited a fire, which quickly grew and headed in all directions fanned by high winds.

Within four days others joined the Shoshone Forest firefighters, some coming as far away as southern California. The Recreation Center became their command post, where meals were prepared, and where 195 weary firefighters slept in tents on the rodeo grounds. Their mission was to stop the fire whose erratic direction threatened ranches and homes along Bennett Creek.

On July 28th with 60% of the fire contained, the responsibility for fighting the fire was turned back to the Shoshone Forest crews and the other firefighters left. By then the fire had consumed over 6,800 acres. It wasn't until late August that the skies were finally free of smoke, after welcome rains finally put an end to the remaining fires in the Beartooth Mountains above Clark. [16]

Clark and Pioneer residents can be proud of our facility and its programs, and be thankful to those who worked so hard to make this long-sought community center, a reality. We can also be grateful to the past and current members of the Board of Directors who oversee the day-to-day operations and needs of this community asset.

The Clark Reunion – or Jubilee Days

One of the events, which centers today at the Clark-Pioneer Rec facility is the annual Jubilee Days. Plans for this celebration were formulated at a meeting in September 1987 at the home of Wilda Hoefer. At that time Vern Spurgin, a former resident of Clark, had returned for a visit from his present home in Alaska. At the Hoefer home were also Juanita Moore of Clark and Ruby Stidham Vaught, also a former resident who lives in Cody.

In discussing past times in the area, those four individuals formulated a plan to create an annual celebration which would highlight and honor the memory of the area pioneers. They called their celebration, the Clark Reunion, and planned to hold their first one the following summer. Vern Spurgin donated $50 for the ladies to help pay for postage to notify old-timers of the planned celebration in 1988. [17]

The first celebration was called the Clark Reunion and was held at the Clark School with a picnic at Edelweiss. After the Recreation Center was completed the celebration was moved there.

Today the annual June event is called Jubilee Days and includes a Saturday parade of local residents in vintage cars, on horseback, or on floats. That afternoon old-timers gather in the gym to enjoy lunch and to see and visit with old friends and neighbors. Then later that evening a potluck dinner is enjoyed by residents and guests climaxed with an evening program. Sunday morning activities include church services followed by an all-day rodeo in the Clark arena.

Chapter 27 Notes:

[1] "Clark Squib," *Park County Enterprise,* August 24, 1910, p. 1.

[2] Here from Clark," *The Cody Enterprise,* April 3, 1935, p. 8.

[3] "Lower Clark Fork," *The Cody Enterprise,* April 17, 1935, p. 6.

[4] "Who Can Use Clark School?" *The Powell Tribune,* August 10, 1989, pgs. 1 & 3.

[5] Ibid.

[6] Barbara and Elmer Bunn, interview with the author, Clark, March 30, 2004.

[7] "Minutes of Meeting at Tolman's," November 10, 1991.

[8] C. Edward Webster, II, Temporary Secretary, "Minutes of Initial Meeting of the Clark Pioneer Recreation Project," Clark School, November 17, 1991.

[9] "Evie's Thoughts Submitted to the Board of Directors, December 5th meeting, 1991."

[10] "Minutes of the December 5, 1991 Clark-Pioneer Recreation Project Board meeting".

[11] "Articles of Incorporation for Clark Pioneer Recreation Project, A Wyoming Domestic Nonprofit Corporation," signed by incorporator, C. Edward Webster II of Cody, Wyoming on 5th day of December 1991 and filed December 10, 1991 with the Wyoming Secretary of State.

[12] Letters from Donald R. Williams, Children's Recreation Society of Philadelphia to Clark Pioneer Recreation Project, dated March 2, 1992 and March 25, 1992; and "Clark Pioneer Recreation Project, History of Your Rec Center," non-dated document.

[13] Agreement between Clark Pioneer Recreation Project and AgriStructures, Inc. & Steel Structures, dated April 1, 1992.

[14] Warranty Deed dated April 6, 1992 and filed on April 16, 1992 in Park County Book 205, p. 961.

[15] Warranty Deed dated June 10, 1997, and filed as Park Co. Document 1997 – 3353.

[16] "Blaze Near Clark, Wyoming, Goes Through and Out of Canyon," *Billings Gazette,* July 19, 2003, p. 1; "Few on Fire Scene in Cody Forests," *Billings Gazette,* July 20, 2003, p. 1; "Winds Fan Clark Fire," "Firefighters Savor Job," and related stories, *Cody Enterprise,* July 21, 2003, p. 1; "Help Arrives at Cody Fire," *Billings Gazette,* July 21, 2003, p. 1; "Deep Lake Fire Slowly Eases," and related stories, *The Powell Tribune,* July 22, 2003, p. 1; "Fire Could Threaten Structures," *Cody Enterprise,* July 23, 2003, p. A-7; "Fire Update – Firefighters Are Hopeful of Getting Clark Blaze Stopped," *The Powell Tribune,* July 24, 2003, p. 1 and p. 20; "Cost to Fight Fire Nears Million," *Cody Enterprise,* July 28, 2003, p. 1; and "Crews Leaving Clark Blaze," *Cody Enterprise,* July 30, 2003, p. A-5.

[17] Wilda Hoefer, interview with the author, Clark, April 1, 2001.

The Clark-Pioneer Recreation Center